Police Corruption
and Police Reforms in
Developing Societies

Police Corruption and Police Reforms in Developing Societies

Edited by
Kempe Ronald Hope, Sr.
Policy Group
Development Practice International

CRC Press
Taylor & Francis Group
Boca Raton London New York

CRC Press is an imprint of the
Taylor & Francis Group, an **informa** business

CRC Press
Taylor & Francis Group
6000 Broken Sound Parkway NW, Suite 300
Boca Raton, FL 33487-2742

First issued in paperback 2020

© 2016 by Kempe Ronald Hope, Sr.
CRC Press is an imprint of Taylor & Francis Group, an Informa business

No claim to original U.S. Government works

ISBN-13: 978-1-4987-3187-4 (hbk)
ISBN-13: 978-0-367-59813-6 (pbk)

Visit the Taylor & Francis Web site at
http://www.taylorandfrancis.com

and the CRC Press Web site at
http://www.crcpress.com

Contents

List of Figures   ix
List of Tables   xi
Preface   xiii
Editor   xvii
Contributors   xix

Section I

THEORETICAL AND ANALYTICAL PERSPECTIVES

1   **An Analytical Perspective on Police Corruption and Police Reforms in Developing Societies**   3

KEMPE RONALD HOPE, Sr.

2   **Confronting Police Corruption in Developing Societies: The Role of the Rule of Law**   33

JOHN MUKUM MBAKU

3   **Emphasizing Anticorruption Training as a Reform Tool to Curb Police Corruption in Developing Societies**   51

KEMPE RONALD HOPE, Sr.

Section II
DEVELOPING SOCIETIES
CASE STUDIES: AFRICA

4   Ghana: Reducing Police Corruption and
      Promoting Police Professionalism through
      Reforms   65
      JOSEPH R.A. AYEE

5   Kenya: Police Corruption and Reforms to Control It   85
      KEMPE RONALD HOPE, Sr.

6   South Africa: A Schizophrenic System for
      Combating the Scourge of Police Corruption   109
      CORNELIS ROELOFSE

7   Cameroon: Police Corruption and the Police
      Reforms Imperative   125
      POLYCARP NGUFOR FORKUM

Section III
DEVELOPING SOCIETIES CASE
STUDIES: ASIA-PACIFIC

8   Hong Kong: Police Corruption and Reforms   143
      DENNIS LAI HANG HUI

9   India: Nature of Police Corruption
      and Its Remedies   157
      ARVIND VERMA

10   Royal Solomon Islands: Rainbows across the
      Mountains—The Issue of Police Corruption   179
      GARTH DEN HEYER

Section IV
DEVELOPING SOCIETIES CASE STUDIES: LATIN AMERICA AND CARIBBEAN

11   **Argentina: Revisiting Police Corruption and Police Reforms in a Captive State**   **197**
        GUILLERMINA SERI

12   **Trinidad and Tobago: Crime, Police Corruption, and Police Reforms**   **207**
        NATHAN W. PINO

Section V
CHAPTER SUMMARIES

13   **Chapter Summaries**   **229**

Index   **237**

List of Figures

Figure 1.1   Police Aggregate Bribery Index for East African
                 Countries, 2010–2014   12

Figure 5.1   Kenya Police Aggregate Bribery Index, 2007–2014   91

Figure 6.1   Socialization Process in Systems Approach   113

List of Tables

Table 1.1   Types and Dimensions of Police Corruption   6

Table 1.2   Classification and Examples of Corrupt Police Behaviors   7

Table 1.3   Selected Developing Societies Where the Police Are
                Perceived as the Most Corrupt Institution, 2013   11

Preface

Much of the literature on police corruption and police reforms is dominated by case studies of those societies classified as developed. However, under the influence of globalization, developing societies have become a focal point of scholarly interest and examination. This book contributes to that interest and examination through its focus on a wide variety of developing societies, spanning several continents. Consequently, it is also intended to make a contribution to changing the developed society dominance in the literature on police corruption and police reforms.

A generalized understanding of police corruption—its causes, consequences, and reform efforts to control it—is not fully possible without completely considering and assessing diverse perspectives derived from understanding the basic realities of different societies and the issues and processes of policing those societies face. This book therefore provides critical analyses of the nature, extent, causes, and consequences of police corruption and misconduct in developing societies and the police reforms that either have been embarked upon or are necessary to control and mitigate the deleterious effects of this corruption and misconduct among the police corps.

This book offers a comprehensive and authoritative account of what we know about the causes and consequences of police corruption and the lessons learned from the police reform efforts that have been undertaken to control said corruption using the experience of a wide cross section of developing societies. The editor and contributors bring a wealth of practical experience to bear on their analyses in their respective chapters. That experience encompasses professional policing activities in the line of police duty, as police reform advisers and police trainers, and/or in policing research. The book is also written in an easy-to-read format that can be readily understood by the uninitiated as well.

The book is comprised of 5 sections with 13 chapters. Section I contains three chapters that cover theoretical and analytical perspectives. In Chapter 1, the editor, Kempe Ronald Hope, Sr., provides an analytical review and assessment of the police corruption phenomenon and problem in developing societies and the police reforms that either have been embarked upon or are necessary to control and mitigate the deleterious effects of this corruption and misconduct among the police corps. In addition to drawing on the author's vast practice experience as a police reform adviser to several governments, the chapter also reviews the literature with the coverage of such topics as what is police corruption, the causes of police corruption, the key indicators of police corruption, the consequences of police corruption, and the required principal elements of police reforms to control police corruption in developing societies. In Chapter 2, John Mukum Mbaku reflects on the role and importance of the rule of law to control police corruption. Drawing on constitutional political economy theoretical constructs, he argues that to deal effectively with police corruption, each society must provide itself with governing processes and institutions that guarantee the rule of law. In Chapter 3, Kempe Ronald Hope, Sr. sets out a basic training framework and approach as a reform tool for curbing police corruption in developing societies. It outlines learning goals and training objectives, proposes a training approach model, suggests training content and coverage, and indicates the expected outcomes from the training approach and process.

Section II kicks off the developing societies case studies with a focus on Africa. It contains the largest number of chapters at four, reflecting the depth and magnitude of the police corruption phenomenon and the ongoing quest for successful police reforms in that region. Chapter 4, authored by Joseph R.A. Ayee, demonstrates and emphasizes that the Ghanaian experience with police corruption and police reforms reinforces the lessons that police corruption is symptomatic of the level of systemic corruption existing in a society and that, like all public sector reforms, the successful implementation of police reforms depends on political leadership, will, and commitment. Chapter 5, also by the editor, probes the nature and extent of police corruption in Kenya, providing a coherent picture and understanding of the police corruption problem and environment in the country. It then outlines and analytically reviews and assesses the outcomes of the recent police reforms that have been implemented and offers recommendations on the way forward for curbing police corruption in the country. Chapter 6, by Cornelis Roelofse, explores what he terms the schizophrenic system for combating the scourge of police corruption in South Africa by outlining the key policy inconsistencies and contradictions where words and actions often do not correspond and political and administrative interference is commonplace. He draws on systems theory and reciprocal moral dualism to undergird his analysis. In Chapter 7, Polycarp Ngufor Forkum presents a critical analysis of the depth and intensity of police corruption and misconduct in Cameroon and then examines the police reforms that either have been embarked upon or are imperative to control and mitigate the deleterious effects of this malpractice and misconduct among the country's police corps.

In Section III, the spotlight shifts to case studies of the Asia-Pacific developing societies. In Chapter 8, Dennis Lai Hang Hui identifies the key features of the current types of police corruption in Hong Kong and provides an overview and analysis of the institutional structure for combating it. It extends existing theoretical analyses to develop an institutional explanation in accounting for the scale and features of police corruption in Hong Kong. Chapter 9 by Arvind Verma investigates the nature of police corruption in India and argues that the democratic polity explains why it exists, why it is unable to control it, and finally how democracy in India is generating new mechanisms to combat all police and other corrupt practices. Chapter 10 by Garth den Heyer dissects the role of the Royal Solomon Islands Police Force (RSIPF) and the major reform issues the organization is facing within the context of the Solomon Islands civil conflict and in the wider context of the influence of corruption that is part of the island's culture.

In Section IV, the final set of case studies is concerned with Latin America and the Caribbean. Chapter 11 by Guillermina Seri inquires into the question of police corruption in Argentina as a salient sign of governmental implosion and a facilitator of the expansion of the captive state and considers the factors that are obstacles blocking the possibility of lasting police reforms. In Chapter 12, Nathan W. Pino surveys the historical, economic, and political context within which policing in Trinidad and Tobago (T&T) occurs, followed by an overview of the crime problems facing the country. Police corruption in T&T is documented, as well as the various reform efforts attempted over time, including more recent developments in policing in the country before concluding with an analysis of what is needed for sustainable and democratic reform of the police in the country.

The final part of the book, Section V, provides a thorough summary of all of the chapters of the book. It offers readers the ability to quickly scan a comprehensive description of the contents of each chapter.

Kempe Ronald Hope, Sr.

Editor

Kempe Ronald Hope, Sr., formerly with the United Nations, is the Director of the Policy Division, Development Practice International, Oakville, Ontario, Canada. Professor Hope has also been a technical adviser to several governments on anticorruption policy, including developing national anticorruption plans as well as police anticorruption and reform strategies, and a professor of development studies at several universities in North America, Africa, and the Caribbean. His books include *The Political Economy of Development in Kenya* (Bloomsbury Publishing, 2012); *Poverty, Livelihoods, and Governance in Africa: Fulfilling the Development Promise* (Palgrave Macmillan, 2008); *From Crisis to Renewal: Development Policy and Management in Africa* (Brill Publishers, 2002); *Corruption and Development in Africa: Lessons from Country Case Studies* (Palgrave Macmillan, 2000), with B. Chikulo; *AIDS and Development in Africa* (Haworth Press, 1999); *Public Administration and Policy in Botswana* (Juta Publishers, 1998), with G. Somolekae; *Structural Adjustment, Reconstruction and Development in Africa* (Ashgate Publishers, 1997); *African Political Economy: Contemporary Issues in Development* (M.E. Sharpe Publishers, 1997); *Development in the Third World: From Policy Failure to Policy Reform* (M.E. Sharpe Publishers, 1996); *Development Finance and the Development Process* (Greenwood Press, 1987); *Economic Development in the Caribbean* (Praeger Publishers, 1986); *Guyana: Politics and Development in an Emergent Socialist State* (Mosaic Press, 1986); *The Dynamics of Development and Development Administration* (Greenwood Press, 1984); and *Development Policy in Guyana: Planning, Finance, and Administration* (Westview Press, 1979).

Contributors

Joseph R.A. Ayee is a Professor and an independent consultant in Accra, Ghana. He is the first Emeka Anyaoku Visiting Professor of Commonwealth Studies, University of London; immediate past deputy vice chancellor, University of KwaZulu-Natal, South Africa; and a former rector, MountCrest University College, Accra. He was also head, Department of Political Science, and dean, Faculty of Social Studies, University of Ghana, Legon, from 1995 to 2000 and 2002 to 2009, respectively. His publications include *Changing Perspectives on the Social Sciences in Ghana* (Springer, 2014), with S. Agyei-Mensah and Abena Oduro; *The Public Policy Making Process in Ghana: How Politicians and Civil Servants Deal with Public Problems* (Edwin Mellen Press, 2012), with Frank Ohemeng, Barbara Carroll, and Alexander Bilson Darku; and *Reforming the African Public Sector: Retrospect and Prospects* (CODESRIA, 2008).

Garth den Heyer is an Inspector with the New Zealand Police. He is also a senior research fellow at the Police Foundation, Washington, DC. Dr. den Heyer has extensive experience in police and security sector reform issues in postconflict societies, including in the Solomon Islands, Timor-Leste, Bougainville, and Afghanistan. Dr. den Heyer is a qualitative researcher whose interests include police organizational reform and performance, and police service delivery effectiveness. His books include *Civilian Oversight of Police: Advancing Accountability in Law Enforcement* (CRC Press, 2015), with Tim Prenzler; *Economic Development, Crime, and Policing: Global Perspectives* (CRC Press, 2014), with Frederic Lemieux and Dilip K. Das; *The Role of Civilian Police in Peacekeeping: 1999–2007* (Police Foundation, 2012); and *Use of Econometric Modeling and Analysis to Support Operational Policing* (VDM Publishing, 2009).

Polycarp Ngufor Forkum holds the rank of Commissioner of Police and currently heads the Human Rights Unit of the National Advanced Police School–Yaoundé, Cameroon. He is a member of the World Bank think tank on governance and anticorruption and the South African–based African Policing Civilian Oversight Forum (APCOF). He doubles as both the Central African and the Cameroon Chapter president of the Association of the Alumni of the Centre for Human Rights–University of Pretoria. He is also the Cameroon Chapter president of the alumni of the African Centre for Peace and Security Training (ACPST) of the Institute of Security Studies (ISS–South Africa). His research interests include human rights and policing, public perception of the police, gender, peacebuilding, peacekeeping, conflict prevention/resolution, and governance (corruption). He is the author of *Police Corruption in Cameroon and Uganda: A Comparative Analysis* (Lambert Academic Publishing, 2012).

Dennis Lai Hang Hui is a Lecturer in the Department of Social Sciences at the Hong Kong Institute of Education, Hong Kong, China. His main research interests include police legitimacy and police accountability.

John Mukum Mbaku is a Brady Presidential Distinguished Professor of economics, the Willard L. Eccles Professor of economics, and a John S. Hinckley Fellow at Weber State University, Ogden, Utah. Professor Mbaku is also a nonresident senior fellow at the Brookings Institution, Washington, DC, and an attorney and counselor at law, licensed to practice in the supreme court of the State of Utah and the U.S. District Court for the District of Utah. His research interests are in public choice, constitutional political economy, sustainable development, law and development, international human rights, intellectual property, rights of indigenous groups, trade integration, and institutional reforms in Africa. His most recent books are *Governing the Nile River Basin: The Search for a New Legal Regime* (Brookings Institution Press, 2015), with Mwangi S. Kimenyi; *Corruption in Africa: Causes, Consequences, and Cleanups* (Lexington Books, 2010); *Multiparty Democracy and Political Change: Constraints to Democratization in Africa* (Africa World Press, 2006), with Julius Omozuanvbo Ihonvbere; and *Culture and Customs of Cameroon* (Greenwood Press, 2005).

Nathan W. Pino is a Professor of sociology at Texas State University, San Marcos, Texas, where he conducts research on international police reform efforts, sexual and other forms of extreme violence, and the attitudes and behaviors of college students. Professor Pino's books include *Globalization, Police Reform, and Development: Doing it the Western Way?* (Palgrave Macmillan, 2012), with Graham Ellison, and *Democratic Policing in Transitional and Developing Countries* (Ashgate, 2006), with Michael Wiatrowski.

Cornelis Roelofse is a Professor of criminology and criminal justice at the University of Limpopo, Polokwane, South Africa. Professor Roelofse is the deputy president of the All Africa Criminal Justice Society (a society that he launched in 2012); a board member of the Criminological and Victimological Society of Southern Africa, responsible for the portfolio of policing; and also a member of the Board of the Policing Association of Southern Africa. He is also a consultant on security and risk assessment and has advised a number of companies in South Africa and was chair of the 2010 International Police Executive Symposium (IPES) in Malta. Professor Roelofse is the subeditor of *Just Africa*—Journal of the All Africa Criminal Justice Society and serves on six other editorial boards in South Africa, and Western and Eastern Europe. He has published on security, policing, and crime prevention and has developed new theoretical perspectives such as reciprocal moral dualism for police behavior, encroachment theory on organized crime, and other theoretical developments in crime prevention.

Guillermina Seri is an Associate Professor in the Department of Political Science at Union College, Schenectady, New York. Professor Seri's research interests include policing, policing use of force, police discretion, executive/police prerogatives, discretionary power and governance, citizen security, democratic police reform, comparative politics, Latin American politics, democratization, and experiences with different forms of accountability, especially (but not only) throughout Latin America. She is the author of *Seguridad: Crime, Police Power, and Democracy in Argentina* (Bloomsbury Publishing, 2012).

Arvind Verma is an Associate Professor in the Department of Criminal Justice and Associate Director of the India Studies Program at Indiana University, Bloomington, Indiana. Professor Verma has also been a member in the Indian Police Service and served for many years in the state of Bihar, holding several senior positions in the organization. His research interests are in policing, criminal justice policy issues, Indian police, research methods, mathematical modeling, and geographical information systems. He is a consultant to the Bureau of Police Research and Development, Government of India, and a continental editor (Asia) for *Police Practice and Research: An International Journal.* His books include *Policing Muslim Communities: Comparative International Context* (Springer, 2012), with Farrukh B. Hakeem and M.R. Haberfeld; *Global Community Policing: Problems and Challenges* (CRC Press, Taylor & Francis Group, 2012), with Dilip K. Das and Manoj Abraham; *The New Khaki: The Evolving Nature of Policing in India* (CRC Press, Taylor & Francis Group, 2010); *Understanding the Police in India* (Lexis-Nexis Butterworth, 2009), with K.S. Subramanian; *Indian Police: A Critical Evaluation* (Regency Publications, 2005); *Police Mission: Challenges and Responses* (Scarecrow Press, 2003), with Dilip K. Das; and *Organized Crime: World Perspectives* (Prentice Hall, 2002), with Jay Albanes and Dilip K. Das.

Theoretical and Analytical Perspectives

I

An Analytical Perspective on Police Corruption and Police Reforms in Developing Societies

1

KEMPE RONALD HOPE, Sr.

Contents

What Is Police Corruption? 5
Causes of Police Corruption 8
    Recruitment and Training 9
    Resources 9
    Systems of Accountability 10
    Cultural Traditions 10
Key Indicators of Police Corruption 10
Consequences of Police Corruption 11
Controlling Police Corruption through Reforms 14
    Preventive Measures 15
        Recruitment and Selection Procedures 15
        Ethics and Integrity Training 16
        Capacity Development in Democratic Policing 18
        Use of Ethics and Integrity Officers 19
        Declaration of Assets, Property, and Liabilities and
        Lifestyle Audits 19
        Counteracting and Managing Conflicts of Interest 20
        Pay and Conditions of Service 21
        Good Conduct Recognition and Rewards 21
        Enhanced Command Accountability and Responsibility 22
        Use of Civilian Oversight Institutions 23
    Punitive Measures 25
        Increased Detection and Investigation 25
        Punishment as Deterrent 26
Conclusions 27
References 28

Police corruption exists in some form in almost all police services across the globe. However, in most developing societies, this corruption tends to be pervasive and generally reflects the prevailing extent of corruption in those societies at large and the failure or nonperformance of governance institutions in curbing such corruption. In fact, the extent and nature of police corruption in any developing society is a direct reflection of the state of corruption in that society. And because of the deleterious effects and consequences of police corruption in such societies, as shown in this book, police reforms have become an imperative and taken on added significance not only for improving policing to serve the interests of the public but also for enhancing the overall governance environment in said societies.

In fact, in many developing societies, police corruption has degenerated into lawless predatory policing that is defined here as the devotion of police activities primarily to the personal enrichment and self-preservation of the police themselves rather than to the protection of the public. The police therefore enforce law and order according to their own self-interest. Kaplan (2013, pp. 101–102) has illustrated this state of affairs in Nigeria, for example, as follows:

> Taxi drivers, market traders, and shopkeepers routinely encounter armed police officers demanding bribes. Victims who report a crime to the police discover that the police refuse to investigate unless the victim pays for the privilege. Meanwhile, criminals with thick wallets bribe the police to avoid arrest or prosecution, to influence the outcome of a criminal investigation, or even to turn the investigation against the victim. Senior police officers take a cut from the money extorted by junior officers. The same pattern of pervasive corruption and of governments unable to tackle it extends across much of the developing world.

Although police corruption is a form of police misconduct, corruption is different from other forms of police misconduct because of its principal motivation: achievement of personal/private or organizational gain or advantage. In that regard, it is therefore best to adopt a broad functional approach, rather than seeking to define police corruption in generic terms, and thereby encompass what is popularly understood by police corruption and corrupt police. As Kleinig (1996) notes, the advantage of this approach is that it enables many acts and practices that may never show themselves as corrupt to be included within a definition of police corruption, for example, doing what one is duty bound to do solely for personal advancement or private gain. It takes into consideration that motivation is the key to understanding police corruption (Kleinig 1996). The motivation behind an act is corrupt when the primary intention is to further private or organizational advantage.

What Is Police Corruption?

The broad functional definition of police corruption being applied in this work is the following: police corruption is any action or omission, a promise of any action or omission, or any attempt of action or omission committed by a police officer or a group of police officers, characterized by the police officer's misuse of the official position and motivated in significant part with the achievement of personal/private or organizational gain or advantage (Punch 1985, 2011; Kleinig 1996; Newburn 1999; Ivković 2005).

This way of defining police corruption goes beyond the usual quid-pro-quo assumption and thus allows us to include behavior that could be otherwise classified as extortion, robbery, burglary, theft, or overzealous policing with the aim of personal advancement (Wood 1997; Newburn 1999). Moreover, this broad functional definition acknowledges that police corruption can be identified as deviant, dishonest, improper, unethical, or criminal behavior by a police officer (Roebuck and Barker 1974; Prenzler 2009). In fact, as Williams (2002) notes, this broader approach can now include related offences, such as outrageous police shootings or incidents of brutality that blatantly violate human rights and that should also come under the rubric of corruption since they reflect a police culture that subverts official standards of accountability.

The best known typology of police corruption, as derived from Barker and Roebuck (1973), Roebuck and Barker (1974), Newburn (1999), and Punch (1985, 2011), is depicted in Table 1.1. Obviously, when police officers engage in corrupt activities without the cover of their police role, they are merely criminals. Police corruption, as it is generally accepted, necessarily involves an abuse of position, and what is corrupted is the special trust invested in the occupation of *police officer* and therefore the special trust enjoyed by all police officers. The typology of police corruption can be further grouped into categories as follows: (1) scale and organization, (2) predatory forms, (3) subversion of justice, and (4) gifts and discounts. However, as argued by Neild (2007, p. 3), "the principal array of police corruption is probably more easily classified and understood in terms of the motives, ends, and the scale of corruption," and this is presented in Table 1.2.

A number of the behaviors exhibited in Table 1.2 enter into more than one column, reflecting the wide variety in level of gain, means and actors involved, and beneficiaries of police corruption. There has also been a further division of corrupt police officers in general into two lots. In one lot, there are the so-called *grass eaters* who are passively corrupt police officers that engage in minor (low-level or petty) corruption such as accepting unsolicited money (Knapp 1972; Ross 2012). These kinds of actions are usually reactive (opportunistic ethical violations) and are usually not frowned upon by other police

Table 1.1   Types and Dimensions of Police Corruption

Type	Dimensions
Corruption of authority	When an officer receives some form of material gain by virtue of their position as a police officer without necessarily violating the law *per se*. For example, free drinks, meals, services, or discounts.
Kickbacks	Receipt of goods, services, or money for referring business to particular individuals or companies, in tendering processes, and for appointment of recruits.
Opportunistic theft	Stealing from arrestees, traffic accident victims, crime victims, and the bodies or property of deceased citizens.
Shakedowns or extortion	Acceptance of a bribe for not following through a real or threatened criminal violation. For example, a traffic officer accepts a cash payment in order not to issue a legitimate or threatened speeding fine.
Protection of illegal activities	Police protection of those engaged in illegal activities (e.g., prostitution, drugs, pornography) enabling the business to continue to operate.
The fix	Undermining of criminal investigations or proceedings, or the deliberate loss of police files, dockets, or evidence.
Direct criminal activities	A police officer commits a crime against a person or persons or property (such as embezzlement) for personal gain in clear violation of both police service and criminal norms.
Internal payoffs	Prerogatives available to police officers (e.g., holidays, shift allocations, promotions) are bought, bartered, and sold.
Flaking and padding	Planting of or adding to evidence such as in narcotics cases.

Sources: Slightly modified from Barker, T. and Roebuck, J.B., *An Empirical Typology of Police Corruption*, Thomas, Springfield, IL, 1973; Roebuck, J.B. and Barker, T., *Soc. Probl.*, 21(3), 423, 1974; Punch, M., *Conduct Unbecoming: The Social Construction of Police Deviance and Control*, Tavistock, London, U.K., 1985; Punch, M., *Police Corruption: Deviance, Accountability and Reform in Policing*, Routledge, Abingdon, U.K., 2011; Newburn, T., *Understanding and Preventing Police Corruption: Lessons from the Literature*, Police Research Series Paper 110, Home Office, London, U.K., 1999.

officers. In the other lot, there are the *meat eaters* who are police officers that actively engage in major (grand) corruption, such as drug dealing crimes or participating in shakedowns, on a regular basis, and they are proactive in their endeavors (Knapp 1972; Punch 2011; Ross 2012).

Both the historical and current literature show that when confronted with allegations of corruption for which there is much supporting evidence, police agencies tend to generally claim that the problem is limited to a small number of corrupt officers who are quite unrepresentative of the wider ethical standards exhibited by the police service as a whole (Newburn 1999; Ross 2012). This is the *bad apples* theory or "pockets of corruption" theory and is relatively true in many police services. However, whatever the magnitude, where there is police corruption, it also leaves a negative taint against the reputation of those officers with high moral standards and integrity as public

Table 1.2   Classification and Examples of Corrupt Police Behaviors

Petty Individual Corruption	Bureaucratic Corruption	Criminal Corruption	Political Corruption
Minor bribes from ordinary civilians (traffic police in particular)	Contracting and purchasing kickbacks, sweetheart deals, etc.	Bribes or kickbacks from known criminals	Manipulating criminal investigations
Gifts and free services	Theft of assets and police resources including salaries, benefits, and lower-rank pay	Extorting regular payoffs from criminal groups/gangs, etc.	Initiating false investigations
Selling information such as criminal files		Providing support for criminal activities with equipment, information, cover-ups, etc.	Providing confidential information to politicians
"Losing" court dockets, evidence, etc.	Selling information such as criminal files		
Theft while searching		Direct participation in crime and organized crime (drug trafficking, kidnapping rings, arrest for ransom)	Suppressing freedom of speech and association (such as public demonstrations and strikes)
Keeping seized contraband	"Losing" court dockets, criminal records, evidence, etc.		Undertaking or covering up extrajudicial killings
Helping prisoners escape	Irregular and unlawful issuing of gun licenses and other permits	Theft of seized contraband	
Use of police resources for personal matters (such as police vehicles used to run family errands)	Undermining internal investigations and discipline	Protection of illegal economic activities (such as resource extraction)	Suppressing political dissent/freedom of information/legitimate political party activities
	Bribes and kickbacks required for recruitment, graduation from training, assignments, and promotions		Leaking information to illegal groups

Source: Neild, R., *USAID Program Brief: Anticorruption and Police Integrity*, USAID, Washington, DC, 2007, p. 3.

perception tends not to make a distinction between the two types of officers, those that are corrupt and those that are not. In fact, public perception tends to see beyond the *bad apples* and look at where it occurs or is nurtured: the barrel. Hence, for the public it is not just a matter of *bad apples* but one of a *rotten barrel*. Consequently, police corruption cannot simply be dismissed by the brass as the product of a few *bad apples* as an easy way out in explaining corruption in a police service (Newburn 1999; Swope 2001; Loree, 2006; Ross 2012).

Moreover, police officers are held to a higher standard of behavior by society because they are stewards of the public trust and are empowered to lawfully apply force and they can also remove constitutional privileges when lawfully justified. They take an oath of office, are expected to comply with professional codes of ethics, and are subject to various laws, rules, regulations, and standing orders. Yet police corruption can be pervasive, continuing, and not bounded by rank. In fact, irrespective of rank, some areas of policing (such as traffic law enforcement and drug law enforcement) are more prone to corruption than others.

From the foregoing, we can summarize as follows:

- Police corruption is a continuing international problem. There is evidence of corrupt practices from all stages of police history across the globe.
- Police corruption can be pervasive. Corrupt practices are found in some form in a great many police services in all societies.
- Police corruption is not simply a problem of the lower ranks. Corruption has been found at all levels of a police organization.
- Police corruption can cover a wide number of activities.
- There are some forms of policing, or areas of a police organization, which are more at risk of corruption (Newburn 1999; Loree 2006; Neild 2007).

Causes of Police Corruption

As noted by Newburn (1999), the literature has remained fairly consistent in identifying the causes of police corruption in developed societies as being the function of two groups of causal factors, namely, (1) constant factors and (2) variable factors. These two factors were first identified by Sherman (1974). The constant factors are those invariable or fixed factors that facilitate corruption, such as discretion and peer group secrecy; and the variable factors vary with societal norms and circumstances and influence the constant factors, such as organizational structure and opportunities for corruption.

However, in developing societies, the causes of police corruption are a lot less complicated and much more obvious to any citizen of those societies or any keen outside observer. In developing societies, police corruption tends to arise primarily from deficiencies in four major areas: (1) recruitment and training, (2) resources, (3) systems of accountability, and (4) cultural traditions (Williams 2002).

Recruitment and Training

Police services in which corruption is rife generally have weaknesses in recruitment and training. Consequently, some recruits bring or succumb to dangerous criminal tendencies that undermine confidence in law enforcement and prove not to be a good fit for police duty. In many developing societies, police recruitment itself is a corrupt activity where huge sums of money change hands through influence peddlers or in direct payments to senior police officers who are expected to guarantee recruitment and selection of those who are willing to pay bribes or on whose behalf bribes are paid. Some police services also lack the capacity and capability to conduct thorough background checks or to administer psychological assessments to determine the suitability of recruits for police work. Nyarko (2014), for example, found that a major contributory factor to corruption in the Ghana Police Service is the service's failure to thoroughly investigate the background of those being recruited and to perform psychological tests that measure their stability for employment as police officers.

Training, and particularly ethics and human rights training, is also another area that is very deficient in most police academies and other training institutions in developing societies. There isn't enough attention paid to the type of training that can instill the necessary ethics the public expects police officers to always display. Yet, ethics training is necessary to provide police trainees with an understanding of ethics and ethical behavior as it affects daily policing in their societies and to instill high standards of honesty, integrity, and ethical behavior when performing their policing duties.

Resources

The lack of resources, such as adequate pay and the basic equipment to function as police officers, for example, can lead to some of those police officers engaging in corruption (Neild 2007). In Mexico, low pay and the opportunity to make money were credited as the principal factors responsible for the police engaging in graft, bribery, and extortion (Botello and Rivera 2000; Williams 2002). Similarly, in India it was found that the salary structure and nature and hours of duty are considerably responsible for police corruption (Lamani and Venumadhava 2013). For Nigeria, Vogl (2012) reported that most of the country's policemen earn less than US $200 a month and many have to pay for their own fuel and telephones. Also for Nigeria, Ojo (2014) determined that poor pay and the lack of modern policing equipment were major contributory factors to police corruption.

Systems of Accountability

The key issue here is whether there are adequate controls over police officers, and are there accountability systems to effectively stem police corruption? To a major extent, police corruption reflects a lack of command and leadership accountability. Basically, police corruption emerges where supervisors turn a blind eye to the warning signals of police misconduct (negligence) or engage in such misconduct themselves (complicity) (Williams 2002). It then prospers in environments where civilian oversight is inept.

Cultural Traditions

In some developing societies, cultural mores have discouraged professional police standards from developing. As a result, the police tend to lack a strong tradition in law enforcement beyond self-aggrandizement (Williams 2002). Bayley and Perito (2011, p. 6) have observed, for example, that: "In developing countries… bribery becomes a transaction fee for doing any business with the police. It afflicts everyone, not just criminals, and it implicates all police officers." Moreover, many police services have become captive of their own organizational culture where conformity to said organizational culture has become much more important than demonstrating ethical behavior. Prenzler (2009, p.23) has noted that one "main area of theory related to police misconduct concerns the concept of organizational culture," and Verma (1999), in a study of India, found that the extensive police corruption in that country is embedded in the culture and organizational norms that have encouraged and sustained venal practices.

Key Indicators of Police Corruption

One of the best known indicators of police corruption is derived from the perception surveys undertaken by Transparency International (TI). Those surveys generally indicate that citizens in a wide variety of developing societies perceive corruption and overall misconduct in their police as one of the principal corruption problems in their societies. Table 1.3 provides a selected list of those societies where the police are perceived as the most corrupt institution in said societies based on 2013 data. The perception scores are based on a scale of 1–5, where 1 means not at all corrupt and 5 means extremely corrupt. The global aggregated perception score is also provided for comparison purposes.

Table 1.3   Selected Developing Societies Where the Police Are Perceived as the Most Corrupt Institution, 2013

Developing Society	Perception Score	Developing Society	Perception Score
Bangladesh	3.9	Papua New Guinea	4.4
Cameroon	4.4	Philippines	4.0
Ghana	4.7	Sierra Leone	4.3
Indonesia	4.5	Solomon Islands	4.4
Jamaica	4.5	South Africa	4.4
Kenya	4.8	Sri Lanka	3.8
Kyrgyzstan	4.6	Tanzania	4.5
Liberia	4.8	Uganda	4.5
Malawi	4.7	Venezuela	4.4
Malaysia	4.0	Zambia	4.7
Mexico	4.6	Zimbabwe	4.5
Mozambique	4.4	Global	3.7

Source: TI (Transparency International), *Global Corruption Barometer 2013*, TI, Berlin, Germany, 2013, pp. 35–38.

Another popular indicator of police corruption is bribery. Here again TI leads the way in producing credible data through its regional and country surveys. Most country and regional bribery indices show that the police are the leading institution in demanding and accepting bribes when compared to other institutions (TI 2013). These bribery indices are compiled from surveys that capture bribery corruption as experienced by ordinary citizens in their interaction with officials of both public and private organizations. Among the most comprehensive and current bribery indices available are those for the East African region. In that region, the share of bribery (an indicator that measures the proportion of actual bribes paid to an institution as a percentage of all the bribes reported to have been paid by the sampled population) is generally highest among the police. Figure 1.1 shows the aggregate bribery index for the police for the period 2010–2014 illustrating that the police in East Africa are among the most bribery prone of the institutions or sectors in the region. The aggregate bribery index is comprised of likelihood, prevalence, impact of bribery, share of bribe, and the average amount that are combined into one indicator. This indicator is scaled from 0 to 100, with 100 being the worst score (TI-Kenya 2012, 2013, 2014).

Consequences of Police Corruption

Acts of corruption by people in or with power have long shaken public faith in government, but the loss of public faith is particularly acute when those acts

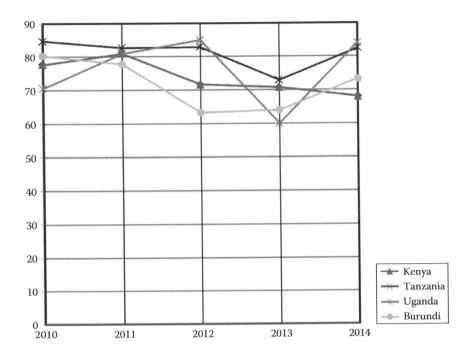

Figure 1.1 Police Aggregate Bribery Index for East African Countries, 2010–2014. (Author based on data from TI (Transparency International)—Kenya, *The East African Bribery Index 2010*, TI-Kenya, Nairobi, Kenya, 2010; TI (Transparency International)—Kenya, *The East African Bribery Index 2011*, TI-Kenya, Nairobi, Kenya, 2011; TI (Transparency International)—Kenya, *The East African Bribery Index 2012*, TI-Kenya, Nairobi, Kenya, 2012; TI (Transparency International)—Kenya, *The East African Bribery Index 2013*, TI-Kenya, Nairobi, Kenya, 2013; TI (Transparency International)—Kenya, *The East African Bribery Index 2014*, TI-Kenya, Nairobi, Kenya, 2014.)

involve the police. That is so because the public relies on the police to uphold the law, protect the community, and assist it in times of need. The police are also the most visible arm of government for most citizens and a yardstick by which they measure authority. When a police officer acts illegally, he or she dishonors both himself or herself and the law and the justice system he or she represents (Newburn 1999; Bayley 2002; Loree 2006). Therefore, as Ivković (2005, p. 3) observed, "the problem of police corruption extends well beyond the rule-violating behavior of a few officers. Police corruption distorts police work, encourages the code of silence, promotes resistance to accountability, and undermines the legitimacy of the police and the government."

Moreover, and as Beyerle (2014, p. 187) observes, "police corruption is a particularly destructive form of injustice and oppression that undermines the rule of law, human rights, and the legitimacy of the State. Police corruption harms the lives of regular people, creating conditions of fear and impunity in dictatorships and fragile states, as well as in emerging and established democracies." The costs of police corruption are therefore high. Police corruption erodes the public trust and its cooperation in crime prevention, detection, and investigation; it diverts resources and thwarts operational capacity; it sustains organized crime and the victimization of vulnerable groups (Loree 2006). The police can and should investigate corruption cases and enforce anticorruption laws, yet if they themselves are corrupt, government-wide anticorruption efforts may be profoundly crippled. When the police build corrupt political alliances, they may contribute to antidemocratic practices (Neild 2007).

Consequently, there is considerable agreement, and based on lessons learned from many countries, that the most severe consequences of police corruption are to be found in its negative impact on the relationship between the police and the public—the community. Perceptions, attitudes, and relationships are affected whether the corruption is low level but well known in the community, and involves the acceptance of gratuities or minor kickbacks or whether it is the cause of major, well-publicized incidents. Police corruption, widely reported, can have a significant impact on public perception and confidence in the police.

In fact, public sector corruption, including police corruption, has not only a financial impact on taxpayers, but more importantly, it has a significant negative impact on the legitimacy of government in the eyes of citizens (Loree 2006; Neild 2007). In societies that purport or aspire to be democratic, this is particularly negative and trust in politics and politicians suffers accordingly. Because of the unique powers of the police in democratic societies, accorded them by the citizens through their government, police corruption is even more significant in the eyes of citizens. When police act beyond the law, they lose their moral authority (Bayley 2002). Police corruption may also have an impact on the institutions of government (Loree 2006). When there is an erosion of public confidence in the police, the ability for government to fulfill its legitimate aims also becomes decimated and nation-building suffers (Harrison 1999; Loree 2006; Bayley and Perito 2011). "The maintenance of public confidence in the police is important in democratic societies and police corruption can seriously threaten it" (Punch 2000, p. 322).

As Loree (2006, p. 19) noted, the results of studies "that examined how the public viewed police gratuities support the claim that acceptance of gratuities undermines confidence in the impartiality of the police and is incompatible with the concept of democratic policing." The public does expect high standards of conduct from the police in democratic societies. It follows therefore that a professional police service that expects to maintain its legitimacy must be prepared willingly to accept their obligation to adhere to these high standards and not overlook the fundamental notion that the police are empowered by the community to serve the community (Crooke 2001; Loree 2006).

Police corruption can also increase the crime rate and may even contribute to the development of large-scale organized crime (Williams 2002). The police corruption–crime nexus allows increased consumption of illegal services (such as prostitution) and goods (such as drugs, illegal alcohol) (Andvig and Fjeldstad 2008). Furthermore, this nexus can have a negative impact on economic growth by discouraging foreign direct investment as a country's international reputation is stained (Hope 2012, 2014).

Finally, in terms of consequences, police corruption at any level, but especially low-level corruption by individual officers, may very well affect other unit or team members who do not agree but who feel the cultural pressure of the "code of silence" not to speak out since loyalty to fellow officers tends to be a key feature of police culture, irrespective of whether criminality is involved (Skolnick 2002, 2008; Williams 2002; Westmarland 2005; Prenzler 2009; Quinn 2011). The code of silence—sometimes called a blue wall, curtain, cocoon of silence, or the blue code of silence—refers to a police subculture of keeping silent regarding fellow officers' unethical behavior. This is a strong informal agreement among police officers that no officer will report the misconduct of a fellow officer, or claim any knowledge of such misconduct, or even cooperate with any investigations against them. In this way, secrecy becomes a protective armor shielding the police service as a whole from public knowledge of infractions. According to Skolnick (2002, 2008), such an unrecorded code has been noted as a feature of policing across continents, wherever scholars or commissions of inquiry have studied police corruption. Due to this code of silence, too many good police officers have learned to tolerate bad police officers and too many bad apples have escaped consequences as a result (Quinn 2011). Consequently, the work of the unit may well be compromised as individuals lose trust and confidence in each other. In the worst case, others may be drawn into the process, thereby exacerbating the problem for the organization and for the community.

Controlling Police Corruption through Reforms

To mitigate the effects of police corruption, many developing societies have embarked on police corruption control measures usually through police reform programs. These reform programs, or recommendations for such programs, usually entail a combination of preventive and punitive measures that are, in turn, classified as internal controls or external oversight approaches, and their objectives are generally intended to accomplish, among other things, the following:

- To demonstrate zero tolerance for police corruption
- To prevent, as much as possible, the occurrence of police corruption and unethical behavior within the police service culture and organization at all levels
- To articulate an ethics and integrity framework into anticorruption objectives to influence and instill a robust corruption prevention culture in the police
- To improve the police service's image and reputation and build community confidence domestically and internationally through a demonstrated fight against corruption
- To provide and refine standards and processes to investigate and manage police corruption and unethical behavior
- To provide guidance on how the police service aims to counter corruption among its officers
- To influence the maintenance of sustained political will and leadership support as the most important factors for success in addressing the police corruption problem

Preventive Measures

The primary goal of the preventive measures to police corruption is to change the underlying structures that encourage corruption and to create an institutional environment that decreases incentives and opportunities for corrupt practices at all levels of the police service. Preventive measures are designed to avoid deliberate or unintended police corruption events or results. The key preventive measures that have been implemented, or recommended for implementation, tend to revolve around (1) recruitment and selection procedures, (2) ethics and integrity training, (3) capacity development in democratic policing, (4) the use of ethics and integrity officers (EIOs), (5) asset declarations and lifestyle audits, (6) counteracting and managing conflicts of interest, (7) pay and conditions of service, (8) good conduct and recognition rewards, (9) enhanced command accountability and responsibility, and (10) use of civilian oversight institutions.

Recruitment and Selection Procedures

The basic approach here has been to take initiatives to improve the screening and selection methods and standards of police recruits. Appointment procedures, in general, have been made much more open, fair, based on merit, and transparent to recruit the candidates with the highest professional qualifications and ethical standards and remove some of the influence peddling and bribery that occurs for gaining recruitment or appointment. Lessons learnt from South Africa and Singapore, for example, point to the importance of an open, fair, transparent, and gender-neutral recruitment process (Quah 2006, 2014; Newham and Faull 2011). Other global evidence also shows that police officers with the lowest incidence of misconduct scored highest on background checks at the time of their recruitment, while those with the highest incidence of misconduct scored lowest on background checks at the time of their recruitment (Roberg and Kuykendall 1993; Quah 2006). This perhaps suggests the need for higher cutoff background scores for police recruits.

As part of the process of recruiting new police officers, the selection procedures and policies have also become important elements of police reforms in developing societies. Inadequate screening criteria for candidates can, and have, resulted in some police officers lacking the skills or incentives to comply with high standards of integrity. This has led to the introduction of new or improved background checks on candidates before they are admitted into the police services. A thorough background check/investigation is one of the most important aspects of the selection process as it is a means of assessing the character and general suitability of a candidate for police work as determined by past experience and lifestyle (Roberg and Kuykendall 1993). Basically, the background check or investigation is based on the extensive personal history provided by the candidate or obtained through other legal and legitimate sources, which enables a selection committee to assess whether the candidate would be honest and reliable and make a contribution to the police service if he or she is recruited (Roberg and Kuykendall 1993). Family and personal background and lifestyle factors, relationships, and so on that could make a police officer susceptible to corruption or compromise the officer are considered.

The use of background checks is, undoubtedly, a form of vetting. This type of police vetting can be regarded as assessing integrity to determine suitability for employment as a police officer. Some police services have also developed and administer integrity-based psychological assessments and/or psychometric tests (DCAF 2012). These assessments or tests are used as an additional tool to assist with selection. International best practice and lessons learned indicate that such assessments have been shown to provide useful and objective information about a candidate and can help identify those most and least suited to the complex job of policing. They allow for the screening of applicants to determine personality factors that might be related to, or predict, corrupt behavior.

Ethics and Integrity Training

Training is an integral part of the process of becoming a police officer and progressing through the ranks as an ethical police officer. Many police services have either developed, revamped, or reemphasized their ethics and integrity modules of their training of recruits. Similarly, new ethics and integrity training programs have been developed for senior police officers as well as other ranks. Indeed, ongoing ethical training, linked to the realities of police work in the respective developing societies, is necessary if there is to be a significant long-term impact on mitigating police corruption. The learning goals are to ensure that the police employees have high standards of honesty, integrity, and ethical behavior when performing their policing duties and to make unambiguously clear to all trainees that even one act of unethical behavior can negatively reflect not only their own professional image but also on that of the entire police service.

In that regard, many reputable police training institutions, such as the European Police College (CEPOL), offer ethics training to police officers from around the globe. One such very credible and prestigious course offered by CEPOL is the Common Curriculum on Police Ethics and Corruption (CCPEC). The CCPEC focuses on the knowledge, attitudes, and skills of police officers and is divided into four sections: (1) role of police in a democratic society, (2) position of ethics in the police organization and day-to-day police work, (3) managing police ethics and prevention of corruption, and (4) risk management in the field of police ethics and prevention of corruption (CEPOL 2014).

The foregoing notwithstanding, training alone is not sufficient to ensure that actual police practice will accord with policy and professional standards (Punch 2000). Lessons of experience have shown that the leadership provided by senior police officers, and the management and supervision of police staff, are also vital factors (Ayres and Corderman 2008). Particularly in the developing society context, more senior officers in the hierarchy need to provide role models for their juniors and demonstrate the required ethical standards in their everyday work. They need to make it clear that they also expect their subordinates to act in accordance with these ethical standards and they need to be active in monitoring that all police conduct complies with these ethical standards and with human rights (den Boer and Pyo 2011).

Nonetheless, ethics training will provide a critical and necessary element of the reforms geared at curtailing unethical police behavior. Consequently, although ethics training cannot serve as a substitute for screening in the hiring process or an individual police employee's personality or character, it can reinforce the values and expectations of a police service and the public and thus strengthen decision making by identifying ethical dilemmas and problem-solving approaches. Moreover, best international practice and further research surveys continue to indicate that only properly trained police officers are able to adequately respond to ethical dilemmas of their profession. Not only do they need to be well acquainted with the principles of police ethics and trained in ethical decision making, they also need clear standards of ethical conduct in their profession (den Boer and Pyo 2011).

As Roelofse (2012) also notes, in assessing police behavior in South Africa, the importance of ethics training for the police in promoting moral behavior is that it further leads to the ideal situation of the police and society working in a reciprocal beneficial relationship to enhance service delivery and morality.

Capacity Development in Democratic Policing

Capacity development is defined here as the enhancement of the competency of individuals and institutions to engage in activities in a sustainable manner for positive development impacts. It is the process whereby people, organizations, and society as a whole unleash, strengthen, create, adapt, and maintain capacity, over time, in specific areas (Hope 2011). Investing in capacity development must now become a critical aspect of the reforms for democratic policing in developing societies, to improve capacity for what can be recognized as a key activity for farsightedness and sustainability in the quest to control police corruption.

The basic tenets of democratic policing require the police to, among other things, uphold the law, be accountable to democratic oversight institutions outside their organization that are specifically designated and empowered to regulate police activity, be accountable to the communities they serve, be ethical and transparent in their activities, give the highest operational priority to protecting the safety and rights of individuals, be representative of the community it serves, and seek to build professional skills and conditions of service that support efficient and respectful service delivery to the public (Stone and Ward 2000; Bayley 2001, 2002, 2006; Pino and Wiatrowski 2006; OSCE 2011). In other words, democratic policing entails appropriate action that involves finding a balance between serving the State (which is also required to serve the public interest), serving the public, and police professionalism (Bayley 2006; den Boer and Pyo 2011; UNODC 2011; DCAF 2012).

When grounded in human rights, it is the preferred model championed by virtually all groups, organizations, and experts involved in or promoting police reforms (Ellison and Pino 2012). Moreover, as also averred by Ellison and Pino (2012, p. 2),

> A willingness to conform to the principles of democratic policing in... is important as an end in itself—to prevent human rights abuses, provide a minimal level of citizen security and so forth, but also more intangibly in that fair and effective policing contributes to the very foundations of political order that democratic freedoms so often depend.

It is this salient importance of democratic policing that requires capacity development in developing societies. In societies such as those in Asia, democratic policing has been one of the biggest objectives as well as one of the most controversial issues for a long time (den Boer and Pyo 2011).

To accept and implement the tenets of democratic policing therefore requires the development of capacity in said democratic policing. This would allow the police to send a strong signal to all within and outside the police service that "because of their high professional standards—they will perform well, be open and approachable, and not tolerate the abuse of power, corruption, neglect of duty ... or any misconduct, nor will they cover up any acts of wrongdoing" (OSCE 2011, p. 29).

Use of Ethics and Integrity Officers

EIOs have been introduced in some police anticorruption reform programs in many developing societies and usually in the framework of an internal affairs unit, internal affairs branch/bureau, internal affairs office, or office of professional standards, which now exist to enact a measure of accountability and quality control over police officers and their actions including through investigations and prosecutions. Information comes to these institutions through civilian review boards, public complaints, and the criminal investigations of officers. Violations pertain to written policies, codes of conduct, procedures, and criminal laws (Ross 2012). In many cases, like in Kenya, these units, branches, bureaus, or offices are also decentralized or required to be decentralized to regions outside of capital and commercial cities.

Declaration of Assets, Property, and Liabilities and Lifestyle Audits

Corruption in any employment sector, like terrorism, thrives on a lack of reliable information. Consequently, many police services such as Singapore, Jamaica, and India, for example, are now turning to more robust collection of information using the declaration of assets, property, and liabilities (usually referred to simply as asset declaration, declaration of indebtedness, or financial disclosure) as a significant tool for preventing police corruption. The principles underlying these declarations, in international best practice as they apply to the police, are (1) to increase transparency and the trust of citizens in the police, by disclosing information about assets that shows they have nothing to hide; (2) to help police managers prevent conflicts of interest among police officers and to resolve such situations when they arise, in order to promote integrity within the police; and (3) to monitor wealth variations of individual police officers, in order to dissuade them from misconduct and protect them from false accusations, and to help clarify the full scope of illicit enrichment or other illegal activities by providing additional evidence (OECD 2011).

Consistent with asset, indebtedness, and financial declarations are lifestyle audits. These audits will continue to be used and the information provided in the assets and financial declarations will be taken into comparative consideration. A lifestyle audit can be simply defined as a study, or the tests

that are performed, to determine if the lifestyle of an employee is commensurate with that person's known income stream (Powell n.d.). It is essentially an
amalgamation of reports from a variety of sources and databases that would
provide management as well as investigators with a snapshot into certain
aspects of the life of an employee (Powell n.d.). Some of the areas covered
in a basic lifestyle audit include properties, motor vehicles, and company
registrar information. These areas are usually publicly available data that
anyone can access. Sometimes, the only clue to illicit activities is a sudden
unexplained change in an employee's lifestyle. Lifestyle audits are, therefore, a critical management tool to identify police employees who, based on
extravagant lifestyles, may potentially be engaging in corrupt or other illicit
activities. These audits are a legitimate corruption prevention and detection
mechanism.

Counteracting and Managing Conflicts of Interest

A conflict of interest (COI) is defined here to mean a situation that has the
potential to undermine the impartiality of a police service employee because
of the possibility of a clash between that employee's self-interest and professional interest or public interest. It is therefore a situation in which a police
service employee is in a position to be influenced, or appears to be influenced, by his or her private interests, when doing his or her job. A COI can
involve avoiding personal disadvantage as well as gaining personal advantage
(NSWPIC 2012). In other words, it is where police personnel have private-
capacity interests that could improperly influence the performance of their
official duties and responsibilities. That is, a COI may allow a police employee
to avoid a loss, expense, or something else that has a negative impact on his
or her personal or private interests.

Many police services in developing societies now have COI policies in
place. In Hong Kong, for instance, members of the police, and their supervisors, are required to be aware of potential conflicts of interest that may
arise when their private interests compete or conflict with the interests of
the police force or their official duties. Officers are also required to formally
declare all such interests (HKPF 2009).

An effective police COI policy entails a framework that allows a police
employee to deal with conflicts of interest by being able to (1) identify the
conflict, (2) avoid the conflict (where practical), (3) report the conflict,
(4) cooperate in the management of the conflict, and (5) monitor the conflict until it is resolved with a supervisor. In each of these stages, there is a
responsibility on the police employee (as the person with the COI) to take
appropriate action to deal with the conflict in the public interest. However,
while it remains the responsibility of the individual police employee to identify conflicts of interest, other circumstances may lead to the identification
of a COI including complaint investigations, information from colleagues,

other intelligence holdings and investigations, and corruption prevention strategies.

Pay and Conditions of Service

Although there have been recent and ongoing efforts to improve the pay and working conditions of police officers in developing societies, these are still generally regarded as inadequate. Where such inadequacies exist, they provide negative incentives to police officers and there is an increased risk of widespread corruption. One of the most basic conditions proven to be related to police corruption is salary (Neild 2007). If police officers are not paid proper salaries and have poor benefits (e.g., housing), there is a greater likelihood of corruption. Therefore, police salaries should be commensurate with the skills required for their assigned tasks and the inherent risks involved. Low police salaries also contribute to low esteem and lack of motivation.

In that regard, one of the key tools required for police reforms in developing societies and to aid in tackling the police bribery problem, in particular, is to regularly review and improve salaries and benefits. Pay increases should focus, in particular, on the worst paid lower ranks and try to reduce undue wage differentials between senior and junior police officers. This need for better paid police officers has been recognized by several analyses and should be given more attention by the authorities in developing societies (see, e.g., Neild 2007; Hope 2013; Quah 2014).

Also related to conditions of service, and a matter that also significantly affects police morale, is the need for appropriate resources and assets to be provided so that police officers can meaningfully undertake their duties. For example, in some police services, the police lack proper communication gear such as two-way radios. Many police officers then have to use their own phones at their own cost to conduct police business. These are work survival tactics at their own expense, yet they are to be held accountable. This, in turn, leads them to rationalize their need to subsidize their existence through the taking of bribes. It is a state of affairs that can only be mitigated through the authorities giving priority to improved police budgets or donors making equipment contributions to these police services.

Good Conduct Recognition and Rewards

Systems of recognition and rewards for good conduct are also being used or have been recommended for use by police services in developing societies through the use of a recognition and reward policy (RRP). This is intended to serve as the opposite of punishment as a deterrent that is discussed below. Where police officers are found to have behaved and acted with integrity and professionalism, they will be rewarded. As Quah (2014) notes, in the context of Singapore, to minimize corruption and deter those police officers who are not involved in corrupt practices from doing so, honest and incorruptible officers must be recognized and rewarded. For example, documented refusal to accept a bribe or refusal to engage in any other corrupt or unethical conduct will or should be recognized and rewarded. Rewards include or should include, among other things, good conduct letters, medals and certificates, salary increments, and potential promotion depending on the nature and scale of the situation to which an officer or officers reacted to uphold their integrity and professionalism and that of their police service.

The RRP must or should also provide an opportunity to recognize police officers who deliver excellent service and go the extra mile in an ethical manner. It must serve to reward behavior that serves the development of a culture of integrity and no tolerance of unethical behavior of any kind. The standards to be contained in a RRP must or should provide the framework for recognizing and rewarding police officers to ensure that the policy is applied fairly and consistently across a given police service. It must or should be designed to ensure that best use is made of recognition and reward initiatives in the fight against police corruption and to motivate police officers and improve their morale. Police officers who are recognized and rewarded will represent good examples of what can be achieved with good behavior and act as role models to others. When police supervisors or commanders emphasize and reinforce specific behaviors, police officers have a better understanding of how to repeat their successes, maximize rewards, and avoid unethical behaviors and failures.

Enhanced Command Accountability and Responsibility

Accountability and responsibility are critical elements of democratic policing and for gaining police legitimacy and public trust in the police. Command accountability and responsibility are key aspects of the means to control police corruption because they reinforce the significance of leadership and, particularly so, given that the police, just like any other disciplined service, is regimental in adherence to the ranking order. Command accountability and responsibility must therefore be enhanced.

Command accountability—which also entails command responsibility—means that commanders (however defined) are accountable for everything done or failed to be done under their command (Doty and Doty 2012). That means being accountable for both negative and positive consequences. A commander can delegate authority, for example, but not responsibility. Authority refers to who is in charge, while responsibility refers to who is accountable (Doty and Doty 2012). Police commanders have a responsibility to set a command climate wherein subordinates will act ethically even in the absence of their commanders. Consequently, all police commanders should be acutely aware that everything they say (or don't say) and do (or don't do) is being seen and internalized by their subordinates (Doty and Doty 2012).

They must therefore lead by example. Command accountability and responsibility illustrate where the buck stops on matters of police ethics and integrity. Moreover, as Bayley and Perito (2011, p. 10) have so eloquently observed:

> Reform starts at the top; it does not percolate up from the bottom. If the top leadership in the police does not visibly and persistently lead reform, then change will not occur. Leaders must articulate what is expected, create opportunities to reinforce the message… throughout the organization, especially with the rank and file, and raise public expectations about what police practices will be. Even in the face of significant contextual obstacles, managerial insistence on change, coupled with discipline, can change traditional behavior. This requires senior leaders to accept responsibility for organizational behavior, never excusing endemic corruption as being the fault of a few "bad apples". It follows that all supervising officers, especially those on the front line, must be held to account for the misbehavior of their subordinates. Police organizations are quasi-military; rank matters and directions are commands.

Undoubtedly, there is less corruption and there is a stimulation of ethical conduct when the police leadership insists on compliance with ethical standards in their organization. As observed by Calderon and Hernandez-Figueroa (2013) and Crawshaw et al. (1998), the crucial task of police leaders is to command and manage police organizations so that they become and remain driven by an ethos of excellence; an ethos that is conducive to lawful and ethical behavior, humanity, and high standards of professional competence; and an ethos that is hostile to the notion of corruption.

Use of Civilian Oversight Institutions

In recent times, many developing societies have moved toward the establishment and use of independent civilian oversight institutions as a key element of their police anticorruption strategies. As Quah (2014) observed with respect to Singapore and Hong Kong, for example, those two societies have succeeded in curbing corruption by rejecting the British colonial government's method of relying on the police for corruption control and relying instead on independent anticorruption agencies. In some developing societies, such as Kenya, for instance, these oversight institutions have also been given punitive powers.

Police operations must be transparent and open to public scrutiny. The police do not operate in a vacuum and need to be held accountable, like any other government department, by both external state and nonstate oversight stakeholders and bodies, for their use of public resources and actions that they claim are in the public interest. Consequently, there is now a system of layered civilian oversight of the police in most developing societies. This is indeed a good thing as experts usually regard a layered system of policing oversight comprising internal and external oversight mechanisms as more effective than either in the absence of the other (see, e.g., Calderon and Hernandez-Figueroa 2013).

As a model of accountability, civilian oversight refers to the actual mechanics of holding police accountable for their conduct. It refers to the entire system of ensuring policing services are delivered in a manner that is conducive to the public good and in accordance with modern standards of justice. Generally, civilian oversight involves people outside the justice system or citizens/civilians taking responsibility for holding police officers to account (Bourke n.d.; Finn 2001; Miller 2002; Stone and Bobb 2002; Calderon and Hernandez-Figueroa 2013). Civilian oversight therefore involves a network of multiple checks and balances on the police that go well beyond complaints (Miller 2002). The reason people think civilian oversight and police complaints are one and the same is often due to the fact that demands for greater accountability frequently follow a specific incident of police misconduct, triggering a complaint and a wider debate for stronger oversight. However, this is not to deny the importance of an effective complaint process (Bourke n.d.).

Civilian oversight falls along a continuum of reactive and proactive approaches to police accountability. Reactive models are used after an incident has taken place, including complaints, investigations, justifications, and sanctions (Bourke n.d.; Calderon and Hernandez-Figueroa 2013). Reactive measures focus on identifying a specific *bad apple*, ignoring larger systemic and structural problems that may have led to the incident. Generally, it tends to suggest that misconduct by police officers must be analyzed in individual terms, so that the appropriate organizational response to individual misconduct is to deal with that individual separately, akin to removing a *rotten apple* from a barrel in order to avoid tainting the other apples (Bourke n.d.). This leads into the other end of the continuum, proactive measures of civilian oversight. This form of oversight seeks to directly influence policies that promote standards of ethics and behavior. Rather than waiting for an incident to occur, measures are taken to avoid and deter misconduct (Bourke n.d.; Calderon and Hernandez-Figueroa 2013).

Police oversight mechanisms in developing societies have a major task to monitor police performance, in terms of effectiveness, organizational structure, and compliance with ethical and human rights standards, and the judgment of these external stakeholders influences the perception of ethical conduct and can also be in the position to correct police performance as was found to be the case in Asia, for example (den Boer and Pyo 2011).

Consequently, civilian oversight of the police is a governance measure designed to improve police accountability. It refers to the ongoing monitoring of police activities with a view toward holding a police service accountable for the services it provides, the policies under which it operates, and the conduct of its members. It involves people from outside the police taking a role in calling the police to account for their actions, policies, and organization covering broad areas of police practice. It is an essential component of a democratic society. Effective civilian oversight and governance of the police is necessary to ensure that the police service uses its powers and authority in a manner reflecting respect for law and individual rights and freedoms (Walker 2001; Miller 2002; Sen 2010). Ultimately, the task is one of striking a balance between police independence to conduct investigations and maintain order—without undue political or other influences—and the need for accountability to the public.

Punitive Measures

Punitive approaches to controlling police corruption are practical applications of the deterrence theory. The intent is to increase the detection, investigation, and punishment of corrupt police officers for deliberate misconduct, to deter all police officers from engaging in corrupt activities, and thereby to promote a positive culture of ethics and integrity for a police service. Some of the detection measures will also have preventive effects on corruptive police behavior, for example, random integrity testing.

Increased Detection and Investigation

In many developing societies, efforts have been stepped up to detect and investigate police corruption through intelligence gathering and other information methods such as public complaints or whistle-blowers, by proactively looking for general indications of corrupt activities through surveillance, through *sting* operations and undercover tactics, or through integrity tests whereby police officers are given an opportunity to commit corrupt acts. Officers who fail the test are or should be summarily arrested.

Integrity tests are not meant specifically to collect evidence, although such tests automatically generate evidence in cases where individuals fail them. The purpose of integrity tests is to identify corrupt individuals or groups by creation of an artificial situation that replicates the normal day-to-day situations that officers experience during which the integrity of the officers targeted will be tested. It therefore creates a realistic condition or situation designed to generate a reaction by an individual or individuals so that their conduct, behavior, and professional standards can be assessed.

The purpose of *sting* operations is to infiltrate corrupt groups or approach corrupt individuals, collect evidence, and identify and arrest offenders. Sting operations are deceptive operations that could be best described as a construction made by the police whereby they offer people opportunities to commit a crime (corrupt activity) with the purpose of catching the offender *in the act*.

Undercover operations are used to infiltrate corruption networks and corruption-prone areas to gather information to facilitate integrity testing, sting operations, future investigations and arrests, and prosecution to deter unethical and corrupt conduct.

Investigation is the process that will take place after the offence has been detected. It determines the merits of a case, gathers the facts, and provides the more concrete evidence required for conviction and for unravelling corruption networks or syndicates.

Punishment as Deterrent

For many developing societies, police corruption is being made a high-risk activity. That is, a high risk that the perpetrators will be caught and severely punished. In other words, all those police officers who are engaged in corruption would receive the harshest available punishment. Where the corruption is a criminal offence, it is being or should be prosecuted regardless of who is involved. Some corruption is being dealt with through internal disciplinary procedures. However, when police officers are suspected of having engaged in activities that meet the threshold of a criminal offence, they are being or should be prosecuted and if necessary sentenced. To implement a policy of punishment as deterrent also requires that those police officers engaged in corruption be dealt with not only severely but transparently. *Naming and shaming* should occur so that other police officers learn what constitutes inappropriate behavior from their colleagues' misconducts and that these actions will not be tolerated. It also gives officers confidence that inappropriate behavior will be addressed and the public will be made fully aware of the occurrence of corrupt behavior by the police and the punishment that has been meted out (DCAF 2012).

The prosecution and conviction of corrupt police officers serves a number of important functions. First, enforcing criminal law irrespective of the individuals involved is a fundamental requirement in any society based on the rule of law. The courts can ensure that there is legal accountability for the actions of police officers. Second, by ensuring that criminal law is enforced against police officers, the courts can help to tackle the *culture of impunity* that generally surrounds police corruption in developing societies (DCAF 2012). A culture of impunity refers to the prevailing view among police officers that they can violate the law without being punished. The successful prosecution and conviction of corrupt officers will serve as a deterrent against future corruption. Third, by prosecuting and convicting police officers guilty of corruption, the courts will send a clear message to the public that the police are not above the law and will be held accountable. This is particularly important because public trust in the police is limited; in the long term, the successful prosecution of police officers for corruption can help to build public confidence in the police. Fourth, the investigation and prosecution of officers involved in corruption will help to reveal more systemic problems within a police service, which can then be addressed by one of the other institutions responsible for oversight and control of the police. For example, the oversight body or bodies may use the conviction of one or more officers for corruption as a basis for initiating a broader investigation into a police service or one of its units; and, in this context, the oversight may also review the police service's internal anticorruption mechanisms.

Conclusions

Police corruption has become recognized to be a major problem in most developing societies, and many of those societies have embarked on police reforms or are considering police reform recommendations encompassing a number of preventive and punitive internal and external measures to control said corruption and mitigate its deleterious effects as discussed above.

The debilitating current and long-term effects of police corruption in developing societies therefore remain the driving force influencing the need to curb corrupt police practices. But it must be understood by all, including civil society, the media, and development partners alike, that controlling police corruption requires adequate time, resources, and dedication. As desirable as they are, there are no *quick fixes* possible. In fact, this work does not claim that police corruption can be eliminated altogether. However, police corruption can, and must, be considerably reduced, and its most serious consequences must be countered. Many have indicated that the omnipresence of this corruption problem in developing societies means that it is unsolvable or that nothing much can be done about it. Nothing is more removed from the truth. The cases of Hong Kong, Georgia, and Singapore, for example, highlight how determined police administrations, continuous political commitment, and an anticorruption approach with wide alliances between the public, private, and civil society sectors, including the media, can make a huge difference (DCAF 2012). Moreover, the public is fed up with the current culture of impunity that surrounds police corruption as well as corruption in general in most developing societies.

Nonetheless, even where strong success has been recorded, such as in Singapore and Hong Kong, the systems that led to success in those societies cannot simply be airlifted to another country to have the same effect. One size does not fit all. Reform efforts must be tailored specifically to individual differences and societal fit, notwithstanding the universal points of best practice that can and must be adopted. Moreover, as Reber (2014) astutely observed, police reforms remain a difficult, costly, and time-consuming task that is also inherently political and depends enormously on local political will to succeed in environments where police services tend to be among the most resistant to change.

References

Andvig, J. C. and O.-H. Fjeldstad. 2008. *Crime, Poverty and Police Corruption in Developing Countries.* WP 2008: 7. Bergen, Norway: Chr. Michelsen Institute.

Ayres, R. M. and D. S. Corderman. 2008. *Ethical, Character Driven Leadership: How to Become a Premier Law Enforcement Agency.* http://www.neiassociates.org/storage/EthicalDrivenLeadership-combined.pdf (accessed June 9, 2014).

Barker, T. and J. B. Roebuck. 1973. *An Empirical Typology of Police Corruption.* Springfield, IL: Thomas.

Bayley, D. H. 2001. *Democratizing the Police Abroad: What to Do and How to Do It.* Washington, DC: National Institute of Justice, US Department of Justice.

Bayley, D. H. 2002. Law enforcement and the rule of law: Is there a trade-off? *Criminology and Public Policy* 2(1): 133–153.

Bayley, D. H. 2006. *Changing the Guard: Developing Democratic Police Abroad.* New York: Oxford University Press.

Bayley, D. H. and R. Perito. 2011. *Police Corruption: What Past Scandals Teach about Current Challenges.* Washington, DC: United States Institute of Peace.

Beyerle, S. 2014. *Curtailing Corruption: People Power for Accountability and Justice.* Boulder, CO: Lynne Rienner Publishers.

Botello, N. A. and A. L. Rivera. 2000. Everything in this job is money: Inside the Mexican police. *World Policy Journal* 17(3): 61–70.

Bourke, C. n.d. Police complaints, civilian oversight, democracy. http://www.scaddingcourt.org/Bill103summit/pdfs/Police%20Complaints%20Civilian%20versight%20Democracy.pdf (accessed August 8, 2014).

Calderon, E. L. and M. Hernandez-Figueroa. 2013. *Citizen Oversight Committees in Law Enforcement.* Fullerton, CA: Center for Public Policy, California State University, Fullerton.

CEPOL (European Police College). 2014. Common curricula—Police ethics & prevention of corruption. https://www.cepol.europa.eu/education-training/trainers/commoncurricula/ethics-corruption (accessed September 12, 2014).

Crawshaw, R., B. Devlin, and T. Williamson. 1998. *Human Rights and Policing Standards for Good Behaviour and a Strategy for Change.* The Hague, the Netherlands: Kluwer Law International.

Crooke, G. W. 2001. Professionalism in policing v. corruption. Presentation to the *15th International Conference of the International Society for the Reform of Criminal Law,* Canberra, Australian Capital Territory, Australia, August 26–30.

DCAF (Geneva Centre for the Democratic Control of Armed Forces). 2012. *Toolkit on Police Integrity.* Geneva, Switzerland: DCAF.

den Boer, M. and C. Pyo. 2011. *Good Policing: Instruments, Models and Practices.* Singapore: Asia-Europe Foundation and Hanns Seidel Foundation Indonesia.

Doty, J. and C. Doty. 2012. Command responsibility and accountability. *Military Review* 92(1): 35–38.

Ellison, G. and N. W. Pino. 2012. *Globalization, Police Reform and Development: Doing It the Western Way?*. Houndmills, U.K.: Palgrave Macmillan.

Finn, P. 2001. *Citizen Review of Police: Approaches and Implementation.* Washington, DC: National Institute of Justice, US Department of Justice.

Harrison, B. 1999. Noble cause corruption and the police ethic. *FBI Law Enforcement Bulletin* 68(8): 1–7.

HKPF (Hong Kong Police Force). 2009. *Ethics and Integrity in the Hong Kong Police Force.* Hong Kong, People's Republic of China: HKPF.

Hope, K. R. 2011. Investing in capacity development: Towards an implementation framework. *Policy Studies* 32(1): 59–72.

Hope, K. R. 2012. *The Political Economy of Development in Kenya.* New York: Bloomsbury Publishing.

Hope, K. R. 2013. Tackling the corruption epidemic in Kenya: Toward a policy of more effective control. *The Journal of Social, Political, and Economic Studies* 38(3): 287–316.

Hope, K. R. 2014. Kenya's corruption problem: Causes and consequences. *Commonwealth & Comparative Politics* 52(4): 493–512.

Ivković, S. K. 2005. *Fallen Blue Knights: Controlling Police Corruption.* Oxford, U.K.: Oxford University Press.

Kaplan, S. D. 2013. *Betrayed: Politics, Power, and Prosperity.* New York: Palgrave Macmillan.

Kleinig, J. 1996. *The Ethics of Policing.* Cambridge, U.K.: Cambridge University Press.

Knapp, W. 1972. *Report of the Commission to Investigate Alleged Police Corruption.* New York: George Braziller.

Lamani, R. B. and G. S. Venumadhava. 2013. Police corruption in India. *International Journal of Criminology and Sociological Theory* 6(4): 228–234.

Loree, D. J. 2006. *Corruption in Policing: Causes and Consequences: A Review of the Literature.* Ottawa, Ontario, Canada: Research and Evaluation Branch, Community, Contract and Aboriginal Policing Services Directorate, Royal Canadian Mounted Police.

Miller, J. 2002. Civilian oversight of policing: Lessons from the literature. Presentation to the *Global Meeting on Civilian Oversight of Police,* Los Angeles, CA, May 5–8. http://www.vera.org/sites/default/files/resources/downloads/Civilian_oversight.pdf (accessed August 12, 2014).

Neild. R. 2007. *USAID Program Brief: Anticorruption and Police Integrity.* Washington, DC: USAID.

Newburn, T. 1999. *Understanding and Preventing Police Corruption: Lessons from the Literature.* Police Research Series Paper 110. London, U.K.: Home Office.

Newham, G. and A. Faull. 2011. *Protector or Predator?: Tackling Police Corruption in South Africa.* Monograph Number 182. Pretoria, South Africa: Institute for Security Studies.

NSWPIC (New South Wales Police Integrity Commission). 2012. Conflicts of interest policy and procedure. http://www.pic.nsw.gov.au/files/File/Conflicts%20of%20Interest%20Policy.pdf (accessed July 19, 2014).

Nyarko, J. A. 2014. Corruption and the police service in Ghana. Paper prepared for the Center for Research for Development and Change. http://www.academia.edu/7639601/CORRUPTION_AT_INSTITUTIONAL_LEVEL_-_THE_CASE_OF_GHANA_POLICE_SERVICE (accessed September 12, 2014).

OECD (Organization for Economic Cooperation and Development). 2011. *Asset Declarations for Public Officials: A Tool to Prevent Corruption*. Paris, France: OECD Publishing.

Ojo, M. O. D. 2014. The Nigeria police and the search for integrity in the midst of diverse challenges: An effective police management approach. *International Journal of Police Science & Management* 16(2): 87–100.

OSCE (Organization for Security and Co-operation in Europe). 2011. *International Police Standards: Guidebook on Democratic Policing*. Geneva, Switzerland: DCAF.

Pino, N. W. and M. D. Wiatrowski. 2006. The principles of democratic policing. In *Democratic Policing in Transitional and Developing Countries*, eds. N. Pino and M. D. Wiatrowski, pp. 69–98. Aldershot, U.K.: Ashgate.

Powell, S. n.d. Lifestyle audits are a critical management tool to identify fraud. http://documents.lexology.com/ae0e573a-4da1-41e1-9a50-7278870d4796.pdf (accessed July 9, 2014).

Prenzler, T. 2009. *Police Corruption: Preventing Misconduct and Maintaining Integrity*. Boca Raton, FL: CRC Press/Taylor & Francis.

Punch, M. 1985. *Conduct Unbecoming: The Social Construction of Police Deviance and Control*. London, U.K.: Tavistock.

Punch, M. 2000. Police corruption and its prevention. *European Journal on Criminal Policy and Research* 8(3): 301–324.

Punch, M. 2011. *Police Corruption: Deviance, Accountability and Reform in Policing*. Abingdon, U.K.: Routledge.

Quah, J. S. T. 2006. Preventing police corruption in Singapore: The role of recruitment, training and socialization. *The Asia Pacific Journal of Public Administration* 28(1): 59–75.

Quah, J. S. T. 2014. Curbing police corruption in Singapore: Lessons for other Asian countries. *Asian Education and Development Studies* 3(3): 186–222.

Quinn, M. W. 2011. *Walking with the Devil: The Police Code of Silence: What Bad Cops Don't Want You to Know and Good Cops Won't Tell You*. Minneapolis, MN: Quinn and Associates Publishing and Consulting.

Reber, M. A. 2014. *Challenges with Assessing Impact in International Police Reform and Assistance*. Occasional Paper No. 1. Stockholm, Sweden: International Forum for the Challenges of Peace Operations.

Roberg, R. R. and J. Kuykendall. 1993. *Police and Society*. Belmont, CA: Wadsworth Publishing Company.

Roebuck, J. B. and T. Barker. 1974. A typology of police corruption. *Social Problems* 21(3): 423–437.

Roelofse, C. 2012. Theoretical reflections on police behavior, an expansion of reciprocal moral dualism. *Acta Criminologica*, Special Edition No. 2: 136–154.

Ross, J. I. 2012. *Policing Issues: Challenges and Controversies*. Burlington, MA: Jones and Bartlett Learning.

Sen, S. 2010. *Enforcing Police Accountability through Civilian Oversight*. New Delhi. India: Sage Publications.

Sherman, L. W. ed. 1974. *Police Corruption: A Sociological Perspective*. New York: Doubleday.

Skolnick, J. H. 2002. Corruption and the blue code of silence. *Police Practice and Research: An International Journal* 3(1): 7–19.

Skolnick, J. H. 2008. Corruption and the blue code of silence. In *Contemporary Issues in Law Enforcement and Policing*, eds. A. Millie and D. K. Das, pp. 45–60. Boca Raton, FL: CRC Press/Taylor & Francis.

Stone, C. and M. Bobb. 2002. Civilian oversight of the police in democratic societies. Presentation to the *Global Meeting on Civilian Oversight of Police*, Los Angeles, CA, May 5–8. http://www.vera.org/sites/default/files/resources/downloads/Civilian_oversight_2.pdf (accessed August 12, 2014).

Stone, C. and H. Ward. 2000. Democratic policing: A framework for action. *Policing and Society: An International Journal of Research and Policy* 10(1): 11–45.

Swope, R. 2001. Bad apples or bad barrel? *Law and Order* 49(1): 80–85.

TI (Transparency International). 2013. *Global Corruption Barometer 2013*. Berlin, Germany: TI.

TI (Transparency International)—Kenya. 2010. *The East African Bribery Index 2010*. Nairobi, Kenya: TI-Kenya.

TI (Transparency International)—Kenya. 2011. *The East African Bribery Index 2011*. Nairobi, Kenya: TI-Kenya.

TI (Transparency International)—Kenya. 2012. *The East African Bribery Index 2012*. Nairobi, Kenya: TI-Kenya.

TI (Transparency International)—Kenya. 2013. *The East African Bribery Index 2013*. Nairobi, Kenya: TI-Kenya.

TI (Transparency International)—Kenya. 2014. *The East African Bribery Index 2014*. Nairobi, Kenya: TI-Kenya.

UNODC (United Nations Office on Drugs and Crime). 2011. *Handbook on Police Accountability, Oversight and Integrity*. New York: United Nations.

Verma, A. 1999. Cultural roots of police corruption in India. *Policing: An International Journal of Police Strategies & Management* 22(3): 264–279.

Vogl, F. 2012. *Waging War on Corruption: Inside the Movement Fighting the Abuse of Power*. Lanham, MD: Rowman & Littlefield Publishers.

Walker, S. 2001. *Police Accountability: The Role of Citizen Oversight*. Belmont, CA: Wadsworth.

Westmarland, L. 2005. Police ethics and integrity: Breaking the blue code of silence. *Policing and Society: An International Journal of Research and Policy* 15(2): 145–165.

Williams, H. 2002. Core factors of police corruption across the world. *Forum on Crime and Society* 2(1): 85–99.

Wood, J. R. T. 1997. *Final Report of the Royal Commission into the New South Wales Police Service: Volume 2: Reform*. Sydney, New South Wales, Australia: Government of the State of New South Wales.

Confronting Police Corruption in Developing Societies

The Role of the Rule of Law

2

JOHN MUKUM MBAKU

Contents

Elements of the Rule of Law.. 35
Confronting Police Corruption: A Role for the Rule of Law....................... 37
    Supremacy of Law... 38
    Voluntary Acceptance of and Respect for the Law.............................. 39
    Judicial Independence... 41
    Openness and Transparency... 42
    Predictability.. 44
    Protection of Human Rights... 44
Rule of Law and Reform Strategies for Reducing Police Corruption........... 45
Conclusion... 46
References... 47

Throughout virtually most of the developing world, corruption remains one of the most important constraints to economic and human development. In addition, corruption contributes significantly to a lot of the multifarious problems (e.g., exploitation of children, drug trafficking, government impunity, ethnic cleansing, and the senseless massacre of vulnerable groups—children, women, religious minorities, and the poor) that these societies currently suffer from and to the failure of many governments to perform their constitutionally mandated functions and provide citizens with certain public goods and services. In many developing societies, corruption is a major constraint, not only to economic growth and development but also to the maintenance of peace. For example, corruption in Mexico, specifically among the Mexican national police, has been blamed for the failure of the government to maintain law and order and provide adequate and full protection to the person and property of citizens (Davis 2006; Uildriks 2009, 2010; Ionescu 2011; Ochoa and Jiménez 2012). The police, an institution whose constitutional function is to protect citizens, maintain law and order, and enhance democratic living, has in Mexico and, indeed in many other developing and transition societies, become instead an agent of a significant level of the violence directed at citizens.

Of course, Mexico is not the only developing society that suffers from police corruption. Good and effective policing is not just the heart or bedrock of the rule of law and democratic living but also the basis for peaceful coexistence, especially in societies such as those in Africa that have significant levels of ethnic and religious diversity (Mbaku 2013a). Unfortunately, throughout Africa and other developing regions of the world, pervasive corruption has destroyed the legitimacy of the police as an institution for the maintenance of law and order, endangered peaceful coexistence, and created conditions that have forced individuals and groups to resort either to self-help associations (e.g., ethnic or religious associations) or take the law into their own hands.

For instance, during the last several decades in Nigeria, self-help associations (including vigilante groups), designed to maintain law and order and insure moral living, have emerged to become important vehicles for security of the person of individuals and their property in many communities throughout the society. In fact, Nigeria's police and legal institutions have become so corrupt and dysfunctional that many citizens have taken the law into their own hands and now rely on vigilantism and other forms of community policing as a way to protect themselves. In many neighborhoods, criminals and criminal gangs have taken control of the streets and, with the help of the police, actually extort money and other resources from citizens. In some parts of Nigeria, the police have become agents of many criminal gangs, in the same way that the Mexican police have, during the last several years, become partners with drug-trafficking gangs (see, e.g., Smith 2007; Pratten 2008; Kirsch and Grätz 2010; Longmire 2010).

This chapter deals specifically with how the rule of law can be used to minimize police corruption in developing societies. It employs Buchanan's (1994) constitutional political economy model, which provides insight into how "societies formulate, select, and amend the rules that regulate their sociopolitical interactions" (Mbaku 2013b, p. 965) to show that police corruption is a form of rule subversion and that the most effective way to deal with it is to restructure a society's institutional arrangements and provide appropriate constraints on the state—specifically, a governing system that guarantees the rule of law. Adam Smith (1976 [1887], p. 106) called these rules "laws and institutions." The latter have a significant impact on, as well as determine, the outcomes that result from sociopolitical interaction. Brennan and Buchanan (1985, p. 14) note, however, that although rules provide individuals with the wherewithal to maximize their values, including wealth creation, they do so in a context in which they do not prevent others from similarly attaining their own goals and objectives. Hence, in providing members of society with the tools to organize their private lives and maximize their values, rules also serve the "negative function of preventing disastrous harm" (Brennan and Buchanan 1985, p. 14).

Although governance systems in developing societies have improved significantly during the last several decades, many people in these societies still face rules that empower their governments to "oppress, exploit, and infantilize them" (Mbaku 2013b, p. 966). In other words, despite the significant democratic gains of the last several decades, laws and institutions in many developing societies still do not adequately constrain the state, and as a result, public servants (including the police) and political elites are able to act with impunity and engage in behaviors (such as corruption) that constrain economic growth and development, as well as violate the fundamental rights of citizens. Thus, in Buchanan's political economy model, the pervasiveness of police corruption—and indeed other forms of political opportunism (e.g., rent seeking)—can be seen as the successful subversion of existing rules by police officers to generate extralegal income and other benefits for themselves. Therefore, the most effective way to minimize and/or eradicate police corruption is to reconstitute and reconstruct the state through democratic constitution making and other rule of law processes to provide institutional arrangements that adequately constrain the state and hence minimize impunity on the part of its agents, such as the police.

Elements of the Rule of Law

The heart of the rule of law is its ability to adequately and effectively constrain the state and the government in their actions. The government must conform with or obey the law (Chemerinsky 2007, p. 6). Put another way, the law is supreme and no one, including those who hold positions in the government, and that includes the police, is above the law. As argued by Justice Anthony M. Kennedy, Associate Justice of the U.S. Supreme Court, "the law rests upon known, general principles applicable on equal terms to all persons. It follows that the Law is superior to, and thus binds, the government and all of its officials" (Quoted in Stein 2009, p. 299). The first element of the rule of law, identified for the purposes of this chapter, is the *supremacy of law.*

A society cannot maintain the rule of law if its citizens "do not [accept] and respect the law" (ABA n.d., p. 5). In any society, if the majority of citizens do not accept and respect the law, it would be extremely difficult for the government and its agencies (including the police) to effectively perform the job of maintaining law and order. Why? Policing to force compliance with the law would be "extremely costly and the government would likely be forced to devote a significant portion of national income to compliance activities, a process that can reduce expenditures on important sectors of the economy such as health and human capital development" (Mbaku 2013b, p. 988). The second element of the rule of law, then, is that *the majority of citizens must accept and respect the law.*

Many legal systems around the world have contributed significantly to the development of modern rule of law jurisprudence. Several of the definitions of the rule of law put forth by various jurists and legal scholars share the assertion that there can be no free society without law administered through an independent judiciary. Chemerinsky (2007, p. 8), for example, has argued that in order to provide a practical definition for the rule of law, one needs to address eight key propositions, which include the following: "An independent judiciary is essential to the rule of law." Also, in its definition of the rule of law, the United Nations has argued that "the 'rule of law' refers to a principle of governance in which all persons, institutions and entities, public or private, including the State itself, are accountable to laws that are publicly promulgated, equally enforced and independently adjudicated,…" (UN 2004, p. 4). Thus, the third element of the rule of law is *judicial independence.*

The law and a legal system function effectively only if citizens are aware of the law and understand, appreciate, and respect the law. The government can help its citizens understand and appreciate the law through the implementation of broad-based education programs at schools, community centers, and other communication mediums. In addition, the "laws [must be] applied predictably and uniformly" (ABA n.d., p. 5) and not arbitrarily or capriciously. The fourth and fifth elements of the rule of law are, respectively, *openness and transparency and predictability.*

As a legal principle, the rule of law developed in the United States centers "around the belief that a primary purpose of the rule of law is the protection of certain basic rights" (ABA n.d., p. 5). Similarly, the decolonization projects of the immediate post–World War II period in the former European colonies were based on the desire of the citizens of these territories to rid themselves of externally imposed institutional arrangements and replace them with locally designed laws and institutions. The hope was that each new society would provide itself with institutional arrangements that guarantee the rule of law. The constitutions that therefore brought these former colonies to independence were expected to "adequately constrain the state, effectively preventing public servants and political elites from engaging in corruption, rent seeking, and other forms of opportunism; and to guarantee the protection of fundamental and human rights, as well as provide citizens with the wherewithal for self-actualization" (Mbaku 20013b, p. 991). Consequently, the sixth and final element of the rule of law is the *protection of the fundamental rights of citizens.*

Confronting Police Corruption: A Role for the Rule of Law

By far, the most important constraint to poverty alleviation and the improvement of the living standards of people in the developing societies today is corruption, which includes police corruption. Impunity by police officers is especially insidious. As Chapter 1 shows, the search by corrupt police officers for extralegal income has become a major obstacle to entrepreneurship, especially among historically marginalized groups (such as women, rural inhabitants, and ethnic and religious minorities). The pervasiveness of police corruption in many developing societies is due, *inter alia*, to the fact that the laws and institutions that exist in these societies do not adequately constrain the state and, hence, the police are able to benefit from various forms of impunity, including from corruption. Specifically, the constitutions that many of these societies currently have do not guarantee the rule of law, nor do they provide necessary mechanisms, such as the separation of powers and checks and balances, to realize those guarantees. As a consequence, there have not been viable and effective mechanisms available to citizens in these societies to adequately check the excesses of the police and other agents of government.

Of course, although the rule of law has the potential to effectively minimize engagement by the police in corruption, the latter can seriously undermine the rule of law. This is especially true in societies that do not have a democratic culture and are still struggling to establish or are in the process of establishing a governing process undergirded or characterized by the rule of law. In such a political environment, the entrenched groups that currently benefit from corruption are likely to oppose any efforts to uphold the rule of law. Yet, without the latter, a society is not likely to be able to deal effectively and fully with police corruption as well as corruption by other public officials.

One of the assumptions of Buchanan's (1994) constitutional political economy is that most people's behavior is governed by self-interest and that "given the opportunity, they are likely to engage in opportunism to maximize their private interest even if doing so imposes net costs on others (i.e., reduces the welfare of others)" (Mbaku 2010, p. 358; see also Brennan and Buchanan 1985). Brennan and Buchanan (1985, p. ix) have therefore argued that the most effective way to deal with this quagmire is to design and adopt rules that provide legal mechanisms for the coordination of the activities of individuals and the peaceful resolution of the conflict that arises from sociopolitical interaction. Such rules should adequately constrain the state and prevent its custodians from engaging in corruption and other forms of economic and political opportunism.

But will self-interested individuals—especially members of politically entrenched groups—willingly undertake the necessary institutional reforms to provide and implement rules capable of adequately constraining the ability of the police to engage in corruption? As evidenced by the collapse of many authoritarian and dictatorial political regimes in many parts of the world, starting with the disintegration of the Soviet Union, the demise of apartheid in South Africa, and the subsequent successful democratization efforts in many of these societies, it is quite possible for the people to overcome the endeavors of entrenched groups and engage in democratic (i.e., people driven, inclusive, participatory, and bottom-up) institutional reforms to produce laws and institutions for effective governance in general and police corruption control in particular. Sustained pressure from grassroots organizations, coupled with assistance from external actors, can create an environment that is conducive to effective institutional reforms (see, e.g., Mbaku 2010). Below, we revisit the elements of the rule of law and show how the failure of societies to guarantee each of them can contribute significantly to the pervasiveness of police corruption.

Supremacy of Law

Where the law is supreme, the police are adequately constrained by the law and hence will generally not be able to engage in blatant corruption and other growth-inhibiting behaviors. Throughout the developing societies today, the police tend to consider themselves to be above the law and regularly engage in various extralegal activities to enrich and advantage themselves at the expense of those who are legally bound to serve (Mbaku 2013b, p. 1033).

For example, in a study of bureaucratic corruption in Cameroon, Jua (1991, p. 166) determined that "public discussion and/or criticism of the alleged acts of some members of the ruling class is still taboo." In fact, in Cameroon, as is the case in many other societies in Africa, police officers openly engage in corrupt activities without fear of prosecution (see also the Cameroon case study in this volume). In their study of corruption in Nigeria, Erero and Oladoyin (2000, p. 280) stated that "the amusing but sad dimension here is that these police officers in Nigeria even give change. For instance, where a driver does not have the required bill, say a 10 currency note and he gives out a 50, the policeman at the check point, will give back 40 in change without any sense of shame. It is that bad now in Nigeria."

Also, in recent pronouncements, the South African Police Service (SAPS) has publicly admitted that hundreds of its members are convicted criminals (Rademeyer and Wilkinson 2013; Smith 2013). The SAPS actually revealed that it uncovered evidence to indicate that there were actually 1448 serving police officers who were convicted criminals. Despite the fact that senior management at the SAPS told the public at the time of this revelation that all criminal elements within the police service would be eliminated, by the end of 2014, that process had yet to be fully undertaken. Police reform in

South Africa, as in other societies, remains a very contentious issue, and it appears that policymakers do not seem to have the political will to bring about the necessary reforms (see also Peters 2013).

The tendency for police officers to act above the law is not limited to any specific developing societies or regions. For example, researchers have uncovered arrogant and blatant extortion of resources by police from rural families in Cambodia and urban households in India (Andvig and Fjeldstad 2008), rampant abuse of the fundamental rights of citizens by extremely corrupt police in Mexico (Meyer 2014), and complicity of police forces in lynchings and extrajudicial killings in Latin America (Prado et al. 2012).

In August 2012, South Sudan, which had gained independence the year earlier, found itself "engulfed in scandals over top officials allegedly looting the treasury" (Burnett 2012, p. 1). The multifarious problems that South Sudan is facing, especially corruption by the police and other public officials, are due to the failure of the new nation to provide itself with institutional arrangements that guarantee the supremacy of law. Unless a society provides itself with such constraining mechanisms, police corruption impunity will remain pervasive.

Thus, one of the most important ways to deal effectively with police corruption is for each society to provide itself with institutional arrangements that guarantee the supremacy of law. Under such a legal system, all citizens, including those who serve in government, are subject to the society's "known and standing" laws (Dicey 1914 [1885], p. 181). The governing process in a society whose constitution guarantees the supremacy of law does not grant its police or other public servants and politicians wide discretion to either make their own laws or subvert existing ones to maximize individual private interests. Consequently, the police, like other citizens, would have to respect existing laws, subject themselves to them, and avoid engaging in any form of economic or political opportunism, including corruption. Of course, the system must have within it effective mechanisms to bring to justice those police officers that attempt to, or actually, subvert the laws for their own benefit.

In the words of English jurist and legal scholar Albert Dicey, the existence of the rule of law, including especially supremacy of law, implies "that no man is above the law, but that every man, whatever his rank or condition, is subject to the ordinary law of the realm, and amenable to the jurisdiction of the ordinary tribunals.... With us, every official, from Prime Minister down to a constable or collector of taxes, is under the same responsibility for every act done without legal justification as any other citizen" (Quoted in Dickinson 1921, p. 34).

Voluntary Acceptance of and Respect for the Law

In any society, it is quite difficult to enforce the law and maintain peaceful coexistence if the majority of citizens do not voluntarily accept and respect the law. As argued by the American Bar Association, "it is very difficult for a nation to maintain the rule of law if its citizens do not respect the law" (ABA n.d., p. 5). While government coercion can be used to force compliance with the law, ironically with the help of the police, such a legal and institutional framework is "extremely costly and difficult to maintain and sustain" (Mbaku 2013b, p. 1000). However, if most citizens voluntarily accept and respect the law, they would most likely comply, significantly minimizing compliance costs. In fact, as argued by the ABA (n.d., p. 5), "the rule of law functions because [the majority of citizens] agree that it is important to observe the law, even if a police officer is not present to enforce it."

In many developing societies, citizens (including the police) view their legal and judicial institutions as "alien impositions designed for the benefit of the ruling elites—and not for helping the people govern themselves, organize their private lives, and deal with daily problems and conflicts" (Mbaku 2013b, p. 1036). Many of these individuals have rejected these laws and institutions and have made maintaining law and order quite difficult and expensive. When citizens view their governments and institutions as alien impositions, they are less likely to serve the necessary function of checking the exercise of government power and making certain that the government operates efficiently, is transparent and accountable, and provides the people with necessary public goods and services. In fact, within such an environment, civil society and their organizations are likely to devote their efforts, not to checking on government, but on extracting as much resources as possible from the government for the benefit of their members. In fact, when police officers and other public servants embezzle, with impunity, public resources, and/or extort payments from organizations and individuals seeking government services, and they engage in such behavior for their benefit and that of their families/ethnic groups, the latter may actually welcome such impunity, even though it is detrimental to the general societal welfare. Here, government and the resources that it controls are seen simply as alien entities that can be fully exploited for the benefit of the group. Thus, a police officer who engages in corrupt activities, including stealing public resources, is only considered bad (or criminally liable) by his kin if he or she does not share those looted resources with members of his or her kin.

But what about marginalized and deprived groups? Would these groups not want to make certain that the governance system is reformed so that it can guarantee the rule of law? The evidence from many developing societies is that groups (e.g., religious and ethnic groups), which have had an opportunity to undertake institutional reforms, have usually manipulated the process to produce outcomes that benefit them and not those that enhance the rule of law (Mbaku 2013b).

Judicial Independence

If police officers engage in criminal activities, including extortion of resources from citizens, the judiciary should be called upon to prosecute such corruption and appropriately punish the guilty parties. If the judiciary is either pervaded by corruption or is not independent enough to be able to perform its constitutionally assigned functions, it cannot contribute positively to the minimization of corruption, especially that committed by the police. At the very minimum, judicial independence requires (1) security of tenure of judicial officers, (2) financial security free from arbitrary interference by the executive in a manner that could affect judicial independence, and (3) institutional independence with respect to matters of administration bearing directly on the exercise of the judicial function and judicial control over the administrative decisions that bear directly and immediately on the exercise of the judicial function.

Given the critical role played by the judiciary in maintaining law and order, including the control of corruption, a society that does not have an effective judiciary—that is, one that is not subservient to the executive—cannot expect to deal fully with the corruption of its police. In order for the judiciary to serve as an effective check on the exercise of executive power, it must be a coequal partner, with the executive and legislative branches, in governance. In other words, there must be judicial independence. If the judiciary is subservient to or under the executive, the latter can use it to maximize its interests and those of its benefactors and supporters. Of course, in response, groups within the society that consider themselves marginalized and deprived by public policies may resort to violent mobilization, a process that can severely exacerbate political and economic instability and seriously impede national integration, economic growth, and human development.

If the judiciary does not have the capacity or independence to adequately and effectively check on the activities of the police and other public servants, these individuals are most likely to engage in corruption and other extralegal activities. Many researchers have determined that judicial independence is rarely realized in practice in many developing societies (see, e.g., Prempeh 2006). As argued by Prempeh (2006, pp. 1304–1305), many governments in Africa, for instance, are being pressured by "international donors and creditor nations to demonstrate their democratic credentials" and provide their economies with a "formal constitutional guarantee of judicial independence." However, in reality, "judicial independence remains vulnerable to political control" (Prempeh 2006, p. 1305) as the judiciary systems in these societies are unable to maintain the independence guaranteed them by national constitutions. This is due to the fact that very important aspects of judiciary independence are missing in these societies. These include, *inter alia*, the fact that these judiciaries lack the authority to have control over their own budgets since "the power of the purse is vested either with the executive or legislative branches" (Mbaku 2013b, p. 1038). In a study of the judiciary in Cameroon, for example, Fombad (2012) determined that the president of the republic not only has the power to *guarantee* the independence of the judiciary but also directly controls all the finances of the judiciary.

Prempeh (2006, p. 1305) has argued that the continued dependence of judiciaries in Africa on the executive and legislative branches is worsened by "the fact that the judiciary has historically been severely under-resourced, leaving it with inadequate and outmoded technology, dilapidated and over-crowded courthouses and offices, and underpaid judges and staff." The lack of independence has severely hampered the ability of the judiciary in many developing societies to function effectively, and without such effectiveness, it is not possible for the judiciary to contribute positively to the eradication of police corruption or corruption in general.

Openness and Transparency

One of the most important ways to minimize police and other corruption is to make certain that public policies are undertaken in an open and transparent manner. First, openness and transparency can significantly improve the efficiency of the public sector. Second, they can also force state custodians (including the police and political elites) to be more accountable to both the constitution and the people, a process that significantly minimizes corruption, including that by the police.

The failure to maintain openness and transparency in government communications significantly enhances corruption. If the police operate out of sight of public scrutiny, they are likely to engage in corrupt activities. As argued by Gerring and Thacker (2004, p. 316), "openness and transparency, which we may understand as the availability and accessibility of relevant information about the functioning of the polity, is commonly associated with the absence of corruption. Since corruption, by definition, violates generally accepted standards of behavior, greater transparency should discourage corrupt actions, or at least facilitate appropriate mechanisms of punishment (legal, administrative or electoral)."

In a political system in which the government communicates openly and makes records of its activities freely available to citizens, corruption is likely to be minimized. Of course, the information must be provided to the people in a relatively accessible manner and form. For example, while placing information on Internet websites significantly improves access, this is not necessarily so in a society where most citizens do not have access to the Internet. In addition, if government information is made available to the people in languages that they do not understand, they are not likely to use it effectively to organize their private lives and/or check on the exercise of government power.

Unless the design of public policies is carried out in an open and transparent manner, some groups within the society are likely to complain that these policies do not reflect their values and interests. If the public policy process is undergirded by openness and transparency, various groups, especially those that have historically been marginalized, including women, ethnic and religious minorities, as well as rural inhabitants, which often complain that public policies marginalize them, are not likely to resort to violent and destructive mobilization. This is especially so if, as a result of government's open approach to policy design and implementation, "these groups either had the opportunity to participate fully and effectively in the design process, or were aware of how the laws were made and why" (Mbaku 2013b, p. 1012).

But what exactly are openness and transparency as they relate to the performance of the public function, including especially that of the police? With respect to government actions, including those of the police, openness and transparency should be understood as "the availability and accessibility of relevant information about the functioning of the polity" (Gerring and Thacker 2004, p. 316). For the citizens of developing societies, openness and transparency in the performance of the public function are important because they enhance the ability of individuals, who are interested in a given public policy or think or believe that the government action might affect them, "to understand and appreciate how that decision was made or arrived at and why" (Mbaku 2013b, p. 1013). When public officials (e.g., the police) make decisions or undertake actions that affect the lives of citizens (e.g., public policies on safety and security), transparency is very important.

Throughout many developing societies, impunity and arbitrariness and capriciousness, especially on the part of the police, are quite pervasive. In such societies, openness and transparency can serve two important, separate but related functions. As argued by Stirton and Lodge (2001, p. 476), "the first is to ensure that public service providers [including the police] respect both the positive and negative rights of individuals." They argue further that this instrumental justification for transparency of public services comes close to the traditional principles for good governance. Consequently, the more strictly we are watched, the better we behave (Stirton and Lodge 2001). The second purpose "relates more directly to democratic theory, which values participation by individuals in the decisions that affect them" (Stirton and Lodge 2001, p. 476). Such participation by the people in governance generally and policy design and implementation specifically should improve accountability of the police and minimize police corruption.

Predictability

Many jurists and legal experts are agreed that one of the most important elements or characteristics of the rule of law is that the law must not and never be administered in a capricious and arbitrary manner. Citizens must be able to "expect predictable results from the legal system" (ABA n.d., p. 5). By *predictable results*, legal scholars mean that "people who act in the same way can expect the law to treat them in the same way" (ABA n.d., p. 5; see also Chemerinsky 2007, pp. 6–8). If police corruption affects the way cases are investigated and adjudicated, predictability of the law is violated. For one thing, where, through corruption, the police are able to impact the outcomes of judicial proceedings (e.g., by manufacturing evidence to favor those accused individuals who have bribed them or destroying evidence detrimental to accused individuals paying bribes), the legal system is compromised and can no longer deliver predictable results. Here, the law is administered capriciously and arbitrarily, favoring those who bribe the police.

It is important to note, however, that while adherence or fidelity to precedent is critical for achieving legal stability, it might be necessary to give up adherence to precedent for public policy reasons. In other words, if the courts determine that doing so would advance important societal objectives, they should seriously consider it. What is important is that while fidelity to precedent is critical for achieving legal stability and predictability, the latter must not be achieved at the expense of rendering the law so rigid that it becomes "impervious to changing societal norms and practices" (Lindquist and Martinek 2011, p. 7). Legal predictability and stability are important for the maintenance of the rule of law. The latter, of course, is part and parcel of any effective anticorruption program. For where there is legal stability, police corruption and other types of corruption is likely to be minimized.

Protection of Human Rights

Corruption in general and police corruption in particular are especially damaging to the protection of human rights. In many developing societies today, corruption is a major constraint to the ability of people to access critical public services that enhance the protection of their fundamental rights. Police corruption can deny the poor necessary protection from harm by state and nonstate actors, a situation that often results in significant abuses of human rights. In fact, police corruption in many developing societies is responsible for a lot of criminal activities (e.g., human trafficking, including the sexual exploitation of children), which directly affect the fundamental rights of many people.

Throughout most developing societies, police impunity has contributed significantly to the abuse of the rights of thousands of individuals.

During the last several years, researchers have determined a link between corruption and human rights. Mary Robinson, former UN Commissioner for Human Rights, has argued that "analyzing corruption in the light of its impact on human rights could well strengthen public understanding of the evils of corruption and lead to a stronger sense of public rejection" (TI 2004, p. 8). It is now clear that corruption can affect much more than economic efficiency and the creation of wealth. In addition to making it much more difficult for entrepreneurs to engage in productive activities, corruption can deny individual's access to life-saving services, which are supposed to be provided by the government through the police and others. Hence, it is important that each society provide itself with institutional arrangements that guarantee the rule of law in order to fully ensure the minimization of police corruption and the protection of human rights.

Rule of Law and Reform Strategies for Reducing Police Corruption

Over the years, various reports, some commissioned by international and national organizations and others by independent researchers, have made over 200 recommendations for reducing police corruption (see, e.g., Bayley and Perito 2011). Some of them include making significant changes to "police culture, management, recruitment and training, disciplinary processes, and external environment" (Bayley and Perito 2011, p. 6). One recommendation that seemed to pervade virtually all of the reports is the idea that an external oversight committee or commission be constituted and placed in charge of overseeing the activities of the police, including especially the "monitoring of police misbehavior" (Bayley and Perito 2011, p. 6).

Establishing external oversight committees to monitor the activities of the police has been tried in many developing societies during the last several decades. Unfortunately, the results have not been very encouraging. The failure of these committees or commissions to effectively reduce police corruption has been due, *inter alia*, to the lack or absence of, in these societies, institutional arrangements that can adequately constrain public servants, including those who serve on these oversight commissions.

The problem has been, and continues to be, the fact that these approaches to police corruption control in developing societies constitute a consensus for societies that have relatively stable and effective legal and judicial institutions. Put another way, these recommendations assume conditions that do not exist in developing and transition societies, including especially those that have, during the last several decades, been embroiled in ethnic, religious, and other forms of sectarian conflict (e.g., Nigeria, Liberia, Afghanistan,

Iraq, Rwanda, Kenya, Pakistan, Sierra Leone). In most of these societies, existing institutional arrangements do not adequately constrain the government, allowing state custodians to engage in various forms of opportunism, including corruption. In other words, these societies do not have governing processes undergirded by the rule of law. Creating an independent oversight committee or commission to monitor police activities will only be effective if those who serve in it are fully and effectively constrained by the law. It is the case that in many developing societies, such oversight committees or commissions are usually subject to manipulation by the executive. This is due to the fact that the budgets, personnel policies, and the institutional environment within which these committees or commissions are required to operate in are usually controlled by the government.

While many of the reforms recommended by experts to deal with police corruption are necessary conditions, they are not sufficient. Sufficiency requires institutional arrangements that guarantee the rule of law. These are laws and institutions that adequately constrain the state. For unless the police are fully and effectively constrained by the law, any effort to deal with police corruption would fail.

Conclusion

Police corruption remains one of the most significant constraints to political, economic, and human development in many developing societies today. Many of these societies have made significant efforts to clean up police corruption and corruption generally, but have failed in terms of their outcomes. In this chapter, we have argued that while the various reforms implemented in the developing societies to deal with corruption are necessary, they are not sufficient conditions. Sufficiency requires that each one of these societies provide itself with institutional arrangements that guarantee the rule of law. Such institutions should fully and effectively constrain the police and political elites and prevent them from engaging in corruption and other growth-inhibiting behaviors.

It is important to note, however, that having a constitution that guarantees certain rights and provides for the functioning of a government is not enough to ensure that the police will not engage in corruption. These *parchment barriers* must be supported, undergirded, or secured by "a competent and balanced governing process" (Best 1992, p. 37). In other words, in each society, the people must provide themselves with a strong, effective, and competent government, while at the same time retaining the ability to control the government so that its custodians do not act with impunity and engage in corruption and other forms of opportunism. Where a competent and effective government does not exist and where the people do not have the wherewithal and necessary legal mechanisms to control their government, as is the case in many of today's developing societies, impunity and corruption, including that by the police, will remain rampant, and many citizens may be forced to opt for alternative ways (e.g., vigilantism and other forms of community policing) to protect themselves and their property.

References

ABA (American Bar Association). n.d. Part I: What is the rule of law? http://www.americanbar.org/content/dam/aba/migrated/publiced/features/Part1DialogueROL.authcheckdam.pdf (accessed December 30, 2014).

Andvig, J. C. and O.-H. Fjeldstad. 2008. *Crime, Poverty and Police Corruption in Developing Countries.* WP 2008: 7. Bergen, Norway: Chr. Michelsen Institute.

Bayley, D. H. and R. Perito. 2011. *Police Corruption: What Past Scandals Teach about Current Challenges.* Washington, DC: United States Institute of Peace.

Best, J. A. 1992. Fundamental rights and the structure of government. In *The Framers and Fundamental Rights*, ed. R. A. Licht, pp. 37–56. Washington, DC: American Enterprise Institute.

Brennan, H. G. and J. M. Buchanan. 1985. *The Reason of Rules: Constitutional Political Economy.* Cambridge, U.K.: Cambridge University Press.

Buchanan, J. M. 1994. *The Economics and the Ethics of Constitutional Order.* Ann Arbor, MI: University of Michigan Press.

Burnett, J. 2012. At age one, a tattered reputation for South Sudan. http://wcbe.org/post/age-one-tattered-reputation-south-sudan (accessed December 30, 2014).

Chemerinsky, E. 2007. Toward a practical definition of the rule of law. *Judges' Journal* 46(4): 4–8.

Davis, D. E. 2006. Undermining the rule of law: Democratization and the dark side of police reform in Mexico. *Latin American Politics and Society* 48 (1): 55–86.

Dicey, A. (1914 [1885]). *Introduction to the Study of the Law of the Constitution.* London, U.K.: Macmillan.

Dickinson, J. 1921. *Administrative Justice and the Supremacy of Law in the United States.* Cambridge, MA: Harvard University Press.

Erero, J. and T. Oladoyin. 2000. Tackling the corruption epidemic in Nigeria. In *Corruption and Development in Africa: Lessons from Country Case-Studies*, eds. K. R. Hope and B. C. Chikulo, pp. 280–287. London, U.K.: Palgrave Macmillan.

Fombad, C. M. 2012. *Constitutional Law in Cameroon.* New York: Wolters Kluwer.

Gerring, J. and S. C. Thacker. 2004. Political institutions and corruption: The role of unitarism and parliamentarism. *British Journal of Political Science* 34(2): 295–330.

Ionescu, L. 2011. Mexico's pervasive culture of corruption. *Economics, Management, and Financial Markets* 6(2): 182–187.

Jua, N. 1991. Cameroon: Jump-starting an economic crisis. *Africa Insight* 21(3): 162–170.

Kirsch, T. G. and T. Grätz, eds. 2010. *Domesticating Vigilantism in Africa: South Africa, Nigeria, Benin, Côte d'Ivoire, and Burkina Faso.* London, U.K.: James Currey.

Lindquist, S. A. and W. L. Martinek. 2011. Legal stability and economic growth. Paper presented at the *State Politics and Police Conference*, Dartmouth College, Hanover, NH, June 2–4.

Longmire, S. 2010. *Cartel: The Coming Invasion of Mexico's Drug Wars*. New York: Palgrave Macmillan.

Mbaku, J. M. 2010. *Corruption in Africa: Causes, Consequences, and Cleanups*. Lanham, MD: Lexington Books.

Mbaku, J. M. 2013a. What should Africans expect from their constitutions? *Denver Journal of International Law and Policy* 41(2): 149–183.

Mbaku, J. M. 2013b. Providing a foundation for wealth creation and development in Africa: The role of the rule of law. *Brooklyn Journal of International Law* 38(3): 959–1051.

Meyer, M. 2014. Mexico's police: Many reforms, little progress. http://www.wola.org/sites/default/files/Mexicos%20Police.pdf (accessed December 31, 2014).

Ochoa, J. A. and Z. I. Jiménez. 2012. Police force crisis and state legitimacy in México. *Asian Social Science* 8(15): 86–92.

Peters, J. 2013. South Africa's cops are really, really, unbelievably corrupt. Wow, they're corrupt. http://www.slate.com/blogs/crime/2013/02/22/oscar_pistorius_detective_hilton_botha_isn_t_alone_south_africa_s_police.html (accessed December 31, 2014).

Prado, M. M., M. Trebilcock, and P. Hartford. 2012. Police reform in violent democracies in Latin America. *Hague Journal on the Rule of Law* 4(2): 252–285.

Pratten D. 2008. The politics of protection: Perspectives on vigilantism in Nigeria. *Africa* 78(1): 1–15.

Prempeh, H. K. 2006. Marbury in Africa: Judicial review and the challenge of constitutionalism in contemporary Africa. *Tulane Law Review* 80(4): 1239–1323.

Rademeyer, J. and K. Wilkinson. 2013. South Africa's criminal cops: Is the rot far worse than we have been told. *Africa Check*, August 27. http://africacheck.org/reports/south-africas-criminal-cops-is-the-rot-far-worse-than-we-have-been-told/ (accessed December 31, 2014).

Smith, A.1976 [1887]. *An Inquiry into the Nature and Causes of the Wealth of Nations*. Chicago, IL: University of Chicago Press.

Smith, D. 2013. Nearly 1,500 South African police exposed as convicted criminals. *The Guardian* (U.S. Edition), August 15. http://www.theguardian.com/world/2013/aug/15/south-african-police-convicted-criminals (accessed December 31, 2014).

Smith, D. J. 2007. *A Culture of Corruption: Everyday Deception and Popular Discontent in Nigeria*. Princeton, NJ: Princeton University Press.

Stein, R. 2009. Rule of law: What does it mean? *Minnesota Journal of International Law* 18(2): 293–303.

Stirton, L. and M. Lodge. 2001. Transparency mechanisms: Building publicness into public services. *Journal of Law and Society* 28(4): 471–489.

TI (Transparency International). 2004. *Global Corruption Report 2004*. Berlin, Germany: TI.

Uildriks, N. 2009. *Policing Insecurity: Police Reform, Security, and Human Rights in Latin America*. Lanham, MD: Lexington Books.

Uildriks, N. 2010. *Mexico's Unrule of Law: Implementing Human Rights in Police and Judicial Reform under Democratization.* Lanham, MD: Lexington Books.

UN (United Nations). 2004. *The Rule of Law and Transitional Justice in Conflict and Post-Conflict Societies: Report of the Secretary-General.* http://www.unrol.org/files/2004%20report.pdf (accessed December 30, 2014).

Emphasizing Anticorruption Training as a Reform Tool to Curb Police Corruption in Developing Societies

3

KEMPE RONALD HOPE, Sr.

Contents

Learning Goals and Objectives of Police Anticorruption Training 52
    Recruits: Entry-Level Training 54
    Current Employees: On-the-Job/Field/In-Service/Post-Academy
    Training 54
        Senior Police Employees 54
        Other Police Employees 55
Training Approach Model 55
Training Content and Coverage 57
    Recruits: Entry-Level Training 58
    Senior Police Employees 58
    Other Police Employees 59
Conclusion: Anticipated Outcomes 59
References 61

Training is an educational and learning process. Trainees can learn new information, relearn and reinforce existing knowledge and skills, and most importantly have time to think and consider what new options can help them improve their effectiveness at work. Effective training conveys relevant and useful information that inform participants and develop skills and behaviors that can be transferred back to the workplace. The goal of training is to create an impact that lasts beyond the end time of the training itself. The focus is on creating specific action steps and commitments that redirect people's attention on incorporating their new skills and ideas back at the workplace. Training can be offered as skill development for individuals and groups. In general, training involves presentation and learning of content as a means for enhancing skill development and improving workplace behaviors.

In addition, employee confidence is also boosted by training. This confidence is derived from the fact that the employee is fully aware of his or her roles and responsibilities. It helps the employee undertake his or her duties in a better way and even find new ideas to incorporate in the daily execution of their duties. This all leads to the benefit of less employee supervision and vigilant oversight being required as well as to increase employee efficiency and productivity. Moreover, training tends to make employees much more committed to an organization as the employees are provided with learning, potential advancement, and growth opportunities (Frost n.d.).

Police anticorruption training (PACT) is important in developing societies to reorient the culture and thinking vis-à-vis corruption among said police. Consequently, such training must be aimed at all ranks and levels of police employees including both recruits and employees previously hired (Williams 2002). In other words, the ideal situation is to have comprehensive anticorruption training targeted at new recruits and on-the-job training—sometimes referred to as field training, in-service, or post-academy training, targeted at those previously employed.

Moreover, most of the anticorruption training that currently exists for the police in developing societies lacks the appropriate focus and is not provided in the manner of a coherent concentration. In fact, it tends to be delivered primarily in the form of police orientation to existing anticorruption laws or other criminal laws in general. It tends not to provide a thorough understanding of the phenomenon of corruption and how it looks in policing practice in the society, nor does it impart even the basic knowledge and skills on how to adhere to professional standards and avoid the temptation of accepting gifts, favors, or gratuities or engage in other corrupt acts.

This chapter sets out a basic training framework and approach for curbing police corruption in developing societies. It outlines learning goals and training objectives, proposes a training approach model, suggests training content and coverage, and indicates the expected outcomes from the training approach and process.

Learning Goals and Objectives of Police Anticorruption Training

The learning goal of PACT must be to ensure that police employees in developing societies have high standards of honesty, integrity, and ethical behavior when performing their policing duties and therefore to make unambiguously clear to all trainees that even one act of corruption can negatively reflect not only one's own professional image but also on that of the entire police organization (Carty 2009).

Employees will also definitely learn best when the general objectives of their training programs are clearly stated to them. General objectives here refer to the purposes and expected outcomes of training activities. Objectives also provide a rational basis for the evaluation of training. In effect, the objectives set the measures through which effectiveness of training can be judged (Stanislas 2014). If trainees meet the standards proposed in the objectives, then it is reasonable for the training activity to be viewed as a success. Of course, this assumes that the objectives are suitable for the training needs identified in the first place. Training objectives therefore make training evaluation more *objective* (no pun intended), because the assessment is tied to what it sets out to do in the beginning, and not some arbitrarily chosen set of criteria. The following are the general overall objectives that should be applicable to all trainees:

- *To receive information and knowledge* of what police anticorruption standards and strategies are and what they mean for the work of the trainees.
- *To acquire or reinforce skills* so that the functions and duties of the police can be fulfilled effectively with due respect and regard for the need to prevent and mitigate police corruption. Simple knowledge of standards and strategies is not enough to enable trainees to transfer these into appropriate professional behavior. The acquisition of skills should be viewed as a process whereby skills are fine tuned through practice and application.
- *To become sensitized* (to reinforce positive attitudes and behavior), so that trainees accept or continue to accept the need to promote and protect police anticorruption throughout their work and actually do so in the course of their professional duties. The question at issue here is the values of the trainee that have to be reinforced by further training.

However, in addition to the general overall objectives, the specific objectives of PACT will vary slightly given the need to differentiate between new recruits and current employees as well as to actualize and meet different needs with respect to seniority. In other words, the tailoring of training. In that regard, separate training has to be arranged for different categories within the police organization, according to the particular function and context of that subgroup's daily work. For instance, new recruits will need much more in-depth grounding in their respective policing regulations, codes of conduct and ethics, and statutes as well as any other laws pertaining to ethics and integrity. On the other hand, those who are currently employed, and have therefore been through training(s), will need to be reoriented from a field training or in-service or post-academy perspective to keep them in step with best practice principles and new knowledge in police anticorruption methods (Prenzler 2009).

Recruits: Entry-Level Training

The key training objectives in the context of police recruits should reflect the following:

- To formulate anticorruption learning opportunities for new police employees that meet or exceed the training needs of the organization
- To develop and enhance the trainee's learning from the training within the community environment through a series of real-life corruption problem-solving activities
- To produce graduates of the training who are capable of providing responsible, community-focused, noncorrupt police services
- To prepare trainees to use a corruption problem-solving approach throughout their careers by employing problem-based learning/training
- To encourage and reinforce an ethos of legality and of integrity in the police organization
- To inculcate a new orientation and culture toward policing that sees corruption as an unwanted stain on the police organization and a disciplinary offence in breach of police codes of conduct and ethics
- To provide a thorough understanding of the phenomenon of corruption and how it looks in policing practice in the society
- To impart knowledge on how to adhere to professional standards and avoid the temptation of accepting gifts, favors, or gratuities or engage in other corrupt acts

Current Employees: On-the-Job/Field/In-Service/Post-Academy Training

This training will need to be directed at both senior and other police employees. Accordingly, the objectives are somewhat varied. The categorization with respect to seniority, although perhaps obvious, will be the responsibility of each respective police organization.

Senior Police Employees

The key training objectives for the senior employees should include the following:

- To enhance their existing knowledge and skills acquired in previous training in order for them to become more responsive to the demands of anticorruption policing and their responsibilities as senior employees in that regard.
- To develop and enhance their value of integrity, professionalism, and commitment to the people they serve.

- To encourage and allow them to apply their acquired and relevant knowledge of police anticorruption practices into practice and, in particular, with respect to supervising their subordinates in that respect.
- To upgrade and update skills and knowledge with respect to the anticorruption aspects of all current laws and the constitution where applicable.
- To provide remedial training and increase proficiency in those areas of police corruption where deficiencies are identified.
- To broaden the minds of supervisors with respect to police anticorruption strategies. Sometimes, narrowness of outlook may arise in supervisors because of previous or influenced orientation.

Other Police Employees

The key training objectives for other police employees should include the following:

- To fill areas of gaps with knowledge and skills and change all negative attitudes to positive attitudes in confronting police corruption
- To encourage the adoption of a proactive and zero defect culture with respect to police corruption
- To assist employees to function more effectively by exposure to the latest laws, concepts, information, techniques, and development of skills required in police anticorruption practice
- To provide employees with the skill set and tools to identify and demonstrate facility in police anticorruption strategies that are most appropriate to the given situations in society
- To empower employees to take all necessary and required actions where they discover police corruption

Training Approach Model

The suggested training approach to be adapted for the anticorruption training of all trainees in the police organization should be a hybrid of instruction content and the application of problem-based learning (PBL). PBL is a learner-centered teaching model that uses problem-solving as the vehicle for learning (COPS n.d.a, n.d.b). Traditionally, learning has solely involved a trainer or instructor delivering information as content to the learner (the chalk and talk method). PBL, however, entails the presentation of real-life problems that the trainees must attempt to solve. The trainees follow a pattern of discovery whereby they express ideas about resolving the problem, list known facts, decide what information to use (including naming sources for that learning), and develop an action plan to solve the problems (COPS n.d.a, n.d.b).

Clearly, it is critically important that trainees know and apply the proper procedures for responding to police corruption. Yet, it is equally important to understand how to look at such problems in a broader community context. Therefore, much of the effort in this training model ought to focus on process rather than content. The most tangible benefit of this training approach model lies in its application to actual street situations. That is, the creation of opportunities to translate ideas and concepts into practice to enable the participants to focus on real problems they will confront. This model encourages trainees to explore, analyze, and think systemically. The PBL method also encourages trainees to collaborate with their peers and communicate effectively with the community. These are the hallmarks of good police work (COPS n.d.a, n.d.b).

Using the instruction content and the PBL, trainees will confront what they know as well as what they do not know. They will ask questions, do research, and determine what actions to undertake. The following steps are the basis of the problem-solving style:

- The Instructor presents the trainees with real-life problems.
- The trainees work with the problems and consider initial ideas.
- The trainees identify what they know about the problems.
- The trainees identify what they need to know about the problems and seek information from available resources, including relevant community sources.
- The trainees develop an action plan based on their research.
- The trainees evaluate their performance and learn to transfer the new knowledge to future similar types of problems (COPS n.d.a, n.d.b).

Many of the greatest discoveries occur when we fail. Contemporary police writers and leaders call this "failing forward" (COPS n.d.c). Policing services want to minimize mistakes and provide high-quality police services. By using this training model, police employees discover not only positive solutions to problems in the community, but also what does not work. Under the supervision of their Instructor, trainees suggest solutions to problems, some of which may not work. Thus, learning can legitimately take place within the context of "failing forward" (COPS n.d.c). Allowing trainees to explore ideas and make noncritical mistakes fosters an environment of exploration and learning. However, this does not absolve the Instructor of the responsibility to intervene if a trainee or trainees is/are about to make a mistake of a serious nature (COPS n.d.c).

Essentially, what this training model offers is extensive participant involvement. This is vital, and responsibility for learning and teaching is shared by all trainers/instructors and participants. The enterprise might best be described as professional colleagues joining together to address issues of mutual and fundamental importance.

Moreover, learning does not mean information being "injected" into people through provision of facts—it emerges from their own experience. For this reason, participation is the key to the training and education of adults. The passive format of lectures is the least effective means of training for any ethics/integrity-related knowledge and skill acquisition—there must be inter-action, and the more participants are active the more they learn. Training is most effective when the objectives have relevance and meaning for the par-ticipants in terms of their own lives, what they already know, as well as their personal goals. Training is meaningless if it is limited to the delivery of facts and figures. Information must be supplemented by an understanding of why it is important and how it can be used to stimulate anticorruption change. Effective training facilitates this process.

Finally here, it is a fundamental truth that training that is interactive is more effective than lectures because the participants' involvement and expe-riences are actually a part of the learning process. Actively engaged partici-pants are more likely to recall and use the information outside of the confines of the training.

Training Content and Coverage

This PACT approach integrates international best practices in a basic police training curriculum relevant to the police corruption environment in a given developing society. It provides the police leadership and educators of police employees with the building blocks needed to pursue training of both recruits and those already in service to become effective police employees who exhibit, demonstrate, and promote integrity and noncor-rupt behavior.

The PACT should present a set of minimum standards and a core curric-ulum for each group of trainees, providing a platform for improving PACT in line with the principles of democratic policing and the policing laws and codes of respective developing societies. It recognizes that the day-to-day decision making and actions of police employees are based on underlying values, sound judgment, and a set of learned skills and knowledge. And, in that context also, training for police employees should be conducted regu-larly so as to raise awareness and update it—awareness of what is and is not acceptable and what has changed including laws and institutions. Values are not static; what might have been acceptable a generation ago may no longer be tolerated. This dynamism needs to be conveyed to police employees on a regular basis; training only in the early stages of their careers is therefore not sufficient.

Given the differing training objectives for the three groups of trainees identified in this PACT approach, there will of necessity also be some difference in the training content and coverage as discussed below. Also, it must be pointed out here that this training is to be undertaken as a specific stand-alone module as opposed to simply being a part of any existing courses. This is currently necessary given the nature and extent of police corruption in developing societies as well as the current concentrated police reform efforts geared to come to grips with it. The same rationale would apply to any stand-alone module on police ethics which would also normally be covered in the same module with police corruption. In fact, police corruption is one form of unethical police behavior. The core anticorruption curriculum for each group of police employees is set out below.

Recruits: Entry-Level Training

For the new recruits, the following topics will need to be addressed but not necessarily in the order shown:

- What is police corruption
- Forms and types of police corruption
- Conditions that breed police corruption
- Temptations faced by the police
- Direct and indirect police corruption
- Impact of police corruption on democracy and development
- National anticorruption strategy—measures needed to prevent, detect, punish, and eradicate corruption in the society where applicable
- Responding ethically to bribes, corruption, and abuse of power and position
- How to bring justice to those who are corrupt
- Mechanisms such as all laws, policies, codes of conduct, and oversight bodies to monitor the systems and measures established for preventing, detecting, punishing, and eradicating police corruption
- Enforcement personnel and institutions such as the oversight institutions
- Global standards to combat police corruption and combating corruption in general

Senior Police Employees

For the senior police employees, the following topics will need to be addressed and not necessarily in the order depicted:

- The best practices of police in fighting police corruption
- Corruption risk awareness in day-to-day police work
- The role of leadership in maintaining a corruption-free climate
- The police anticorruption strategy (where it exists), current laws, and the various institutions and their statutory roles in curbing police corruption
- Investigative tools and techniques in investigating and preventing police corruption
- Policing in a democratic society

In addition, senior police employees would benefit from exposure to some of the courses addressing police corruption in some of the international training programs. One such very credible and prestigious course, as also noted in Chapter 1, is the Common Curriculum on Police Ethics and Corruption (CCPEC) offered by the European Police College. The CCPEC focuses on knowledge, attitudes, and skills of police officers and is divided into four sections: (1) the role of police in a democratic society, (2) the position of ethics in the police organization and day-to-day police work, (3) managing police ethics and prevention of corruption, and (4) risk management in the field of police ethics and prevention of corruption (CEPOL 2014).

Other Police Employees

The topics to be covered for other police employees are the following and not necessarily in the order shown:

- Current extent and nature of police corruption in and the need to prevent it
- Responding to corrupt and corruptive police employee behavior
- Incorporating noncorrupt behavior in policing
- Policing in a democratic society
- The police anticorruption strategy (where it exists), current laws, and the various institutions and their statutory roles in curbing police corruption

Conclusion: Anticipated Outcomes

One of the key objectives of this PACT approach is to ensure a basic level of knowledge, skills, and key competencies so that the functions and duties of the police can be fulfilled effectively with due respect and regard for the need to prevent and mitigate police corruption. Anything other than this approach will be counterproductive at best. On the other hand, this PACT approach aims to contribute to effective, credible, and sustainable anticorruption behavior to considerably reduce police corruption.

The anticipated PACT outcomes are based on stock taking of strengths and vulnerabilities related to and emerging from training. The vulnerabilities that require attention can usually be classified as (1) an embedded culture of police corruption and (2) a lack of uniform or standardized training. The strengths to emerge from the training are (1) acquisition of skills and knowledge to counteract police corruption and (2) improved awareness of corruption within the police. The ensuing outcomes are (1) improved knowledge and skills in confronting police corruption and (2) built integrity of a critical mass of police employees.

Introducing and sustaining PACT requires both knowledge and champions. Some may exist naturally in the police organization, while many others will be keen to contribute but will lack the knowledge and credibility to act. Among other things, the PACT approach outcomes will result in the provision of counter-corruption education (both ideas and mechanisms) in policing, showing the role of leaders by giving participants confidence that they can bring about institutional change. This will be achieved by developing and enhancing knowledge and understanding in (1) strengthening police integrity and reducing corruption and (2) bringing integrity and corruption-reducing strategies into police management.

The PACT approach suggested here recognizes that good police reform programs reinforce positive behaviors and controls. It is a mistake for anticorruption programs to focus only on constraining illegal or bad behavior. They must also accentuate the positive behavior through training. In police corruption, this means strengthening the knowledge, skills, values, and the codes of conduct by which police employees are required to conduct themselves. Over the longer term, capacity would be developed in positive ethics and integrity values that can influence police behavior.

Consequently, a significant outcome of this PACT approach is the improvement of ethical decision making and behavior that, in turn, will influence the reduction of police corruption (Prenzler 2009). Ethics can be generally defined as the personal values, ideas, or beliefs that influence a person's conduct. It identifies standards and virtues that define what is morally right, good, and proper and guides the good conduct of people (Josephson 2009). Most importantly, ethics is a prescription, not a description. This means ethics directs us and prescribes how we should behave (Josephson 2009; Barker 2011). It is fundamental to what distinguishes humankind from all other living things in the sense of knowing what is right and wrong. Without ethics, we would have no conscience or moral compass. Without ethics, we could not treasure such virtues as truth, justice, compassion, responsibility, and respect, nor could we condemn their opposites.

In the context of the police, ethics is regarded as the standards, values, and principles of conduct that apply to a police officer. Ethics is central to everyday policing. Police ethics is important because of the role of policing in society (Prenzler 2009). That role entails a duty to serve the community; to safeguard lives and property; to protect the innocent against deception, the weak against oppression or intimidation, and the peaceful against violence or disorder; and to respect the constitutional rights of all to liberty, equality, and justice. None of that role can be effectively accomplished through unethical behavior. In fact, the role and functions of the police presupposes ethical behavior.

Police ethics are also important because of the powers of the police that can potentially have negative effects if abused (Prenzler 2009). With these, special powers are expectations of professionalism, ethical conduct, and accountability. Unlike many other occupations, police personnel are expected to maintain high ethical standards. Whether on duty or off duty, at work or at home, the public is watching. Moreover, police ethics is inextricably linked to police legitimacy. As observed by Prenzler (2009, p. 29), "unethical policing is illegitimate policing". Police legitimacy derives from the legitimacy of the entire justice system, and that legitimacy confers an entitlement to be obeyed, for example. Unethical police behavior conflicts with police service values. It also tends to have a negative impact on the police organization by eroding public confidence and trust. Negative interaction with, or observations of, unethical behavior by the police, no matter how isolated, results in the tainting of the opinion of the public about the police in general.

References

Barker, T. 2011. *Police Ethics: Crisis in Law Enforcement*. Springfield, IL: Thomas Books.

Carty, K. 2009. *Good Practices in Basic Police Training—Curricula Aspects*. Vienna, Austria: Organization for Security and Cooperation in Europe.

CEPOL (European Police College). 2014. Common curricula—Police ethics & prevention of corruption. https://www.cepol.europa.eu/education-training/trainers/common-curricula/ethics-corruption (accessed September 12, 2014).

COPS (Community Oriented Policing Services). n.d.a. *A Problem-Based Learning Manual for Training and Evaluating Police Trainees: Training Standard*. Washington, DC: COPS, US Department of Justice.

COPS (Community Oriented Policing Services). n.d.b. *A Problem-Based Learning Manual for Training and Evaluating Police Trainees: Trainee Manual*. Washington, DC: COPS, US Department of Justice.

COPS (Community Oriented Policing Services). n.d.c. *A Problem-Based Learning Manual for Training and Evaluating Police Trainees: PTO Manual*. Washington, DC: COPS, US Department of Justice.

Frost, S. n.d. The importance of training & development in the workplace. http://smallbusiness.chron.com/importance-training-development-workplace-10321.html (accessed September 12, 2014).

Josephson, M. 2009. *Becoming an Exemplary Peace Officer: The Guide to Ethical Decision Making.* Los Angeles, CA: Josephson Institute.

Prenzler, T. 2009. *Police Corruption: Preventing Misconduct and Maintaining Integrity.* Boca Raton, FL: CRC Press/Taylor & Francis.

Stanislas, P. 2014. Introduction: Police education and training in context. In *International Perspectives on Police Education and Training,* ed. P. Stanislas, pp. 1–20. New York: Routledge.

Williams, H. 2002. Core factors of police corruption across the world. *Forum on Crime and Society* 2(1): 85–99.

Developing Societies Case Studies: Africa

II

Ghana
Reducing Police Corruption and Promoting Police Professionalism through Reforms

4

JOSEPH R.A. AYEE

Contents

Brief Country Context.. 66
Short History of the Ghana Police Service.. 67
Constitutional and Legal Frameworks Governing the
Ghana Police Service... 69
Police Corruption.. 71
    Street-Level Bribery and Extortion 73
    Bureaucratic Corruption 74
    Criminal Corruption...74
Police Reforms 76
    Strategies to Promote Internal Accountability.................................. 77
    Strategies to Promote External Accountability.................................. 79
Conclusion: The Ghana Lessons.. 80
References...81

A number of published and unpublished studies have been devoted to the Ghana Police Service (GPS). They may be grouped under three headings. First, some of the studies, which form the largest number of studies on policing in Ghana, have focused on the historiography of policing (Young 1951; Jeffries 1952; Gillespie 1955; Ankama 1984; Anderson and Killingray 1991, 1992; Killingray 1991; Deflem 1994; Pokoo-Aikins 2002); the significance, causes, and types of violence in police operations and role performance (Ansah-Koi 1986; Aning 2002; Tankebe 2008a); and police administration (Ansah-Koi 1987; CHRI 2007). The second group of studies deals with monitoring police performance through their powers, actions, finances, and legal framework (Atuguba 2001; 2003; Aning 2002) and police accountability and types of accountability such as state control, independent external control, internal control, and social accountability (CHRI 2007; Anamzoya and Senah 2011). Police legitimacy and trustworthiness and public trust are influenced by police effectiveness; hence, the absence of trust can hugely undermine the success of the police; some of the factors that have possibly undermined trust in the police include neglect, indifference, incompetence, venality, extortion, discrimination, intimidation, inconsistency, excessive use of force, and brutality (Karikari 2002; Goldsmith 2005; Tankebe 2008b; Boateng 2012). The third group of studies, which seems considerably small compared to the first two groups, is directed at police corruption and reform (Atuguba 2007; CHRI 2007; Quantson 2008; Aning et al. 2013; Nyarko 2014).

Against this backdrop, this chapter builds and extends on these studies and thereby makes a contribution to the debate over police corruption and reform as well as policing generally in Ghana. It also emphasizes that police reform is not only to address police corruption but also to improve police performance and professionalism in the country.

Brief Country Context

Ghana is considered one of the most resilient democracies in West Africa after two and a half decades of military rule and political instability. Since 1992, political governance, which is a necessary crucible for sustaining economic governance, has improved considerably. The incidence of rampant coups during the postindependence era has given way to a stable multiparty democracy. Elections have been held, and there have been peaceful transfers of power between the country's two main political parties, namely, the National Democratic Congress (NDC) and New Patriotic Party (NPP). The December 2012 election was won by the NDC under the leadership of John Dramani Mahama, by a narrow margin of less than 1% (325, 000 votes out of 11 million). The election results were challenged at the supreme court by the opposition NPP, which alleged election irregularities and the cancellation of over 1 million votes. On 29 August 2013, the court dismissed the case and upheld John Mahama as the legitimate elected president. The peaceful adjudication of the election petition and the fact that both political parties accepted the ruling have further consolidated Ghana's democracy. The court case no doubt divided the country along political sympathies rather than on ethnic lines. Notwithstanding this, the risk of instability was muted by calls from civil society, including the clergy and the peace council, for peace to be maintained in the country. However, the outcome of the election has highlighted the need for electoral reforms especially with regard to the appointment and supervision of electoral officers (Ayee 2015; Oduro et al. 2014).

In a turbulent region, Ghana's political stability has been a fundamental asset to foreign investors. Ghana boasts one of Africa's most dynamic press industries and improved its ranking in the 2013 World Press Freedom Index from 41 in 2012 to 30. However, although several high-level corruption cases were publicized in 2013 and 2014, corruption continues to be a significant problem. By 2014, Ghana ranked 61 out of 175 countries in the Corruption Perceptions Index and the eighth in Sub-Saharan Africa with a score of 48 points out of a possible 100 (TI 2014). Commenting on the 2013 ranking, the Ghana Integrity Initiative (GII), a local chapter of Transparency International, had said that no reason could be given for Ghana's score, but that some of the recent corruption issues meant that the country has more to do to fight corruption as scoring below 50 only serves as another reminder that Ghana has not marshaled enough resolve in tackling corruption (Myjoyonline 2013).

A Whistleblowers' Act had been passed in 2006. It is to provide for the manner in which individuals may, in the public interest, disclose information that relates to unlawful or other illegal conduct or corrupt practices of others and for the protection against victimization of persons who make these disclosures. However, a Right to Information Act, a powerful weapon against corruption, is yet to be passed. For over a decade, the bill has been languishing in parliament with the parliamentarians exhibiting no real conviction or courage to pass it. To further reduce corruption, a National Anti-Corruption Action Plan—a 10-year blueprint—was also approved by parliament in 2014 and will be implemented as of 2015.

Short History of the Ghana Police Service

The Ghana Police is a creation of the British colonial government. Professional policing was introduced by the British colonial authorities to the Gold Coast, now the Republic of Ghana, in 1821. Prior to that, policing or maintenance of law and order was organized by the traditional authorities such as the local headsmen and chiefs, who employed unpaid messengers to carry out the executive and judicial functions in their respective communities (Ghana Police Service n.d.).

In 1894, the Institution of Police was formalized with the passing of the Police Ordinance that gave legal authority for the formation of a civil police force (Ghana Police Service nd). The attainment of independence in 1957 saw the Ghana Police Force being renamed the GPS to give it a human face and serve the citizens better (Mensah, 2008). In 1970, the police service was backed by an Act of Parliament—Act 350 of 1970—and this was supported later by other legislative instruments that have given the service a high level of legitimacy. With the enactment of the Police Force (Amendment) Decree in 1974, the GPS was removed from the control of the Public Service Commission and restored to the status of an autonomous organization

(Mensah 2008). Under the British colonial authority, the civilian police force functioned as a state/party/personal service fashioned for the principal goal of provision of security services to the governor and his or her governmental functionaries; provision of security services to private (chartered) companies for the purposes of peaceful, effective, and efficient exploitation of the natural resources of the Gold Coast; and the enforcement of the *rule of law* for particular political, economic, and social ends of the colonialists (Ankama 1984; Aning 2002; Atuguba 2007).

After independence in 1957, there has not been much change in the operations of the Ghana Police. In other words, the nature, character, operations, and structure of modern policing did not change significantly from that of the colonial policing era. The GPS therefore continues to function primarily to protect the lives and property of the politicians first and the citizens second. It also protects the interests of the business class especially the mining companies and the banks. Furthermore, the GPS has been used by politicians for many of their sectarian interests: from its use in the colonial era to keep the citizens under control and compliant, through its use in the early postindependence era to silence political debate and its use under various military regimes as a backup for the military brutality of the citizenry, to its use during constitutional debate eras to arrest, harass, and intimidate political opponents and obstruct their activities (Aning 2002; Atuguba 2007).

The GPS has also remained a centralized organization structured by 2014 into 13 administrative regions, 51 divisions, 179 districts, and 651 stations across the country. The strength of the police service increased progressively from the years leading up to independence and continued until the peak year in 1971. At that time, the police numbered 19,410 personnel that served the total population of Ghana of about 8.5 million (Aning 2002). Currently, the police service is approximately 17,000 serving a population of approximately 25 million.

The modern police service in Ghana performs both crime-related and service-related duties. The crime-related functions are stipulated in Section 1 of the Police Service Act 1970 (Act 350). The act states that it shall be the duty of the police service to prevent and detect crime, to apprehend offenders, and to maintain public order and the safety of persons and property (Republic of Ghana 1970). The service-related functions, which are not stated in the act, include performing motor traffic duties, vetting and issuance of police criminal check certificates, and assisting and helping the female gender to deal with traumatic and psychological problems as a result of sexual abuse (Boateng 2012).

To further strengthen the police capacity to perform these duties, a 5-year (2010–2014) strategic national policing plan was launched in 2010 by the government. The plan represents the second formal attempt by the GPS to fulfill the combined specification of the strategic objectives, national policing targets, and capacity building programs and activities to be implemented over the medium term of 5 years and beyond to 2020 (Mensah 2010).

The purpose of the plan is to enable the GPS to focus on democratic policing practices, as mandated by the constitution, in serving the communities and the people, first, by reviewing the prevailing socioeconomic conditions, stakeholders' expectations, other environmental factors, the strengths and weaknesses of the service, and where the organization is or fits now. The specified direction of the plan commits the GPS to be proactive, anticipate and recognize impending threats, and plan to seize the opportunities available to achieve their mandate. The national policing plan therefore seeks to institutionalize the culture of democratic, noncoercive policing methods to achieve policing objectives, targets, and reporting practices, to tackle crime successfully from local to national levels and across borders (Mensah 2010).

Its principal objectives were:

1. To increase the level of protection of life and property, increase the rates of prevention and detection of crime, and speed up the apprehension and prosecution of offenders so as to enhance public confidence and satisfaction
2. To enhance the capacity of the service by improving its human resources through training and development of personnel and by recruiting appropriate skills and competencies
3. To acquire relevant, modern information and communication technologies that would enable the service to perform its services
4. To establish closer and more mutually beneficial working relationships with external stakeholders to improve the partnership and public image of the police service (Mensah 2010; Modern Ghana 2010).

It was believed and intended that this plan would positively impact crime reduction in Ghana within its stipulated duration. Crime rates in Ghana, as compared to most other African countries, have been relatively low (Boateng 2012).

Constitutional and Legal Frameworks Governing the Ghana Police Service

The GPS is mandated by Article 200 of the 1992 Constitution of the Republic of Ghana and the Police Service Act 1970. The constitution mandates the service to operate on democratic policing principles. Article 200 (1) of the 1992 Constitution requires that the police service shall be equipped and maintained to perform its traditional role of maintaining law and order.

The constitution debars any person or authority from raising any police service except by or under the authority of an Act of Parliament. The GPS is also established in the 1992 Constitution as a public service (Republic of Ghana 1992).

The constitution also sets out the procedure for appointing the Inspector-General of Police and creates the Police Council and the regional police committees, which have key presidential advisory roles on policing and the potential to operate as oversight mechanisms. As well as providing a broad framework for the police, the constitution enshrines the protection and promotion of human rights into Ghana's legal fabric (CHRI 2007).

Ghana's police are defined and empowered by the Police Service Act 1970 (Act 350). Section 1 of that act sets out the functions of the GPS as noted earlier. The act also deals with the structure and conditions of the service and vests the responsibility for day-to-day supervision over the operation and administration of the service in an Inspector-General, subject to any directions by the Minister responsible for the police. The act further details the functioning of the Police Council created under the constitution and sets out a list of possible police misconduct activities and appropriate penalties and also outlines disciplinary procedures.

In addition to the constitution and the Police Service Act, there is also the Police Service Regulations, 2012 (Constitutional Instrument 76), which deal with, among other things, the structure of the GPS, administration, recruitment and enlistment, conditions of service, remuneration, allowances, leave, staff leave, disciplinary offences, retirement benefits, and service awards. Other legal documents that regulate the operations of the GPS as well are:

- The Police Service Instructions, which are a set of conduct guidelines published by the Inspector-General, which also deal with the standards of conduct
- The Security and Intelligence Act 1996, which sets up regional and district security councils, which are committees of the National Security Council—a constitutional provision
- Police Service (Administration) Regulations 1974 (LI 880), which defines standards of conduct
- Police Force (Disciplinary Proceedings) Regulations 1974 (LI 993), which sets out the process for disciplining members of the police service

It is instructive to note two major weaknesses of the constitutional and legal frameworks. First is the failure to set out clear and positive guidelines in terms of police conduct and behavior. Such guidelines are regarded as key components that international good practice considers essential for modern-day police legislation. Modern-day police legislation includes a statement of police values to guide officers and set a benchmark for police behavior. The importance of a statement of values is particularly apparent in Ghana, where police misconduct is a serious issue. Second, none of the documents specifically mentioned corruption. Perhaps the one that might seem to have come closest to dealing with corruption is the Police Service Regulations of 2012 that identifies as one of the major offences an act that amounts to a failure to perform in a proper manner a duty imposed on an officer while one of the minor offences is "to accept directly or indirectly a gratuity, gift, subscription or testimonial without the knowledge and permission of the Inspector-General of Police" (Republic of Ghana 2012, pp. 37, 40).

Police Corruption

Stories of police corruption have become cover-page news; they draw public attention and sell the newspapers. In fact, there seems to be no police agency that is completely free of corruption, and police officers entrusted and empowered to enforce the law can become some of the most aggressive criminals themselves (Ivković 2003).

Like other forms of corruption, learning how much police corruption there is and understanding its characteristics are both basic yet crucial steps toward successful corruption control. Accurate information is necessary to diagnose the extent and nature of the corruption problem, trace the changes in its volume and patterns over time, determine the causes of corrupt behavior, learn about the susceptibility of various types of corrupt behavior to successful control, choose the required degree of interference, design adequate control strategies and mechanisms, estimate the resources necessary, determine the success of the techniques used, and monitor agency performance in corruption control over time.

Consequently, police administrators determined to engage in extensive reforms and invest resources in corruption control without information about the nature, extent, and organization of corruption in the agency are likely to end up wasting time and resources, lowering the morale, strengthening the code of silence, and raising doubts about the ability to manage the organization. Moreover, without accurate measurement of corruption, the degree of success of reforms is often determined on the basis of its political appeal and the absence of subsequent scandals, rather than on the true impact the reforms have had on the actual corruption in the police service. Despite its apparent significance and the vast resources invested in the police, the measurement of police corruption or, for that matter, any other type of corruption, is surprisingly underdeveloped (Jacobs 1999; Ivković 2003).

Although no official nationwide data on police corruption are available in Ghana, the situation regarding measurement of corruption is brighter as surveys have been conducted and official reports have been presented on police corruption generally. In addition, some reforms have been implemented and some police officers have been sanctioned for engaging in corruption.

The GPS is perceived to be the most corrupt public institution in Ghana. For instance, as far back as 1974, the *Final Report of the Commission of Inquiry into Bribery and Corruption* listed the police as the most "corrupt public institution" (Republic of Ghana 1974, p. 8). Also, the results of the Afrobarometer survey (2014) found the GPS to be the most corrupt public institution ahead of other public institutions. The survey focused on trust and perceived corruption in Ghana's public institutions. The result found that some 89% of the respondents said the police service is the most corrupt institution (Armah-Attoh 2014). Other surveys, such as those conducted by the GII, similarly identified the police service as the institution perceived by many Ghanaians to be the most corrupt institution in the country.

Further evidence of this police corruption in Ghana has also been provided by a former Inspector-General of Police, C. K. Dewornu, who admitted that "The Police Service, a human institution, where a lot of people belong to, a few ones may go off the track who misconduct themselves much to the discomfiture of the rest" (Ghanafilla 2014, p. 1). This admission has been further reinforced by a Director General of Public Affairs of the GPS who noted:

> We won't allow ourselves to be corrupted again. We won't take bribes again. We are also appealing to the general public not to corrupt us. People are eager to give us things for our pockets. They shouldn't corrupt us because we have seen people talking about us. We want to tell the people that we are ready to lead a clean life… We are ready to remove any tarnished image that we have acquired. We want to see a new Ghana Police Service that is corrupt-free and ready to serve mother Ghana. (Starrfmonline 2014, p. 1)

It is, however, important to note that even though top police officers indicate that there is corruption in the GPS, it (the GPS) distances itself from the reports and surveys that indicate that the police service is the most corrupt institution in the public sector in Ghana. The GPS has also sometimes been defensive on being portrayed as the most corrupt institution. In reaction to the 2014 Afrobarometer survey, the public relations officer of the GPS dismissed the report as monotonous and inaccurate because to get the true reflection of the real index on the ground, you need to do more random sampling. He was quoted as saying that: "As it stands, the report remains an academic exercise. It is academic because I don't trust it. I think it is not deeply scientific enough to bring out the truth of the situation…. The perception of corruption on the part of the police appears to be entrenched because of the frequency at which the police engage the public" (*The Announcer Newspaper* 2014, p. 1).

As observed by Chêne (2010), police corruption in Ghana may also be classified into three forms, namely, (1) street-level bribery and extortion, (2) bureaucratic corruption, and (3) criminal corruption, as discussed in the following sections below.

Street-Level Bribery and Extortion

There are two forms of street-level corruption. The first one is corruption that involves acts of bribery in the everyday interactions with citizens whereby police officers use their power to obtain money or sexual favors from members of the public in exchange for not reporting illegal activities or expediting bureaucratic procedures. For instance, in September 2014, a former Deputy Minister of communications filed a case of sexual assault and harassment against a senior police officer and three other police officers alleging that they fondled her breasts in the office of a Divisional Commander (Ghana Review International 2014). The GPS is endowed by law with considerable powers and discretion—including the use of coercion and force—providing a strong temptation to engage in corrupt practices. These powers have been misused for personal (or political) purposes.

Street-level corruption has also taken the form of extortion, with some members of the GPS, especially the junior officers often from constable to inspector, demanding payments from civilians whom they threaten to fine or arrest under false pretense, for the sole purpose of collecting a bribe. Some members of the GPS are known to accept bribes from drivers who have expired driver's licenses, flout traffic regulations; and accept bribes to not arrest sex workers, for example. Such forms of corruption are especially common in interactions between traffic police officers and civilians. Other forms of corruption in the daily interactions with citizens involve practices such as extorting regular payment from street vendors, charging for services that are meant to be free, and demanding or accepting a bribe for leaking information, for losing court evidence, or for issuing permits. Corrupt payments are also in-kind and entail free drinks, meals, or other benefits in exchange for preferential treatment. While the individual sums of money involved in such acts of police misconduct may be relatively small, these acts take place with high frequency with serious negative consequences for the overall integrity of the GPS as well as public perception of and trust in one of the most visible institutions of the state. The GPS has also been used to clear the streets of hawkers and squatters in slum areas that have grown in the urban areas, road traffic control, and sometimes the illegitimate function of collection of private debts for the citizenry—functions that have in one way or the other exposed members of the GPS to corruption (Atuguba 2007; CHRI 2007).

Perhaps, it is this street-level bribery and extortion as a result of interaction with the public on a daily basis that may have created the perception of the GPS as the most corrupt public sector institution in Ghana.

Bureaucratic Corruption

Bureaucratic corruption refers to the misuse of internal procedures and bureaucratic processes and resources for private gain. There are many internal processes that have been subjected to abuse as the GPS is an institution with a very large workforce and extensive assets to manage (Boateng 2012).

The Auditor General's reports have pointed out the vulnerabilities in public sector contracting and procurement processes including that of the GPS. They include risks of tender manipulation in exchange for bribes and kickbacks. In addition, some irregular practices have occurred in human resources management, including recruitment, promotion and task assignment, internal disciplinary and investigation processes, preferential shift duties, and holiday and location assignments. Apart from these, there is evidence of the diversion of police resources for personal benefits, with practices ranging from the misuse of police vehicles for private matters to the diversion of salaries or benefit funds or the theft of seized contraband goods. GPS resources have also been misused in cases where some officers of the GPS provided their legitimate services such as patrols in return for free or discounted meals and drinks (Aning et al. 2013).

There are also cases of misconduct contrary to the GPS regulations. For instance, in November 2014, two police officers were seen in photos drinking alcoholic beverages, which went viral on social media. The Police Service Regulations of 2012 classifies drinking alcohol on duty as a disciplinary offence. The rate of police misconduct has resulted in 108 police officers being dismissed from the GPS between 2010 and June 2013 as a result of their involvement in various criminal activities, and an additional 132 personnel of the service were demoted, while 239 were sanctioned during the same period (VibeGhana 2013). Another form of bureaucratic corruption is police–judicial collusion that includes falsification of evidence, the refusal to grant bail, and indefinite or frequent adjournment of cases (Appiagyei-Atua 2006).

Criminal Corruption

Criminal corruption involves the abetment of crime by some members of the GPS either by building their own criminal enterprises, by protecting illegal activities from law enforcement, or by conspiring with criminals to commit crimes. A typical form of collusion between the police and criminals can be gleaned from a recent arrest of two police officers who were extorting monies from people who withdrew cash from automated teller machines. The two officers were believed to be members of a group engaged in such operations (*Daily Graphic* 2014).

In August 2014, two detective corporals, who were being held for robbery, were denied bail by an Accra Circuit Court. The accused officers together with a driver and a businessman were alleged to have apprehended a pharmacist carrying substances suspected to be cocaine. The said substance, estimated to be worth US$ 60,000, was to be used for the production of nasal drop. The accused took the substance and offered it for sale (GhanaWeb 2014).

A number of cases in which cocaine has either disappeared or been replaced with other substances with complicity of senior police personnel have been reported. In 2006, Ghanaian security and law enforcement officials received intelligence reports that a vessel in Ghanaian waters was carrying a shipment of cocaine (Aning et al. 2013). Despite the notification, the officials failed to act on the information in their official capacity. Subsequently, 76 parcels of a total of 77 cocaine parcels were seized and then disappeared and the vessel was set ablaze. Investigations by a government-instituted Commission of Inquiry implicated several individuals including three of the vessel's crewmembers as having aided the importers and owners of the consignment.

Significantly, the investigation also implicated the GPS's Director of Operations (who held the rank of Assistant Commissioner of Police) and a detective sergeant. The commission also discovered other acts of corruption, abuse of office, professional misconduct, and unsatisfactory service on the part of the assistant commissioner and recommended his arrest and prosecution. It also found that the detective sergeant, who possessed important information that could have led to the immediate arrest of one of the traffickers, withheld such information in exchange for a bribe of US$ 3000 (Aning et al. 2013). In response to the commission's report and recommendations, the government of Ghana arrested and prosecuted some of the suspects. Some received sentences of up to 15 years. The most notable exception, however, was the assistant commissioner; he was instead given leave, during which he studied at the Ghana Law School. He was also eventually cleared of any wrongdoing by the Police Council, reinstated, and promoted to the rank of Deputy Commissioner of Police (Ghana Pundit 2009; Myjoyonline 2009).

In 2011, the Bureau of National Investigations implicated the deputy head of the police commercial crime unit for allegedly swapping a 120 kilogram of cocaine exhibit with baking soda that formed the basis for a trial (Myjoyonline 2011). This senior officer was dismissed by the

Police Central Disciplinary Board on the grounds that she held nine meetings with the defendant while that defendant was in custody at the police headquarters. She subsequently filed a petition to the President for reinstatement and gave a press interview in which she pointed out that "I have been sacrificed by the Police Administration to cover up the officers involved" and that "the Police and the BNI (Bureau of National Investigations) have used me as a pawn for their nefarious activities, and they will not go scot free, but pay dearly for it" (GhanaVisions 2012, p. 1). Following her petition, the then Inspector-General of Police relieved the Deputy Chief of the Criminal Investigation Department (CID) and a Deputy Superintendent of Police of their duties. Both had been cited as the main characters in the swapping of the cocaine (Ghana News Agency 2012).

The involvement of some members of the GPS in the narcotics business is worrisome and unfortunate. This emphasizes the point made by Chêne (2010) that when criminal corruption has become institutionalized, it has the potential to lead to a wholesale criminalization of the state that poses a real risk for the stability of many societies, particularly those in developing regions. No wonder, the menace of narcotics has become a big challenge in Ghana, and it has also been politicized with the two main political parties always pointing accusing fingers at each other any time drug dealers get arrested.

Apart from corruption, there are other cases of misconduct such as malingering, illegal arrest and detention, excessive use of force including brutalities, a failure to respond to complaints, drinking alcohol while at work, and other forms of unprofessionalism, which have attracted disciplinary sanctions from the authorities (Aning et al. 2013).

Police Reforms

Police reforms in Ghana can be divided into two categories in the quest to reduce corruption and ensure high performance and professionalism: (1) strategies to promote internal accountability and (2) strategies to promote external accountability (Appiagye-Atua 2006; Anamzoya and Senah 2011).

Internal accountability—or self-regulation—promotes professionalism and responsibility. It largely involves the development of internal systems to monitor performance, maintain discipline, investigate public complaints against the police, investigate allegations of abuse of power or outright corrupt and criminal behavior, and manage any resulting disciplinary procedures. It also involves incentives such as regular and quicker promotions, recognitions, and honors, while disincentives can include dismissal, reduction in rank, reprimand, fines, and withholding or deferment of extra duty.

External accountability mechanisms are the systems, processes, and means by which the police, as individuals and as an institution, can be made responsible for their actions. These mechanisms operate outside the police and complement internal procedures (CHRI 2007; Chêne 2010).

Strategies to Promote Internal Accountability

A number of strategies have been implemented to reform the GPS and to promote effective accountability. They include constitutional and legal frameworks such as the 1992 Constitution; Police Service Instructions; Criminal Procedure Code; Police Service Act; disciplinary proceedings; a public complaints process, which replaced the suggestion box from the early 1970s; Police Intelligence and Professional Standards Bureau since 2005; and Police Service Regulations of 2012. They are meant to promote professional standards of ethical integrity, human resource management, administration, and accountability across the institution involving interventions such as reviewing the GPS's system of incentives, creating effective bookkeeping systems and asset-tracking mechanisms, reinforcing internal controls and supervision, strengthening management and administrative systems, or introducing effective complaints mechanisms; the investigation, prosecution, and removal of tainted police officers; and the creation of effective mechanisms to detect and punish crime (Atuguba 2007).

It has been argued that apart from the 1992 Constitution and the Police Service Regulations of 2012, the legal framework of the GPS needs to be updated to be in tandem with the 1992 Constitution. For instance, the Police Service Act was passed in 1970. A new act will ensure consistency with the provisions of the 1992 Constitution that deal with the supremacy of the constitution over all other laws, human rights and the Directive Principles of State Policy (Chapters 5 and 6), Administrative Justice (Article 23), Due Process (Article 19), Discretionary Powers (Article 296), the public service character of the GPS (Articles 190, 191, and 199), and the chapter on the GPS itself (Chapter 15). In addition, various regulations that govern the GPS, from the legislative instruments that govern the details of police administration and disciplinary procedures, through to the standing orders and squad notes, some dating from the beginning of the twentieth century, to the various service and administrative instructions that are issued periodically by the GPS should also be repealed, reenacted, or reissued as appropriate (Aning 2002; Atuguba 2007).

The efficacy of these strategies has been questioned as they have largely failed to reduce police corruption and malfeasance. This is judged by the number of cases of dismissal, demotions, and other sanctions (Atuguba 2007; Aning et al. 2013).

Six strategies implemented deserve some attention. They are:

1. The introduction of a badge of authority for all police personnel across the country to facilitate easy identification of the police and also to prevent private security personnel from mimicking the police. The silver badge has numbers that are peculiar to individual police personnel to enable the police administration to easily identify officers who engage in misconduct while on duty.
2. The restructuring of the GPS into three major formations—CID, Motor Traffic and Transport Department, and the Patrol Department—in conformity with most policing systems around the world.
3. The launch of a bus shuttle service to convey police personnel from their homes to their various stations or duty posts, which was a measure to boost police morale. The shuttle service is being extended to all districts and units of the police service to ensure that personnel get to work on time (Mensah 2014).
4. The informant reward system instituted by the service to reward individuals who volunteer information to the police leading to major arrests. For example, between January 2012 and August 2014, about 200 informants had been given monetary rewards for supporting the police with information to fight crime. The reward package ranges from approximately US$ 625 to US$ 6250, depending on the gravity of the crime and other factors (Modern Ghana 2014).
5. The institutionalization of Martyrs' Day on 28 November 2014 to be marked every 28th day of November of each year to honor officers who are killed in the line of duty to boost the morale of officers and encourage them to do more.
6. Improved conditions of service, especially an attractive salary range as per the single-spine salary structure (Myjoyonline 2014).

Even though it is too early to evaluate the efficacy of these strategies, there is no doubt that they are meant to intensify the police image-cleansing exercise to elicit more confidence and respect from members of the public. The improved salary structure, for instance, has corrected the distortions between salary levels of the GPS and other public services. This and other improved conditions of service buttress the point that poor terms and working conditions can provide both incentives and opportunities for police officers to resort to corruption. Human resource management is therefore a critical area to consider for minimizing police corruption risks, as it lies at the core of the organization's incentive system (Chêne 2010).

Strategies to Promote External Accountability

The major independent oversight bodies in Ghana are the Police Council, a constitutional body mandated with an advisory role to the President on policing; Regional Police Councils, which support the work of the Police Council and the Commission for Human Rights and Administrative Justice (the all-rounder human rights institution); Parliamentary Committee on Defence and Interior; and civil society organizations (CSOs) including the media. Even though these institutions promote external accountability of the police in their various mandates, they have not by themselves designed and implemented any large-scale reforms. The major means of reforms therefore in the GPS emerge from the reports of commissions/committees of enquiry set up by succeeding governments.

Some commissions/committees of enquiry were set up to deal with corruption, while the rest have dealt with internal procedures, recruitment, brutalities, and professionalism (see, e.g., Republic of Ghana 1974, 1996, 1999). The reforms were generally meant to improve professionalism and performance of the GPS and not necessarily deal with corruption even though tackling corruption may be a by-product.

In spite of the recommendations of the various committees and commissions, there are still weaknesses in the GPS because of shortcomings. These shortcomings include delays in the publication of the reports (and the associated government response), the nature of the government response to the recommendations (which tend to highlight a lack of political will to engage in reform or change), and delays in the implementation of the recommendations—or no implementation of the reforms at all—or the reports that have for the most part gathered dust on the government's shelves (CHRI 2007). The inability to implement the reforms' initiatives has led some analysts to assert, for example, that the lack of administrative and political will to reform the GPS, since it was established almost two centuries ago, had contributed to its inefficiencies and the present lack of confidence in the organization by the public that, in turn, had compelled many people to take charge of their personal security, hence the rush to register guns, the high patronage of private security services, and the frequent resort to mob justice (Atuguba and Aning 2007).

From the surveys of Afrobarometer and other CSOs, it seems clear that internal and external accountability reforms have not minimized corruption in the GPS. The GPS is still perceived as the most corrupt public institution in Ghana, while the record of its handling of narcotic cases has been disappointing. The reaction of the GPS to this perception has been both defensive and, at times, one of admission or concession. On improved performance and professionalism, there are still too many instances of police brutalities and other human rights' abuses of members of the public.

Conclusion: The Ghana Lessons

This chapter has shown that corruption in the GPS may be regarded as a product of both organizational weaknesses and larger systemic issues such as the lack of transparency, the absence of checks and balances, inadequate legal frameworks, weak rule of law and fragile institutions, and unattractive conditions of service. Even though some of the recommendations of commissions/committees of enquiry were implemented, they were not enough to transform the GPS in terms of either considerably reducing corruption or ensuring professionalism and effective performance. In most cases, the recommendations were not implemented at all by successive governments because of their own perception of the GPS.

However, efforts were made to promote internal and external accountability through the integration of both punitive and preventive approaches and coordinate reforms that focus on issues of enforcement and changes in institutional design. Both the constitutional and other legal frameworks and recommendations of committees/commissions of enquiry were meant to remove the underlying structures that encourage corruption and create an institutional environment that decrease incentives and opportunities for corrupt practices. These entailed reforming management systems and the organizational culture of the GPS with measures aimed at promoting integrity at all levels of the police institution, strengthening accountability mechanisms, and engaging with the public through the public complaint mechanism.

Nonetheless, the current state of affairs has seen widespread public discontent with the operations of the GPS. This has sometimes resulted in mob attacks on police officers and their facilities, a situation which has been on the ascendancy (Pokoo-Aikins 2002). Even though this is regrettable, it is not surprising given the level of loss of public confidence in the GPS. Reforms are important for the health and growth of any organization. However, in the case of the GPS, the reforms are incomplete as recommendations made either were not implemented at all or were implemented without the necessary political and bureaucratic support and commitment.

The Ghanaian experience of police corruption and police reforms has reinforced a number of lessons. First, police corruption is symptomatic of the level of systemic corruption existing in the country. Second, the inability to deal with police corruption is due to the lack of transparency, the absence of checks and balances, inadequate legal frameworks and rule of law, and fragile institutions. Third, police reforms may not necessarily be targeted toward corruption but to the overall improved performance and transformation of the institution. In this sense, reforms become a retooling exercise. Finally, like all reforms, the successful implementation of police reforms depends on political and bureaucratic leadership, will, and commitment, which succeeding governments did not demonstrate.

References

Anamzoya, A. S and K. Senah. 2011. Internal control and disciplinary mechanisms in the Ghana Police. In *Police Internal Control Systems in West Africa*, eds. E. E. O. Alemika and I. C. Chukwuma, pp. 16–33. Lagos, Nigeria: CLEEN Foundation.

Anderson, D. M. and D. Killingray, eds. 1991. *Policing the Empire: Authority and Control, 1830–1940.* Manchester, U.K.: Manchester University Press.

Anderson, D. M. and D. Killingray, eds. 1992. *Policing and Decolonization: Politicization, Nationalism and the Police.* Manchester, U.K.: Manchester University Press.

Aning, E. 2002. An historical overview of the Ghana Police Service. In *The Face and Phases of the Ghana Police*, ed. K. Karikari, pp. 7–53. Accra, Ghana: Media Foundation for West Africa.

Aning, K., S. B. Kwarkye, and J. Pokoo. 2013. Getting smart and scaling up: The impact of organized crime on governance in developing countries: A case study of Ghana'. In *Getting Smart and Shaping Up: Responding to the Impact of Drug Trafficking in Developing Countries*, ed. C. Kavanagh, pp. 97–134. New York: NYU Center on International Cooperation.

Ankama, S. K. 1984. *Police History: Some Aspects in England and Ghana.* Essex, U.K.: Silcan Press.

Ansah-Koi, K. 1986. A note on police violence in post-colonial Ghana. *Research Review* 2(1): 39–59.

Ansah-Koi, K. 1987. Police administration in Ghana. *Universitas* 9(11): 23–31.

Appiagyei-Atua, K. 2006. A study of police external accountability in Ghana. A report prepared for the Commonwealth Human Rights Initiative (CHRI), Accra, Ghana.

Armah-Attoh, D. 2014. Perceived corruption escalates, trust in institutions drop: A call for ordinary Ghanaians to get involved in the fight. *Afrobarometer Dispatch* No. 5. http://www.afrobarometer.org/files/documents/dispatches/ab_r6_dispatchno6.pdf (accessed December 7, 2014).

Atuguba, R. A. 2001. Monitoring police performance in Ghana. Paper presented at a *Roundtable on Police and Policing, Organized by the African Security Dialogue and Research*, Accra, Ghana, August 20–22.

Atuguba, R. A. 2003. Police oversight in Ghana. Paper presented at a *Workshop on Security Sector Governance in Africa, Organized by the African Security Dialogue and Research*, Elmina, Ghana, November 24–26.

Atuguba, R. A. 2007. The Ghana Police Service (GPS): A practical agenda for reform. *Policy Analysis* 3(1): 1–15.

Atuguba, R. A. and K. Aning. 2007. Reform police service. http://www.modernghana.com/news/136927/1/reform-police-service.html (accessed December 3, 2014).

Ayee, J. R. A. 2015. Manifestos and agenda setting in Ghanaian elections. In *Issues in Ghana's Electoral Politics*, ed. K. A. Ninsin, pp. 81–111. Dakar, Senegal: CODESRIA Books.

Boateng, F. D. 2012. Public trust in the police: Identifying factors that shape trust in the Ghanaian police. Working Paper No 42 of the *International Police Executive Symposium*, Geneva Center for the Democratic Control of Armed Forces, and Coginta—For Police Reforms and Community Safety. http://www.coginta.org/uploads/documents/2ba342d854f029fbf2ca6105add54c6fda5bb170.pdf (accessed November 29, 2014).

Chêne, M. 2010. Anti-corruption and police reform. http://www.u4.no/publications/anti-corruption-and-police-reform/ (accessed December 3, 2014).

CHRI (Commonwealth Human Rights Initiative). 2007. *The Police, the People, the Politics: Police Accountability in Ghana*. Accra, Ghana: CHRI Africa.

Daily Graphic. 2014. Two policemen arrested for extortion. http://www.ghheadlines.com/agency/daily-graphic/20140124 (accessed December 2, 2014).

Deflem, M. 1994. Law enforcement and British Colonial Africa: A comparative analysis of imperial policing in Nyasaland, the Gold Coast and Kenya. *Police Studies* 17(1): 45–68.

Ghanafilla. 2014. Former IGP admits to corruption in the Police Service. http://www.ghanafilla.net/former-igp-admits-to-corruption-in-police-service/ (accessed November 29, 2014).

Ghana News Agency. 2012. Police sack two over Tehoda cocaine saga. http://omgghana.com/police-sack-two-over-tehoda-cocaine-saga/ (accessed December 3, 2014).

Ghana Police Service. n.d. Brief facts about the Ghana Police Service. http://www.eservices.gov.gh/GPS/SitePages/CID-History.aspx (accessed December 6, 2014).

Ghana Pundit. 2009. Police Council to consider Kofi Boakye's reinstatement'. http://ghanapundit.blogspot.com/2009/07/police-council-to-consider-kofi-boakyes.html (accessed December 3, 2014).

Ghana Review International. 2014. Police officer fondled with my breast—Victoria Hammah. http://www.ghanareview.com/Restyle/index2.php?class=all&date=2014-10-12&id=62047 (accessed December 2, 2014).

GhanaVisions. 2012. DSP Tehoda threatens to spill the beans: I've been sacrificed. http://www.ghanavisions.com/news/headlines/33811-dsp-tehoda-threatens-to-spill-the-beans-i-ve-been-sacrificed.html (accessed December 4, 2014).

GhanaWeb. 2014. Court refuse two Police officers bail. http://www.ghanaweb.com/GhanaHomePage/crime/artikel.php?ID=319821 (accessed November 3, 2014).

Gillespie W. H. 1955. *The Gold Coast Police*. Accra, Ghana: Government Printer.

Goldsmith, A. 2005. Police reform and the problem of trust. *Theoretical Criminology* 9(4): 443–470.

Ivković, S. K. 2003. To serve and collect: Measuring police corruption. *Journal of Criminal Law and Criminology* 93(2–3): 593–650.

Jacobs, J. B. 1999. Dilemmas of corruption control. In *Perspectives on Crime and Justice: 1998–1999 Lecture Series*, eds. M. A. R. Kleiman, F. Earls, S. Bok, and J. B. Jacobs, pp. 73–79. Washington, DC: National Institute of Justice, US Department of Justice.

Jeffries, C. 1952. *The Colonial Police*. London, U.K.: Max Parrish.

Karikari, K., ed. 2002. *The Face and Phases of the Ghana Police*. Accra, Ghana: Media Foundation for West Africa.

Killingray, D. 1991. Guarding the extended frontier: Policing the Gold Coast, 1865–1913. In *Policing the Empire: Authority and Control, 1830–1940*, eds. D. M. Anderson and D. Killingray, pp. 106–112. Manchester, U.K.: Manchester University Press.

Mensah, M. 2008. Ghana @51 special pull out (brief history of Ghana Police Service). http://mamens.blogspot.com/2008/03/ghana-51-special-pull-out-brief-history.html (accessed December 6, 2014).

Mensah, M. 2010. Police to launch a five year strategic plan. http://mamens.blogspot.com/2010/07/police-to-launch-five-year-strategic.html (accessed December 6, 2014).

Mensah, M. 2014. New badge of authority for police personnel. http://graphic.com.gh/news/general-news/15459-new-badge-of-authority-for-police-personnel.html (accessed December 4, 2014).

Modern Ghana. 2010. Police launches strategic plan. http://www.modernghana.com/news/276407/1/police-launches-strategic-plan.html (accessed December 3, 2014).

Modern Ghana. 2014. 200 police informants receive cash reward. http://www.modernghana.com/news/567653/24/200-police-informants-receive-cash-reward.html (accessed December 3, 2014).

Myjoyonline. 2009. Kofi Boakye promoted to DCOP. http://edition.myjoyonline.com/pages/news/201201/79771.php (accessed December 3, 2014).

Myjoyonline. 2011. Cocaine turned baking-soda saga: DSP Tehoda sacked. http://www.modernghana.com/news/425014/1/cocaine-turned-baking-soda-saga-dsp-tehoda-sacked.html (accessed December 3, 2014).

Myjoyonline. 2013. Ghana's new rank in Corruption Perception Index not a reprieve—Vitus Azeem. http://myjoyonline.com/news/2013/December-3rd/ghanas-new-rank-in-corruption-perception-index-not-a-reprieve-vitus-azeem.php (accessed November 29, 2014).

Myjoyonline. 2014. Police Service inaugurates Martyr's Day. http://www.myjoyonline.com/news/2014/November-28th/police-service-inaugurates-martyrs-day.php (accessed December 2, 2014).

Nyarko, J. A. 2014. Corruption and the police service in Ghana. Paper prepared for the Centre for Research for Development and Change. https://www.academia.edu/7639601/CORRUPTION_AT_INSTITUTIONAL_LEVEL_THE_CASE_OF_GHANA_POLICE_SERVICE (accessed November 30, 2014).

Oduro, F., M. Awal and M. A. Ashon, 2014. A dynamic mapping of the political settlement in Ghana. Working Paper 28. http://www.effective-states.org/working-paper-28/ (accessed November 29, 2014).

Pokoo-Aikins, J. B. 2002. *The Police in Ghana, 1939–1999*. Accra, Ghana: J. B. Pokoo-Aikins.

Quantson, K. B. 2008. *Beyond the Frontiers of National Security*. Occasional Papers 37. Accra, Ghana: The Institute of Economic Affairs.

Republic of Ghana. 1970. *Police Service Act, 1970*. Accra, Ghana: Ghana Publishing Corporation.

Republic of Ghana. 1974. *Final Report of the Commission of Inquiry into Bribery and Corruption in Ghana*. Accra, Ghana: Ghana Publishing Corporation.

Republic of Ghana. 1992. *Constitution of the Republic of Ghana, 1992*. Accra, Ghana: Ghana Publishing Corporation.

Republic of Ghana. 1996. *Presidential Commission Report into the Ghana Police Service*. Accra, Ghana: Ghana Publishing Corporation.

Republic of Ghana. 1999. *Government White Paper on Presidential Report into the Ghana Police Service*. Accra, Ghana: Ghana Publishing Corporation.

Republic of Ghana. 2012. *Police Service Regulations, 2012* (Constitutional Instrument 76). Accra, Ghana: Ghana Publishing Company Ltd (Assembly Press).

Starrfmonline. 2014. Don't corrupt us: We won't take bribes again—Police Service. http://starrfmonline.com/1.1913358 (accessed December 7, 2014).

Tankebe, J. (2008a). Colonialism, legitimation and policing in Ghana. *International Journal of Law, Crime and Justice* 36(1): 67–84.

Tankebe, J. 2008b. Police effectiveness and police trustworthiness in Ghana: An empirical appraisal. *Criminology and Criminal Justice* 8(2): 185–202.

The Announcer Newspaper. 2014. Police reject 'unscientific' Afrobarometer report. http://announcernewsonline.com/police-reject-unscientific-afrobarometer-report-p6710-73.htm (accessed December 7, 2014).

TI (Transparency International). 2014. *Corruption Perceptions Index 2014*. Berlin, Germany: TI.

VibeGhana. 2013. Police Service dismisses 108 officers. http://vibeghana.com/2013/07/26/police-service-dismisses-108-officers/ (accessed December 2, 2014).

Young, A. E. 1951. *A Report upon the Gold Coast Police*. Accra, Ghana: Government Printer.

Kenya
Police Corruption and Reforms to Control It

5

KEMPE RONALD HOPE, Sr.

Contents

The Current Policing Institutional Architecture in Kenya: A Brief
Description 86
Nature and Extent of Kenya's Police Corruption... 89
Controlling Police Corruption in Kenya through Police Reforms 97
Conclusions.. 103
References.. 105

As the chapters in Section I have noted, police corruption is found in both rich and poor societies, developing and developed, albeit in different forms and magnitude. Consequently, eradicating police corruption, and the fight against it, remains a key policy agenda of virtually every society across the globe including Kenya.

However, in those societies or countries where police corruption is persistent, such as Kenya, it represents a systemic failure of governance where the principal institutions responsible for ensuring police accountability, the observance of ethics and integrity standards, and enforcing the rule of law are compromised and may themselves be infested with corrupt individuals and syndicates. The result is that a chain environment of personal and collective impunity prevails and police corruption is therefore both perceived and real as running rampant. That, in turn, has considerable negative impacts on justice or security sector development and performance and is a challenge to nation-building, to the maintenance of public order and the rule of law, and to supporting the legitimacy of the State. It further leaves citizens helpless and frustrated and leads to activism (that is not always constructive) on the part of nongovernmental organizations (NGOs) and external actors to advocate on behalf of the citizens for measures to tackle police corruption.

This chapter discusses and analyzes the nature and extent of police corruption in Kenya, within the new and current policing institutional architecture, and then outlines and reviews and assesses the recent police reforms that have been implemented and offers recommendations on the way forward for curbing police corruption in the Kenyan society.

The Current Policing Institutional Architecture in Kenya: A Brief Description

The current policing institutional architecture in Kenya emerged in 2010 following the promulgation of the country's 2010 Constitution. That Constitution provided the overarching legal framework for the transformation of the policing institutional architecture in the country and it was aimed at, among other things, increasing transparency and accountability, improving governance and efficiency, and enhancing professionalism.

Article 243 of the 2010 Constitution established the National Police Service (NPS), which consists of the Kenya Police Service (KPS) and the Administration Police Service (APS) under the overall and independent command of an Inspector-General (IG) with two Deputy Inspector-Generals responsible for the day-to-day management of the KPS and the NPS, respectively. The objectives and functions of the NPS are to (a) strive for the highest standards of professionalism and discipline among its members, (b) prevent corruption and promote and practice transparency and accountability, (c) comply with constitutional standards of human rights and fundamental freedoms, (d) train staff to the highest possible standards of competence and integrity and to respect human rights and fundamental freedoms and dignity, and (e) foster and promote relationships with the broader society (Republic of Kenya 2010).

The NPS Act, 2011 gave effect to the role, functions, and powers of the IG, the KPS, and the APS, respectively. Under that act, the functions of the IG shall be to:

(a) implement policy decisions; (b) audit of police operations and functioning; (c) coordinate all police operations; (d) advise the government on policing matters and services; (e) prepare budgetary estimates and develop a policing plan before the end of each financial year, setting out the priorities and objectives of the service and the justification thereof; (f) determine the establishment and maintenance of police stations, posts, outposts, units, or unit bases in the county and determine the boundaries of the police stations, outposts, or unit bases; (g) determine the distribution and deployment of officers in the service; (h) organize the service at national level into various formations, units, or components; (i) recommend the establishment of, manage and maintain training institutions, centers or places for the training of officers joining the service and other officers; (j) commission research and benchmark against best practices; (k) issue guidelines on community policing and ensure cooperation between the service and the communities it serves in combating crime; (l) provide the command structure and system of the service taking into consideration the recommendation of the service board for the efficient administration of the service nationally; (m) subject to the Constitution and this Act or any written law, cooperate with and implement the decisions of the

Independent Policing Oversight Authority (IPOA) including compensation to victims of police misconduct; (n) designate any police station, post, outpost, unit, or unit base as a place of custody; (o) promote cooperation with international police agencies; (p) establish and devolve the services of the internal affairs units (IAU) that are able and equipped to conduct investigations into police misconduct in a fair and effective manner and report directly to the IG; (q) monitor the implementation of policy, operations, and directions of the service; (r) issue and document service standing orders; (s) cooperate with other public or private bodies to provide reliable police statistics on crime rates, detection rate, public confidence in the police, number of complaints against the police, as well as personnel statistics; (t) act on the recommendations of the Independent Policing Oversight Authority, including compensation to victims of police misconduct; and (u) perform any other lawful act on behalf of the service (Republic of Kenya 2011a).

The KPS is tasked with (a) provision of assistance to the public when in need, (b) maintenance of law and order, (c) preservation of peace, (d) protection of life and property, (e) investigation of crimes, (f) collection of criminal intelligence, (g) prevention and detection of crime, (h) apprehension of offenders, (i) enforcement of all laws and regulations with which it is charged, and (j) performance of any other duties that may be prescribed by the IG under the Act or any other written law from time to time (Republic of Kenya 2011a); while the functions of the APS are (a) provision of assistance to the public when in need; (b) maintenance of law and order; (c) preservation of peace; (d) protection of life and property; (e) provision of border patrol and border security; (f) provision of specialized stock theft prevention services; (g) protection of government property, vital installations, and strategic points as may be directed by the IG; (h) rendering of support to government agencies in the enforcement of administrative functions and the exercise of lawful duties; (i) coordinating with complementing government agencies in conflict management and peace-building; (j) apprehension of offenders; (k) performance of any other duties that may be prescribed by the IG under the NPS Act, 2011 or any other written law from time to time (Republic of Kenya 2011a).

Two other key institutions that were established within the NPS are the Directorate of Criminal Investigations (DCI) and the IAU. The DCI replaced what was previously the Criminal Investigations Department, and its functions are to (a) collect and provide criminal intelligence; (b) undertake investigations on serious crimes including homicide, narcotic crimes, human trafficking, money laundering, terrorism, economic crimes, piracy, organized crime, and cybercrime among others; (c) maintain law and order; (d) detect and prevent crime; (e) apprehend offenders; (f) maintain criminal records; (g) conduct forensic analysis; (h) execute the directions given to the IG by the Director of Public Prosecutions (DPP) pursuant to the Constitution;

(i) coordinate country Interpol affairs; (j) investigate any matter that may be referred to it by the IPOA whose mandate is described in the text below; and (k) perform any other function conferred on it by any other written law (Republic of Kenya 2011a).

The functions of the IAU are to (a) receive and investigate complaints against the police, (b) promote uniform standards of discipline and good order in the service, and (c) keep a record of the facts of any complaint or investigation made to it. The IAU shall investigate misconduct and hear complaints as follows: (a) from members of the service or members of the public, (b) at the direction of a senior officer, (c) on its own initiative, (d) on the direction of the IG, or (e) at the request of the IPOA. The IAU is to be located in separate offices from the rest of the NPS and has the powers to recommend the following disciplinary actions to the IG: (a) the interdiction of an officer; (b) the suspension of an officer; (c) the administration of a severe reprimand or a reprimand to control or influence the pay, allowances, or conditions of service of an officer; or (d) any other lawful action (Republic of Kenya 2011a, 2014). By statute, the IAU therefore has a major role to play in the detection and investigation of police corruption and misconduct.

The 2010 Constitution also established two oversight institutions to be part of the policing architecture. The first, the National Police Service Commission (NPSC), was given effect through the NPSC Act, 2011, and basically, it currently manages the employment and pay matters of the police including vetting and monitors the running of the NPS. The key functions of the NPSC include to (a) recruit and appoint persons to hold or act in offices in the service, confirm appointments, and determine promotions and transfers within the NPS; (b) keep under review all matters relating to standards or qualifications required of members of the service; (c) ensure that the service is efficient and effective; (d) hear and determine appeals from members of the service; (e) receive and refer civilian complaints to the IPOA, the Kenya National Commission on Human Rights, the DPP, or the Ethics and Anti-Corruption Commission (EACC), as the case may be, and where necessary; (f) monitor and evaluate the performance of the service; and (g) receive complaints and recommendations from police associations registered in accordance with the applicable law (Republic of Kenya 2010, 2011b). In the exercise of its powers or the performance of its functions, the NPSC is also charged with the responsibility to "prevent corruption, and promote and practice transparency and accountability" (Republic of Kenya 2011b, p. 11).

The other oversight institution is the previously referred to IPOA. The IPOA was operationalized through the IPOA Act, 2011. The objectives of the IPOA as set out in Section 5 of that Act are to (a) hold the police accountable to the public in the performance of their functions; (b) give effect to the provision of Article 244 of the Constitution that the police shall strive for professionalism and discipline and shall promote and practice transparency and accountability; and (c) ensure independent oversight of the handling of complaints by the Service (Republic of Kenya 2011c).

In order to ensure the achievement of these objectives, the IPOA is empowered under Section 6 of the Act to undertake a number of functions. These are to (a) investigate any complaints related to disciplinary or criminal offenses committed by any member of the police service, whether on its own motion or on receipt of a complaint and make recommendations to the relevant authorities, including recommendations for prosecution, compensation, internal disciplinary action, or any other appropriate relief and shall make public the response received to these recommendations; (b) receive and investigate complaints by members of the service; (c) monitor and investigate policing operations affecting members of the public; (d) monitor, review, and audit investigations and actions taken by the IAU in response to complaints against the police and keep a record of all such complaints regardless of where they have been first reported and what action has been taken; (e) conduct inspections of police premises, including detention facilities under the control of the service; (f) cooperate with other institutions on issues of police oversight, including other state organs in relation to services offered by them; (g) review the patterns of police misconduct and the functioning of the internal disciplinary process; (h) present any information it deems appropriate to an inquest conducted by a court of law; (i) take all reasonable steps to facilitate access to the authority's services for the public; (j) subject to the Constitution and the laws related to freedom of information, publish findings of its investigations, monitoring, reviews, and audits as it sees fit, including by means of the electronic or printed media; (k) make recommendations to the service or any state organ; (l) report on all its functions under the Act or any written law; and (m) perform such other functions as may be necessary for promoting the objectives for which the authority is established (Republic of Kenya 2011c).

Nature and Extent of Kenya's Police Corruption

As previous chapters have pointed out, police corruption is nearly always a function of larger systemic problems caused by the lack of overall transparency, the absence of checks and balances, weak rule of law, and fragile institutions (Neild 2007). Moreover, by any measure or indicator, Kenya is regarded as one of the most corrupt countries in the world (Hope 2012, 2014). For example, based on the percentage of people who report having paid a bribe in 2013 to one of eight services, including the police, Kenya is one of the most corrupt countries in the globe with 70% of Kenyans paying a bribe (TI 2013). Only three other countries had more people paying bribes: Sierra Leone (84%), Yemen (74%), and Liberia (75%) (TI 2013). Consequently, it should not be surprising that a considerable number of reports, studies, surveys, and other publications have observed that corruption is a pervasive and historical part of police functioning in Kenya leading to the Kenya Police remaining somewhat deficient in the areas of professionalism, ethics, integrity, and accountability (Hope 2012, 2014).

Corruption therefore arises in the daily routines of the Kenya Police and is now a matter of some concern with Kenyans having a considerably negative perception of their police. In a report by the Commonwealth Human Rights Initiative and the Kenya Human Rights Commission, it was observed that:

> Kenyans view their police... in one of two ways. First, they see it as an organization in such a corrupt state that it is little more than an institutionalized extortion racket, that uses illegal and violent methods to uphold the status quo and is only paying lip service to reform initiatives. Alternatively, they see it as an institution that is struggling to reform itself and to overcome its history, to become a disciplined and law-abiding police service more suited to the democracy in which it now exists.

CHRI and KHRC (2006, p. 19)

Survey after survey has found that Kenyans estimate that large numbers of the police service are corrupt. In fact, the 2012 *National Survey on Corruption and Ethics* by the EACC found that the Kenya Police overall leads government departments perceived to be very corrupt by 48% of the respondents with the traffic police ranked as the second most corrupt by 19% of those respondents (EACC 2013).

Another prominent indicator of police corruption in Kenya is bribery. The *East African Bribery Index* by Transparency International Kenya shows that the police in Kenya take the lead as the sector most affected by bribery based on an aggregate index. The aggregate index value ranges between 0 and 100 with 100 being the worst score, and the aggregation is a composite index of the individual scores of five indicators. The five indicators are (1) likelihood of encountering a bribery incidence, (2) prevalence of bribery, (3) average size of bribe, (4) share of "national" bribe, and (5) impact of bribery. The aggregate index serves to capture an overall reflection of the bribery pattern in an institution (TI-Kenya 2013, 2014).

Figure 5.1 shows the aggregate bribery index for the Kenya Police for the period 2007–2014. As can be gleaned, the index increased significantly between 2007 and 2010 before beginning to decline each year since, indicating some recent positive movement in the incidence or likelihood of police corruption as perceived by Kenyans. However, on average, 60%–93% of respondents reported a probability of a bribe payment to the police and an average of 52% reported that a failure or refusal to comply with such a bribe demand either resulted, or would result, in their failure to access the service

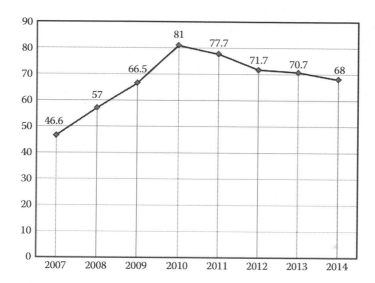

Figure 5.1 Kenya Police Aggregate Bribery Index, 2007–2014. (Based on data from TI (Transparency International)-Kenya, *The East African Bribery Index 2009*, TI-Kenya, Nairobi, Kenya, 2009; TI (Transparency International)-Kenya, *The East African Bribery Index 2010*, TI-Kenya, Nairobi, Kenya, 2010; TI (Transparency International)-Kenya, *The East African Bribery Index 2011*, TI-Kenya, Nairobi, Kenya, 2011; TI (Transparency International)-Kenya, *The East African Bribery Index 2012*, TI-Kenya, Nairobi, Kenya, 2012; TI (Transparency International)-Kenya, *The East African Bribery Index 2013*, TI-Kenya, Nairobi, Kenya, 2013; TI (Transparency International)-Kenya, *The East African Bribery Index 2014*, TI-Kenya, Nairobi, Kenya, 2014.)

or in their incurring punishment (Hope 2014). In fact, as noted by the TJRC Kenya (2013, p. 355), "those who cannot bribe police officers are the ones who are arrested and charged."

By 2014, the average size of the police bribe amount was equivalent to U.S. $55 and the police also accounted for the largest share of the national bribes paid at 43.5% (TI-Kenya 2014). Paying these bribes imposes a direct financial cost, a rent-seeking tax burden, on Kenyans. These are extortion payments that the police collect from their victims, often times, as per a survey conducted by Andvig and Barasa (2011, p. 74), "using imprisonment or the threats of it as their major instrument... [and] these extortion forms constitute more than 80% of the police corruption incidences reported." Other indices by Transparency International showing the perceptions of corruption by institution, for example, further confirm that the Kenya Police are the most corrupt with a perceptions index score of 4.8 with the country's parliament coming second with an index score of 4.0 (TI 2013). For this perception index, the score scale is 1–5, where 1 means not at all corrupt and 5 means extremely corrupt (TI 2013).

The concerns raised about police corruption in Kenya tend to be primarily about, but not limited to, police officers actively misbehaving rather than about any omissions, incompetence, negligence, or poor performance in controlling crime. Accordingly, it seems to be police criminality, plain and simple, that is fuelling the most negative perceptions about the police. In addition to bribery as discussed earlier, criminality includes the perversion of the criminal process, illegal use of force, and abuse of due process. All of this amounts to predatory policing as defined in Chapter 1.

The report by the retired Justice Philip Ransley (commonly known as The Ransley Report) released in 2009 is considered the definitive source and analysis (and rightly so) of what ails the Kenya Police and what reforms are needed to improve the organization's performance overall and for democratic/ethical policing. Among other things, the report found or observed that:

1. Corruption among junior and senior police officers has been rife and has had a debilitating impact on policing and on public trust.
2. There is corruption and nepotism in the recruitment and promotion process perpetrated through interference by influential individuals and instances where recruits paid substantial sums to join the police services. This then presents a basic contradiction in values, in that a police officer, who is expected to uphold law and order, has entered the police force on a corruption platform.
3. Corruption within the police services is widespread and endemic with the tolerance levels for corruption for all ranks being unacceptably high and bribery appearing to be blamed on poor salaries and working conditions of the officers. Allegations of links and collusion with organized criminal groups and drug cartels were also raised by the public as a major concern.
4. The public and other stakeholders accused the traffic department of corruption and complained of the numerous roadblocks, some of which have become permanent features on the roads and which are used by traffic police officers to extort money from motorists and other members of the public. Many police officers were categorical that a majority of police officers manning road blocks and many others performing traffic duties knew nothing about traffic management and operations, while those who have been trained with the objective of taking up traffic duties are deployed elsewhere to perform duties that are completely irrelevant to their training. Nepotism and ethnicity have significantly contributed to corruption in the traffic department.
5. The low salary paid to the police officers contributes highly to their predisposition to corruption, lethargy, and inefficiency in the execution of their duties.

6. The performance of the police has been consistently poorly rated by the public, particularly on violation of human rights, abuse of power, and corruption. This is a matter of great concern to the government, hence the focus of the current reforms.

7. A major security challenge was found to be emanating from the Northern part of the country through Eastern Province of Kenya from Ethiopia and from Somalia through North Eastern and Coast regions of Kenya. The immigration personnel have not coordinated well with the police and there are allegations of rampant corruption in facilitating the trafficking (Republic of Kenya 2009).

Other reports by NGOs and the United Nations Committee Against Torture (UNCAT), for example, have also observed that corruption in the police service in Kenya was hindering efforts to deal with violations of human rights and arbitrary arrest by the police. In a 2009 report, UNCAT stated that

> The Committee urges the State Party [Kenya] to address the problem of arbitrary police actions including unlawful and arbitrary arrests and widespread police corruption particularly in slums and poor urban neighborhoods, through clear messages of zero tolerance to corruption from superior officers, the imposition of appropriate penalties and adequate training. Arbitrary police action must be promptly and impartially investigated and those found responsible punished.
>
> **UNCAT (2009, p. 3)**

Also in 2009, the United Nations Special Rapporteur on extrajudicial, summary, and arbitrary executions accused the Kenya Police of having death squads that hunted down and killed people arbitrarily and brutally (UNHRC 2009). In 2012, the United Nations Human Rights Committee (UNHRC) raised concerns about the slow pace of investigations and prosecutions for allegations of torture and extrajudicial killings by the Kenya Police (UNHRC 2012). The failure to prosecute police officers responsible for human rights violations remains a serious challenge for accountability in Kenya.

In 2013, the IPOA conducted and released a *Baseline Survey on Policing Standards and Gaps in Kenya* to gather firsthand data/information and perceptions of Kenyans, including police officers, on policing standards and factors/challenges affecting effective and efficient policing in Kenya. The survey found, among other things, that

- Thirty percent of respondents had experienced police malpractice including assault/brutality, falsification of evidence, bribery, and threat of imprisonment within 12 months prior to the survey.

The incidence of police malpractice is higher in rural areas at 61% than in urban areas, higher among men (62%) compared to 38% of women, and higher among younger people aged less than 35 years (64%) than those aged above 35 years (34%).

- Only 30% of those who experienced incidences of police malpractice reported the crime to the relevant authorities.
- Among police officers, 53% admitted to have experienced incidences of police misconduct that included bribery (36%), assault (25%), use of excessive force (25%), injuries from a weapon (14%), falsification of evidence (14%), threats of imprisonment (14%), and unwarranted shooting (9%).
- Among the police officers who had witnessed incidences of misconduct, only 32% of them reported such cases to the relevant authorities.
- Police officers who do not report cases of malpractice by their colleagues indicated that they do not do so for fear of reprisals (56%), threats of being transferred (18%), fear of losing their job (13%), because not much action will be taken (5%), and being unaware of where to report (5%).
- For police officers, the most important factors affecting police performance in Kenya is low pay and incentives (54.6%); limited resources including transportation to fight crime (24.7%); corruption (3%); discrimination, ethnicity, nepotism, and favoritism (2,7%); lack of ICT infrastructure (1.6%); lack of proper training (1.2%); and other factors (2.6%).
- The concept of community policing is fairly well known with 56.3% of the public reporting awareness.
- A surprisingly significant proportion (61%) of the public had confidence in the police to effectively discharge their duties.
- About 34.3% of the public have confidence in the IPOA's ability to effectively hold the police accountable for their misconduct, while 13.7% have no confidence.
- The majority of the police officers (62.5%) had confidence in the IPOA and believes that it can deliver its mandate, while 29.3% are somewhat confident. Only 6% are not confident, while 2.1% are not sure (IPOA 2013).

Even more recently, the evidence continues to show the damning nature and extent of police corruption and misconduct in the country. In a 2014 report published by the Independent Medico-Legal Unit (IMLU) in which they examined 1873 deaths resulting from gunshot wounds over the period 2009–2013, it was found that (1) police use of firearms accounted for 67% of those deaths, (2) inadequate documentation did not allow for perpetrator identification in more than 200 cases, (3) the circumstances of police involvement were unclear or absent in over 60% of these fatal shootings, and (4) the reason for the police resorting to deadly force was not given in over 65% of the shootings (IMLU 2014).

Also in 2014, a monitoring report by the IPOA—on a police security operation undertaken in areas of Kenya perceived to be hideouts for immigrants and intended to flush out terrorists and search for weapons and explosives as well as disrupt and deter terrorism and other criminal activities—found that "the operation was marred by widespread allegations of corruption where members of the public were allegedly forced to part with bribes to avoid being arrested and/or detained in unclear circumstances; [and] arbitrary arrests, harassment, assault, unlawful detentions and deportation of individuals" (IPOA 2014a, p. 3).

In addition, the Kenyan newspapers are almost on a daily basis replete with investigative reports of police corruption. Recently, these reports have been concerned with internal police corruption and misconduct such as the rampant cases of victimization, widespread graft, unexplained salary deductions, and dismissals perpetrated by senior officers against the junior ones. Teyie and Menya (2014), for example, reported that junior police officers, who do not cooperate with their seniors in corrupt activities, are being arbitrarily dismissed, transferred, or demoted on questionable grounds. This has led some junior officers to question "if expertise in corruption is a qualification for one to be promoted in the police service" (Teyie and Menya 2014, p. 28).

Other examples of the police corruption menace can be gleaned from the July 2014 attempt by the NPSC to recruit 10,000 police trainees in 1 day. This exercise was troubled with allegations of much shameless bribery and tribalism that moved one commentator to describe it as reaching a new low when it comes to corruption in the police service with the security services having become even more corrupt, politicized, and tribalized since 2013 when a new government came to power (Warah 2014). It had previously been noted by the *Ransley Report* (Republic of Kenya 2009) as indicated earlier and, subsequently, the TJRC Kenya (2013, p. 102) that "during the recruitment exercise, money changes hands. If you cannot part with Ksh 60,000 [approximately US$ 680], your son cannot be employed."

The resultant effect of this botched corrupt recruitment of 10,000 police trainees was that a number of institutions and individuals went to court to prevent the selection results from being implemented and that included candidates who were not selected. Among the institutions that moved to the courts was the IPOA. The IPOA filed a case in the high court seeking to have this police recruitment exercise nullified on the grounds that the exercise was marred by maleficent irregularities, was conducted in a manner that was not in compliance with the Constitution, and hence led to the great hue and cry from members of the public and aggrieved participants (IPOA 2014b).

In a much more elaborate and dramatic statement, entitled *Police Recruitment: A National Shame and a Sham*, the IPOA outlined its findings and subsequent verdict on the recruitment exercise as its rationale for taking the matter to court. Among its findings was that:

> there were reported incidents of influence peddling and conflict of interest. The involvement of NPS senior officers and the Deputy County Commissioners from the stations within or near the recruitment exercise appeared to complicate the exercise. Given the manner in which many of these officers conducted the exercise, it was easy to conclude that these officers could have been compromised long before the exercise.
>
> **IPOA (2014c, p. 2)**

Based on its findings, the verdict by the IPOA was stated as follows:

> Therefore, it is the position of IPOA that the recruitment exercise was not transparent and accountable. There were complaints of discrimination on the basis of ethnicity and undefined criteria which disqualified the candidates in the final stage. The exercise was marred by widespread irregularities and, therefore, could not pass muster in the test of a free and fair undertaking including promoting public confidence in policing.
>
> Arising from this, we recommend the cancelation of the entire exercise, and its repeat with a more transparent process owned by as many stakeholders as possible, before commencement of the exercise. We are confident that the process when started afresh, will create a viable relationship between the public and the police, and further, improve the policing function, and this can only start at the recruitment and selection stage. No other way.
>
> **IPOA (2014c, p. 2)**

In an attempt to head off court action, the NPSC annulled the recruitment in 36 of the 289 centers suspected to have had malpractices in the exercise and to repeat the process. The 36 centers affected 1,215 recruits representing 12% of the total 10,000 recruits. According to the NPSC, the results were annulled for reasons including acts, which are criminal in nature, corruption, and professional misconduct (NPSC 2014). The high court eventually ruled in favor of the IPOA, annulled the entire recruitment process, and ordered that the recruitment be started afresh. In a precedent-setting ruling, the high court said that the July 2014 hiring was tainted with corruption, irregularities, and blatant violation of the Constitution. According to court reporting by Lucheli and Weru (2014, p. 1), the high court found and held "that the National Police Service Commission failed itself, it failed Kenyans, it failed the recruits, it failed the Constitution and it must be told so. The orders that are appropriate in the circumstances is an order quashing the recruitment exercise conducted on July 14 [2014]. [The Court is] satisfied that drastic action must be taken, painful or unpopular as it may be." The NPSC subsequently appealed the court's decision but that appeal was rejected.

However, it was indeed quite interesting and refreshing to notice that the IPOA was vigorously and studiously exercising its civilian oversight role. Perhaps this augurs well for the future as a sign that the policing institutions will be made to comply with the Constitution and all existing policing statutes that have now been put in place in support of said Constitution to bring about a professionalization of the police that significantly eschews corruption. Indeed, the control of police corruption and the professionalization of the NPS must begin at the recruitment and training stages in the quest for the transformation of the NPS into an efficient, effective, accountable, and transparent organization (Hope 2013). In fact, in response to this corruption problem in police recruitment, the NPSC subsequently developed regulations governing the recruitment, selection, and appointment of police officers as outlined in the next section.

In September 2014, further evidence on the extent and nature of Kenya's police corruption emerged when it was revealed by the EACC that they had arrested and charged five traffic police officers for demanding bribes from motorists on a busy traffic thoroughfare in the capital city, Nairobi, where the officers had set up a roadblock checkpoint for the sole purpose of extorting motorists (Star Reporter 2014). Three other officers (accomplices) managed to get away by darting through the traffic and running off leaving some of their police uniform, including hats and sweaters, behind. The five that were apprehended were each found to have an average of Ksh 5000 (approximately U.S. $56) when searched, and which the EACC surveillance detected they had collected within an hour of setting up the roadblock checkpoint (Star Reporter 2014). Based on their surveillance of the traffic police, the EACC estimates that each traffic officer pockets between Ksh 4000 and 8000 (approximately U.S. $45 and $90) daily from extortionary bribes (Star Reporter 2014).

Controlling Police Corruption in Kenya through Police Reforms

While Kenya has engaged in some attempts at police reforms over the past several decades, this work is concerned only with those reforms that led to the current policing institutional architecture—as described earlier—and beyond. A major objective of that police reforms process has been to provide a policy, legal, and institutional framework to enable the transformation of the police service into a professional and accountable security agency that can effectively and efficiently deliver on its mandate. Deliberate efforts were therefore made to establish institutions expected to ensure police reforms that would subsequently result in respect for human rights, accountability, and professionalism among the police.

The catalyst for the current police reforms can be traced back primarily to the recommendations contained in the *Report of the National Task Force on Police Reforms* (The Ransley Report) (Republic of Kenya 2009). The impetus for the appointment of the National Task Force on Police Reforms (NTFPR), in turn, arose mainly from the postelection violence in 2008, which was triggered by the disputed December 2007 presidential election results, and the various agreements that were thereafter struck between the two main contenders for political power who agreed to form a government of national unity (GNU). The inclusion of police reform as an agenda item stemmed from a strong feeling that the level of postelection violence and destruction would have been minimized had the police responded in a professional and nonpartisan manner (Republic of Kenya 2009). Consequently, in their comprehensive agreement, an article entitled "Comprehensive Reform of the Kenya Police and Administration Police" was agreed to by the parties. That article stated that:

> The Parties shall initiate urgent and comprehensive reform of the Kenya Police and the Administration Police. Such reforms shall be undertaken by a panel of policing experts and will include but not be limited to a review of all tactics, weapons, and the use of force, establishment of an independent Police Service Commission to oversee both the Kenya Police and the Administration Police, an Independent Police Conduct authority for both the Kenya Police and Administration Police, creation of a modern Code of Conduct for the Kenya Police and the Administration Police, and achieving ethnic and tribal balance in the Force.
>
> **Republic of Kenya (2009, pp. 2–3)**

In May 2009 and pursuant to the above article and the slow pace of reforms that followed its agreement, the GNU announced the appointment of the NTFPR with a terms of reference (TOR) to

(a) Examine the existing policy, institutional, legislative, administrative, and operational structures, systems, and strategies and recommend comprehensive reforms taking cognizance of the recommendations contained in… other Police related Reports so as to enhance police efficiency, effectiveness and institutionalize professionalism and accountability, (Special focus to be given to recommendations on: Police Service Commission; Independent Police Oversight Authority; Policing Policy; and National Security Policy);

(b) Examine existing competences, skills, knowledge, and attitudes of the Police at all levels and make recommendations aimed at enhancing shared core values, policing excellence and benchmarking against international best practices;

(c) Review the human resource management and development policies with a view to examining current standards and practices in recruitment, deployment, training, career progression, exit, post-exit management and recommend implementation of changes that enhance morale, meritocracy, and professionalism;

(d) Review the tooling, logistical and technological capacity and recommend changes necessary to sustain modern security management, disaster management, conflicts and early warning/rapid response systems, and joint operational preparedness strategy;

(e) Review the state of preparedness of the Police to combat insecurity and other forms of emerging security challenges occasioned by national and international threats such as terrorism, piracy, organized gangs, drug/human trafficking, industrial espionage, cybercrime, money laundering, and economic crimes;

(f) Review and recommend strategies to harmonize and fast-track partnership between the community and security agencies in policing;

(g) Design a continuous monitoring and evaluation mechanism to track police reform gains and consistency of policing needs;

(h) Recommend appropriate institutional arrangement to oversee the implementation of comprehensive police reforms;

(i) Prepare a draft Police Reforms Bill to embrace the comprehensive police reform agenda;

(j) Make any other appropriate recommendations that add value to police reforms; and

(k) Develop a prioritized implementation matrix clearly categorizing the immediate, medium and long-term police reforms and the attendant budgetary requirements.

Republic of Kenya (2009)

The methodology applied by the NTFPR to meet its TOR included benchmarking visits to Botswana, Sweden, and the United Kingdom and Northern Ireland to study their policing structures and different policies and operational approaches toward policing as best practices. In October 2009, the NTFPR issued its Report (The Ransley Report), which became the platform from which a number of police reform measures were codified in the constitution and a new policing institutional architecture emerged. It is through this new policing institutional architecture, as previously described and discussed, that police reforms are being implemented in Kenya.

In addition to the institutional architecture itself, a number of policy changes have been put in place to accelerate the transformation of the NPS into an efficient and effective organization with enhanced accountability, transparency, professionalism, preparedness, and ethics and integrity (NPS 2014). The reforms process has also benefited from donor funding and technical assistance provided through the United Nations Office on Drugs and

Crime (UNODC). The UNODC launched a police reform project in Kenya in October 2013, in cooperation with the government of Kenya, and in partnership with the policing institutions (NPS, NPSC, IPOA) reaffirming the need to strengthen the capacity of law enforcement agencies in order to provide a peaceful and secure society for all Kenyans (UNODC 2013).

The overall goal of the UNODC project, at the time it was initiated, was to create a solid and efficient police sector in Kenya. UNODC (2013) noted that despite efforts in recent years, reforms in the police sector in the country have largely focused on operational and administrative aspects. The project was therefore designed to also target institutional, legal, and policy areas that are necessary for transformation and assist with establishing a transformational framework to govern policing and support effective and sustainable institutional reforms to enhance professionalism, integrity, and accountability within the police (UNODC 2013). This was to be accomplished through the provision of direct technical assistance and advisory services to the NPS, the NPSC, and the IPOA to strengthen their capacity to undertake and sustain their police reforms initiatives (UNODC 2013).

In addition to the establishment of the new policing institutional architecture, and since that establishment, police reforms in Kenya have resulted in the following key achievements:

- A comprehensive review, revision, and updating by the NPS of the police force standing orders to the NPS standing orders encompassing and reflecting all constitutional and national legal frameworks and reflecting best international practices.
- The establishment by the NPS of a centralized command center and operationalization of standard emergency numbers (999/112) for the public to contact the police.
- The development of multiyear strategic plans for the NPS, the NPSC, and the IPOA. These strategic plans provide a road map for each institution's approach to meeting their mandate and articulate strategies for realizing their respective vision and mission for professional, transparent, and accountable policing.
- The development by the NPS of policies related to gender and human rights for policing in Kenya.
- The development by the NPS of a communications strategy.
- The revision and updating by the NPS of the Police Code of Conduct and Ethics including the compliance, enforcement, and disciplinary measures and procedures.
- The development by the NPS of a police anticorruption strategy entailing anticorruption measures categorized into four strategic objectives: (1) promoting a positive police culture of ethics and integrity, (2) enhancing accountability and transparency,

(3) engaging the community, and (4) cooperating with oversight stakeholders and building partnerships.

- The development by the NPS of community policing guidelines and programs based on the national community policing policy and intended to enhance interaction with the public and proactive policing.
- The establishment by the NPS of the Kenya Association of Women in Policing to support female police officers in professional development and networking.
- The improvement of police officers' welfare through the provision of new housing units, group life insurance, and comprehensive medical insurance cover.
- The ongoing acquisition by the NPS of new police vehicles and allocated to police stations with mechanisms put in place for their proper utilization.
- The operationalization by the NPS of the IAU to investigate complaints of misconduct against police officers.
- The establishment by the NPS of County Commands in the 47 counties and formation of 290 NPS police divisions in line with the statutory requirements.
- The implementation of vetting by the NPSC to determine the suitability and competence of police officers or potential police officers to serve, resulting in more than 10 senior police officers being declared unfit to serve largely due to undeclared or unexplained wealth.
- The development by the NPS of new police training programs and curricula in anticorruption and ethics.
- The development by the NPS of a conflict of interest policy.
- An increase in the number of investigations (now conducted by the IPOA) of police misconduct resulting from use of firearms and/or human rights violations and an increase in the number of police officers charged with such violations and prosecuted.
- The development of regulations by the NPSC—approved by parliament at the end of 2014—establishing a more streamlined system for recruitment, selection, and appointment of police officers. These new regulations, aimed at ridding police recruitment of the corruption and nepotism that have historically characterized the recruitment exercise, will now include background checks and will also take into account gender, regional, and ethnic balance (Maina 2014; NPS 2014).

From the foregoing key achievements, one can conclude that Kenya has been making some progress in its police reforms efforts. However, there is much more that needs to be done. In particular, there must be robust and unflinching implementation of the various strategies, policies, training programs, and codes that have been developed for the reform initiatives and that go beyond "reform-speak," to show outcomes success and for that success to be sustained (Osse 2014). The quest for police reforms, with significant donor support, indicates the backdrop of the observed and known defects in or disaffection with the country's police service and its reputation as one of the most corrupt in the world. Police corruption is both a reason for and a barrier to implementing police reforms in Kenya. It is a reason for police reforms because it undermines police ethics, integrity, and accountability as well as national trust and nation-building. It is a barrier to implementing police reforms because the police are seen and regarded as the most corrupt institution in the country with corruption deeply entrenched within it.

Another area that has been observed to be a hindrance to more effective outcomes of the police reforms is the seemingly breakdown in command structure. Despite the establishment of a NPS as a single service, but with two service units (KPS and APS) as described earlier, under the command of an IG, the two service units continue to function as entities that are separate and apart. They issue conflicting orders; they focus on self-preservation and caution rather than on professional policing responses to save lives and property, provide assistance to the public, and apprehend offenders; they maintain separate training facilities and institutions even for nonspecialized trainings; and they do not cooperate on anticorruption initiatives. The IPOA has even been moved to comment as follows in one of its monitoring reports:

> The Authority's enquiries indicate that this discord between the [service] units' command centers permeates even regular day-to-day operations of the police where there is widespread mistrust and rivalry. To some it seems the KPS and APS are in competition to outdo and sometimes undermine each other. This practice affects effective policing.
>
> **IPOA (2014d, p. 13)**

This state of affairs is also mirrored at the county community levels where the policing apparatus lacks harmony and operates with suspicion and deep-rooted personal differences and dislike for each other (IPOA 2014d). This bad blood situation, in turn, influences local policing decisions and responses and thereby jeopardizes the safety and security of local neighborhoods.

Also, notwithstanding all of the measures that have been put in place, the country still has far to go to rid the police of corruption, favoritism in recruitment, brutality, senseless use of firearms by officers leading to the deaths of many Kenyans, and other problems. For instance, survey after survey continues to rank the Kenya Police as the most corrupt institution in the country and one of the most corrupt in East Africa. And, the IPOA is being kept busy with monitoring and investigations of police misconduct in its fulfillment of its mandate to hold the police accountable to the public in the performance of their functions.

Conclusions

Despite the new policing institutional architecture aimed at transforming the police service and the various reform initiatives undertaken through that new architecture, police corruption and other forms of misconduct still arise in the daily routines of the Kenya Police and have emerged as significant problems and matters of concern in the country that have now also garnered significant attention both domestically and internationally (Mount 2014). That concern also reflects the view that the police are entrusted with a diverse set of tasks requiring a high degree of integrity within their services and their oversight. Where this does not function well, police officers may become vulnerable to acting unlawfully and outside of their remit. It is that concern about police corruption and its consequences that are among the reasons the Kenyan government was prompted to embrace police reforms including a significant push to engage policy measures to control said police corruption.

In fact, the police reforms program currently underway in the country aims, among other things, to control police corruption and its negative societal consequences. That reforms program is being spearheaded by, among others, the NPS whose then IG had observed in that regard that:

> Police are the most visible manifestations of government authority responsible for public security. In Kenya, this manifestation has previously been associated with high-handedness, brutality and corruption. This led to the unequivocal call for police reforms... to come up with pragmatic measures to make the police service more responsive and accountable to the people they serve.
>
> **Kimaiyo (2013, p. 1)**

The country's president has also recognized the importance of controlling police corruption and corruption in general for that matter. In that regard, among his speeches he has exhorted police recruits as follows:

> ... I want to make it perfectly clear to you that my government, and the people of Kenya whom we serve, simply will not tolerate corruption. For corruption is an evil in itself, but when it infects those who are supposed to guard us from its effects, then we are speaking of a special kind of wickedness.
>
> It has been said that the corruption of the best is the worst. That saying is certainly true when dishonesty compromises the finest of our youth, charged

with the protection of our common safety. I urge you not to fall victim to it, and I assure you that those who succumb, especially at this critical time, will suffer the most severe penalties that our law can impose.

It is also my place to remind you all that the reforms which the police service is undergoing are motivated, in part, by our desire to clean the force of this vice. It falls to you to support them, both because our laws dictate them, and because they will ease your fulfilment of the duties which you take up today.

Kenyatta (2014, p. 1)

There is also a further vocal consensus among Kenyans that combating police corruption is one of the country's most critical governance and development challenges. The maintenance of public confidence in the police is important in democratic societies or those aspiring to such, like Kenya, and police corruption seriously threatens that. Among other things, the goal of the police reforms in the country is to transform the NPS into an efficient, effective, professional, and accountable security service that Kenyans can trust for their safety and security within a transparent framework that seeks to embed democratic policing.

Police reforms are about change and policing is part of governance at every level. Consequently, the promotion of police reforms must be regarded as an element of good governance interventions. The police are accountable for producing public safety and for behaving respectfully and within the law. In Kenya, police corruption, especially the bribery aspect, creates a double demand on the police by requiring that police officers adhere to higher standards of conduct while also providing higher standards of service. Addressing police corruption in the country is essential to maintaining public order and the rule of law, to support the legitimacy of the state and to maintain or restore public trust in democratic processes and institutions.

Another point of concern emanating from police corruption in Kenya is that related to the insecurity stemming from terrorism and its threats. As Mboya (2014, p. XII) observed:

... Kenya has become a favored target for terrorists. This is largely the case due to the fact that terrorists are aware that our corrupt nature guarantees any indulgence for a small fee. Indeed, many have been able to secure their freedom from the clutches of our security services in precisely this manner!

Undoubtedly, there is a causal connection between corruption in Kenya and the continued security threat the country faces, and counteracting that will require Kenyans to take responsibility for the fight against corruption. It cannot, at this stage, be left entirely to the government. The lessons of history learned have demonstrated that the incubated corruption in the country has broken out into the lawlessness and the insecurity Kenyans must now confront (Mwandia 2014). It is a confrontation Kenyans cannot afford to lose.

Finally, and in fairness, it must also be said that any unbiased analysis would also recognize that the transformation of the police will not and cannot occur overnight. Lessons of experience of police reforms around the globe clearly suggest that such initiatives are long-term processes for which there are usually no quick fixes. It takes considerably more than changing the policing institutional architecture. In the case of Kenya, that change was a necessary but not a sufficient condition, and the authorities have recognized that and responded appropriately with crucial technical assistance being provided by donors. However, police anticorruption efforts will fail and positive outcomes from overall police reforms will not be sustained unless there is full and complete cooperation between the KPS and the APS functioning as a single NPS as envisaged in the Constitution and the NPS Act, 2011.

For the NPS to be effectively managed and to efficiently undertake its responsibilities to the citizens of Kenya, there has to be a consistent, standardized, harmonized, and uniform policy direction that is followed by the entire NPS. Among other things, this must, for example, include the applicability of the Service Standing Orders, the Code of Conduct and Ethics, the police anticorruption strategy, and trainings. For the latter, only for the APS, and in exceptional cases of specialized training relevant to a given specialized unit, should there be allowed a variance that can be coordinated by the APS as provided for in the NPS Act, 2011. Beyond that, under Articles 243 and 245 of the Constitution, the NPS is established as a single entity. It was never intended that the KPS and the APS should operate as parallel or independent police services.

References

Andvig, J. C. and T. Barasa. 2011. Cops and crime in Kenya: A research report. Norwegian Institute of International Affairs (NUPI) Working Paper 794. Oslo, Norway: NUPI.

CHRI (Commonwealth Human Rights Initiative) and KHRC (Kenya Human Rights Commission). 2006. *The Police, the People, the Politics: Police Accountability in Kenya*. London, U.K./Nairobi, Kenya: CHRI/KHRC.

EACC (Ethics and Anti-Corruption Commission). 2013. *National Survey on Corruption and Ethics, 2012: Report*. Nairobi, Kenya: EACC.

Hope, K. R. 2012. *The Political Economy of Development in Kenya*. New York: Bloomsbury Publishing.

Hope, K. R. 2013. Tackling the corruption epidemic in Kenya: Toward a policy of more effective control. *The Journal of Social, Political, and Economic Studies* 38(3): 287–316.

Hope, K. R. 2014. Kenya's corruption problem: Causes and consequences. *Commonwealth & Comparative Politics* 52(4): 493–512.

IMLU (Independent Medico-Legal Unit). 2014. *Guns: Our Security, Our Dilemma!: Enhancing Accountability for Police Use of Firearms.* Nairobi, Kenya: IMLU.

IPOA (Independent Policing Oversight Authority). 2013. *Baseline Survey on Policing Standards and Gaps in Kenya.* Nairobi, Kenya: IPOA.

IPOA (Independent Policing Oversight Authority). 2014a. *Monitoring Report on Operation Sanitization Eastleigh: Publicly Known as 'Usalama Watch.* Nairobi, Kenya: IPOA.

IPOA (Independent Policing Oversight Authority). 2014b. The Independent Policing Oversight Authority (IPOA) files a case to nullify the just concluded police recruitment exercise. *Press Release,* August 5. Nairobi, Kenya: IPOA.

IPOA (Independent Policing Oversight Authority). 2014c. Police recruitment: A national shame and a sham. http://www.ipoa.go.ke/images/press/POLICE%20RECRUITMENT%20JULY%202014.pdf (accessed September 5, 2014).

IPOA (Independent Policing Oversight Authority). 2014d. *IPOA Report Following the Mpeketoni Attacks: 15 and 16 June 2014.* Nairobi, Kenya: IPOA.

Kenyatta, U. 2014. Speech by his Excellency Hon. Uhuru Kenyatta on the Kenya Police Service recruits passing-out parade. Kiganjo Police Training College, Kiganjo, Kenya, April 4.

Kimaiyo, D. M. 2013. Remarks by the Inspector-General of Police during the launching ceremony of the County police reforms forums. Hilton Hotel, Nairobi, Kenya, May 13.

Lucheli, I. and J. Weru. 2014. High Court nullifies police recruitment. *Standard Digital,* November 1. http://www.standardmedia.co.ke/article/2000140061/high-court-nullifies-police-recruitment (accessed November 29, 2014).

Maina, S. B. 2014. Tough new rules for police jobs. *Daily Nation,* December 8: 11.

Mboya, T. 2014. The role we play in a corrupt society. *Weekend Star,* August 16/17: XII.

Mount, S. 2014. *A Force for Good? Improving the Police in Kenya, Tanzania and Uganda.* London, U.K.: Commonwealth Human Rights Initiative.

Mwandia, J. 2014. Systemic corruption and embezzlement began at independence. *Weekend Star,* August 16/17: XIV.

Neild, R. 2007. *USAID Program Brief: Anticorruption and Police Integrity.* Washington, DC: USAID.

NPS (National Police Service). 2014. Status of police reforms. *Daily Nation,* August 27: 51–52.

NPSC (National Police Service Commission). 2014. *Statement by the National Police Service Commission on the Audit of the Police Constables Recruitment Exercise Held on 14th July 2014.* Nairobi, Kenya: NPSC.

Osse, A. 2014. Police reform in Kenya: A process of 'meddling through'. *Policing and Society: An International Journal of Research and Policy.* http://dx.doi.org/10.1080/10439463.2014.993631 (accessed December 24, 2014).

Republic of Kenya. 2009. *Report of the National Task Force on Police Reforms* (The Ransley Report). Nairobi, Kenya: Republic of Kenya.

Republic of Kenya. 2010. *The Constitution of Kenya, 2010.* Nairobi, Kenya: Republic of Kenya.

Republic of Kenya. 2011a. *National Police Service Act, 2011.* Nairobi, Kenya: Republic of Kenya.

Republic of Kenya. 2011b. *The National Police Service Commission Act, 2011*. Nairobi, Kenya: Republic of Kenya.

Republic of Kenya. 2011c. *Independent Policing Oversight Authority Act, 2011*. Nairobi, Kenya: Republic of Kenya.

Republic of Kenya. 2014. *The National Police Service (Amendment) Act, 2014*. Nairobi, Kenya: Republic of Kenya.

Star Reporter. 2014. Five traffic police officers arrested for taking bribes from motorists on Waiyaki way. *The Star*, September 30. http://allafrica.com/stories/201410010389.html (accessed October 12, 2014).

Teyie, A. and W. Menya. 2014. GSU officers accuse seniors of harassment and corruption. *Sunday Nation*, August 17: 28.

TI (Transparency International). 2013. *Global Corruption Barometer 2013*. Berlin, Germany: TI.

TI (Transparency International)-Kenya. 2009. *The East African Bribery Index 2009*. Nairobi, Kenya: TI-Kenya.

TI (Transparency International)-Kenya. 2010. *The East African Bribery Index 2010*. Nairobi, Kenya: TI-Kenya.

TI (Transparency International)-Kenya. 2011. *The East African Bribery Index 2011*. Nairobi, Kenya: TI-Kenya.

TI (Transparency International)-Kenya. 2012. *The East African Bribery Index 2012*. Nairobi, Kenya: TI-Kenya.

TI (Transparency International)-Kenya. 2013. *The East African Bribery Index 2013*. Nairobi, Kenya: TI-Kenya.

TI (Transparency International)-Kenya. 2014. *The East African Bribery Index 2014*. Nairobi, Kenya: TI-Kenya.

TJRC (Truth, Justice and Reconciliation Commission), Kenya. 2013. *Report of the Truth, Justice and Reconciliation Commission: Volume IIB*. Nairobi, Kenya: TJRC Kenya.

UNCAT (United Nations Committee Against Torture). 2009. *Consideration of Reports Submitted by States Parties Under Article 19 of the Convention: Concluding Observations of the Committee Against Torture: Kenya*. New York: United Nations.

UNHRC (United Nations Human Rights Council). 2009. *Promotion and Protection of All Human Rights, Civil, Political, Economic, Social and Cultural Rights, Including the Right to Development: Report of the Special Rapporteur on Extrajudicial, Summary or Arbitrary Executions: Addendum: Mission to Kenya*. New York: United Nations General Assembly.

UNHRC (United Nations Human Rights Committee). 2012. *Consideration of Reports Submitted by States Parties Under Article 40 of the Covenant: Concluding Observations Adopted by the Human Rights Committee at its 105th Session, 9–27 July 2012: Kenya*. New York: UNHRC.

UNODC (United Nations Office on Drugs and Crime). 2013. UNODC launches police reform project in Kenya. http://www.unodc.org/unodc/en/front-page/2013/October/unodc-launches-police-reform-project-in-kenya.html (accessed March 17, 2014).

Warah, R. 2014. Corruption, politics and tribalism have neutered our security services. *Daily Nation*, August 4: 12.

South Africa
A Schizophrenic System for Combating the Scourge of Police Corruption

CORNELIS ROELOFSE

Contents

Background 110
Theoretical Context: Systems Theory and Reciprocal Moral Dualism.........112
   System Approach Contextualized 112
   Reciprocal Moral Dualism 113
Oversight of the Police..115
   National Parliament and Provincial Legislatures 115
   National and Provincial Secretariats for the Police Service 115
   Community Policing Forums 116
   Independent Police Investigative Directorate..117
   Civil Society and the Media 118
Police Leadership Issues 118
   Crime Intelligence Unit 120
Conclusion 120
References..122

At the onset, it is essential to emphasize that police corruption is a secretive phenomenon. Such practices not only are perpetrated in clandestine ways but also often go unreported due to fear and intimidation of those affected and reciprocal benefits derived through bribing. Corruption in the police is not confined to developing societies as this volume makes clear. However, common among all is the fact that corruption is endemic in a sizable majority of police organizations (Newburn 1999). In South Africa, the testimony before the Truth and Reconciliation Commission by a high-ranking officer in the former apartheid police force recounted widespread corruption. Now, more than two decades after the first universal franchise election in South Africa and a completely transformed police service, there is still mounting evidence of grand-scale corruption in the police. In its own documents, for example, the South African Police Service (SAPS) reported that from April 2013 to March 2014, the following number of corruption and fraud-related charges were made against members of the SAPS: corruption (332), fraud (207), aiding an escapee (421), defeating the ends of justice (169), extortion (34), and bribery (9), for a total of 1,172 (SAPS 2014). Other independent research has also reported on findings of unethical behavior and misconduct in the SAPS related to corruption as well as various violent crimes (see, for instance, IRR 2011, 2015).

Looking at the historical backdrop of all these developments, the South African global corruption ranking for 2008, for example, was 54 based on the Corruption Perceptions Index (CPI) for 180 countries compared to 67 out of 175 countries/territories in 2014 (TI 2008, 2014). As can be seen, there has been a gradual downgrading of South Africa according to the CPI. These rankings give us an idea of the scope of corruption but to comprehend what is going on in South Africa, and in the country's policing, the background of political interference must be sketched. Senior prosecutors, high-ranking police officers, and officials seem to have been both victims and perpetrators of grand-scale corruption and cover-ups. In fact, De Vos (2014, p. 1) contends that "the practice of appointing politicians or politically-connected individuals to leadership positions in the National Prosecuting Authority (NPA) has seriously dented the credibility of the NPA... [and] has thus eroded its independence, its credibility and its effectiveness." To this can also be added that by appointing politically connected national commissioners of police, public confidence is dented.

Schizophrenia is a mental condition characterized by inconsistent or contradictory features, elements, and behavior. There is no better way to describe South Africa's approach, and particularly that of the SAPS, to the corruption problem. This chapter explores these inconsistencies and contradictions and concludes with a summary of some hopeful aspects of police anticorruption strategies now being introduced.

Background

It seems as if history is on the side of South Africa's young democracy. A malignant attitude has gripped the politicians that seemingly have the attitude that by destroying apartheid no other evil will ever befall the country again. No matter what wrongs are done, it can always be justified by comparing it with the past. But therein lies the greatest threat for South Africa. Actions do not have to be debated or truly justified, critics can simply be referred to the past, and there is no need to be rational, scientific, or even humane. South Africa's history of apartheid as the rogue political system apparently gives a carte blanche for the future, and therefore, nothing that is done in South Africa can surpass that. It relegates individual, group, and even legal interpretations to a level of moral superiority that needs no justification (Roelofse 2012). In fact, it is an approach used by researchers, practitioners, and politicians alike. Instead of measuring police performance against international standards of conduct, the country's own constitution, and the principles of democratic policing, the approach often taken is to compare police corruption as a specific phenomenon to the encompassing political philosophy of the apartheid past (Faull 2007; Newham and Faull 2011).

To make the foregoing statements about South Africa, borders on political blasphemy but, fortunately, others have also ventured into this arena. De Vos (2010, p. 1), for example, reflects on a letter by former President Mbeki in which the latter said:

> [W]e should not, and will not abandon the offensive to defeat the insulting campaigns further to entrench a stereotype that has, for centuries, sought to portray Africans as a people that is corrupt, given to telling lies, prone to theft and self-enrichment by immoral means, a people that is otherwise contemptible in the eyes of the 'civilized'. We must expect that, as usual, our opponents will accuse us of 'playing the race card', to stop us confronting the challenge of racism.

However, no one denies that Western critics often ignore corruption in their own countries while hammering African states about the latter's corruption. But voices against corruption also come from African critics (see, e.g., the case studies in Hope and Chikulo 2000).

In discussing the aforementioned statement by former President Mbeki, De Vos (2010, p. 1) commented that:

> The letter laid bare some of the deeply problematic ideological assumptions underlying the discourse on corruption in post-apartheid South Africa. It then used this insight – which was not only spot on, but also tapped into a widespread resentment amongst members of the newly emerging post-apartheid elite – to defend what seemed to be indefensible.

This line of argumentation is a tactic that has been used very often to negate valid criticisms against obvious problems in South Africa and to portray the opposing voices as archaic and regressive. As De Vos (2010, p. 1) so aptly states:

> This was a tactic often used by Mbeki in his letters: correctly expose and analyze widespread racist or Afro-pessimistic assumptions, then use the insight to deny the existence of obvious problems or to discredit the valid criticism of progressive voices in our society. He used the same tactic against the so-called 'ultra left'… and against those who pointed out the folly of his HIV stance.

Adding fuel to the fire is the fact that the ruling African National Congress party has a two-thirds majority, in combination with one of its allies, in the National Assembly, and in some provinces, the majority is over 80%. They therefore control the majorities in parliament, provincial legislatures, and municipalities, having majorities in parliamentary standing committees and portfolio committees and in some provinces even all the chairpersonships of committees (including the Standing Committee on Public Accounts). Nepotism and cronyism have, consequently, become the order of the day with ruling party members filling top positions in the government and parastatals. Among other things, this allows for the manipulation of tenders, irregular and unfruitful spending, and protection of incompetence and even criminality.

Corruption can therefore be described as endemic in South Africa. In that regard, the South African Press Association (SAPA) (2014, p. 1) has also reported that a Corruption Watch Executive Director said: "Think of our criminal justice institutions. And think of the impunity enjoyed by leading public sector and private sector individuals, with... the clearest example of impunity enjoyed by the politically powerful."

From the foregoing, the interconnectedness of political meddling and impunity can be clearly seen. Appointments to protect individuals until evidence becomes so damning that action must be taken is repeated time and again. The corruption activities seem to be the hippopotamus that must be kept underwater, and this impacts on policing and the course of justice. The theoretical context of what is happening in South Africa is discussed next and also undergirds this chapter.

Theoretical Context: Systems Theory and Reciprocal Moral Dualism

System Approach Contextualized

A system processes inputs to specific outputs. For example, new recruits are taken from society and then trained in police academies/training colleges. They have a particular orientation and predisposition based on their socialization. They come from particular communities in which they were raised. Simply put, corrupt societies provide corrupt recruits. This is aptly demonstrated by Rademeyer and Wilkinson (2013, p. 1) who reported that during the police recruitment, quantity instead of quality is pursued. They quoted the then SAPS acting Deputy National Commissioner for human resource management as saying that "recruits had found ways to bypass reference checks and fingerprinting . . . there were cases where recruits with criminal records had used other people to substitute for them during the fingerprinting process" and "there are instances where the people who submitted themselves for psychometric assessments were not necessarily the same people who submitted themselves for finger printing." Clearly, such gross police corruption can only be perpetrated with the help of police officers in the recruitment system of the SAPS.

Reciprocal Moral Dualism

Reciprocal moral dualism clearly stipulates the interaction between communities and the police and also the dynamics of the socialization process within the police. Socialization primarily takes place through training and influencing by colleagues. This process can be described best as shown in Figure 6.1.

The theoretical paradigm of reciprocal moral dualism (Roelofse 2012) is embedded in the systems theory and asserts that a young recruit can be introduced into, and influenced by, a police subculture. The recruit is selected through, among other means, psychological testing. Twersky-Glasner (2005, p. 3) writes that this selection process ensures that a certain baseline personality enters the police. This is referred to as the psychological model of predisposition (Twersky-Glasner 2005, p. 65). Once recruited, the rookie police officer is placed in a training center, college or academy; introduced to law, firearms, crowd control, crime prevention, other policing activities, and an "us-and-them" culture; and desocialized from previous experiences and resocialized and institutionalized. This perspective is termed as the anthropological paradigm that suggests that police are members of a unique occupational subculture. They develop trust in colleagues (insiders) and distrust in the public (outsiders). As Figure 6.1 indicates, this process is based on the systems approach, containment (Conklin 1992), and control theory

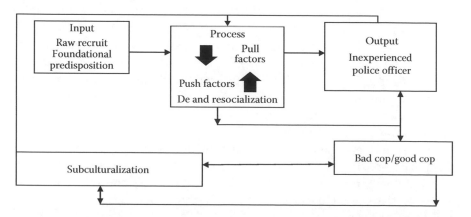

Figure 6.1 Socialization Process in Systems Approach. (From Author.)

(Gottfredson and Hirschi 1990; Welch 1998; Katz 1999). There is interplay of the individual's personality, as shaped by society, and the dynamics of the organizations, other officers, and particular subcultural influences.

Part of the training of new recruits is through contact or on-the-job training with more seasoned or experienced officers. At one level, this can be regarded as teaching the recruits the job at a practical level. On the other hand, seasoned officers may employ practices that are less than ideal or even unacceptable to their managers and society. Consequently, the novice police officer may merely learn bad practice from his or her colleagues. This is particularly important when we consider the transmission of the occupational subculture or general police culture (Sturt 2013).

When recruits are eventually deployed, senior police officers entrench the subculture that becomes the *raison d'être* and eventually *homo politis* emerges. *Homo politis* can be identified as a person in uniform with a tendency to protect the police organization, tends somewhat to secrecy, and identifies with the ideals of police camaraderie. This is where the moral conflict can arise. The dilemma is that the subculturalized police officer with a responsibility and affinity toward fellow officers, but also a responsibility toward the community, can be confronted with opportunities to get involved in cover-ups, bribery, perjury, and even violent behavior or to stand up to peer pressure and uphold basic good morality and human rights. This depends on the constituent personality (predisposition) of the individual. A theory that aptly describes predisposition to crime is Gottfredson and Hirschi's (1990) discussion on general crime theory. The conjecture is that criminal behavior results from a lack of self-control. This "control theory of delinquency" assumes delinquent acts will result when one's bond or connection to society is weak or broken. The broad theory that Gottfredson and Hirschi (1990) developed, according to the interpretation of Katz (1999, p. 1), is that "the general theory of crime assumes that although the individual's personality (i.e., the characteristic of self-control) remains stable through time, the relationship between self-control and crime is amenable to change." In the context of moral dualism, the socialization of community members to be inherently self-controlled is contextualized in the construct of import–export. With endemic corruption, the high levels of violent crime and aggression can be conjectured as being inherent to large sections of society, and police recruits may be prone to such behavior due to their socialization (Roelofse 2012, pp. 145–147).

Society and its organs function in a political system that permeates every aspect of our existence. Police officers as a component of society are also subject to political and community influences, policy, and control. In order to create effective oversight over the police, a number of oversight mechanisms have therefore been created.

Oversight of the Police

South African legislation and SAPS operations require adherence to international standards for civilian oversight over the police. The South African constitution and the Police Act provide for a hierarchy of oversight regimes that have been put in place of which the most prominent are as discussed in what follows below.

National Parliament and Provincial Legislatures

At the national level, oversight is given effect through the Portfolio Committee on Safety and Security. In addition, each of South Africa's nine provinces has a similar portfolio committee for oversight over the provincial component of the national police. Opposition political parties also serve on these committees. At both levels, portfolio committees receive and interrogate reports from the police including an annual report and reports from the Auditor General on financial matters. The portfolio committees also have public hearings, conduct visits and inspections of police facilities, and may call the Minister in charge of the police, the National Police Commissioner, or any staff member or members of agencies such as the Independent Police Investigative Directorate (IPID) to appear before them.

The National Parliamentary Portfolio Committee, for instance, has visited the Central Firearms Registry (CFR) to establish the effectiveness of strategies aimed at addressing corruption allegations and management challenges at the CFR. In 2014, the SAPS management also appeared before the committee to explain their plans to address police corruption allegations. In this regard, it is also worth mentioning that Versluis (2015) reported that a high court had sentenced the Minister of Police, the National Police Commissioner, and the head of the firearms registry to 30 days in prison, suspended for 5 years because they were in contempt of court. This stems from an action brought against them by a private company that applied for firearms licenses and were issued with the wrong ones. Attempts to rectify this situation were futile. Clearly, this is one indication that the national portfolio committee has valid concerns about the CFR.

National and Provincial Secretariats for the Police Service

Section 208 of the South African constitution calls for the establishment of a civilian secretariat to function under the direction of the cabinet member responsible for policing. In that regard, legislation has established national and provincial civilian secretariats for the police service with the following key functions:

- To monitor the performance of the police service and regularly assess the extent to which the police service has adequate policies and effective systems and to recommend corrective measures
- To consider such recommendations, suggestions, and requests concerning police and policing matters as it may receive from any source
- To advise and support the minister in the exercise of his or her powers and the performance of his or her functions
- To provide the Minister with regular reports with regard to the performance of the police service and implementation of and compliance by the police service with policy directives issued or instructions made by the Minister
- To assess and monitor the police service's ability to receive and deal with complaints against its members
- To promote good police–community relations in the provinces
- To conduct or cause any research to be conducted as it may deem necessary
- To monitor the utilization of the budget of the police service to ensure compliance with any policy directives or instructions of the Minister (Republic of South Africa 2011a)

In a statement made at the Accountability and Transformation Conference held in January 2004, the then member of the executive council (MEC) for safety and liaison in Gauteng Province noted that the area of civilian oversight over the police service is one of the critical areas where there has been transformation that has led to major changes within the operations as well as the policy and legislative direction within the broader criminal justice system. However, and despite this stance, the protection of wrongdoers remains evident to this day, and there continues to be a culture of cover-ups exhibited.

Community Policing Forums

The Police Act (Act 68 of 1995) regulates Community Policing Forums and Boards (Republic of South Africa 1995). The act states that the SAPS shall liaise with the community, through community police forums and area and provincial community police boards, with a view to, among other things:

- Establishing and maintaining a partnership between the community and the service
- Promoting communication between the service and the community
- Promoting cooperation between the service and the community in fulfilling the needs of the community regarding policing
- Improving the rendering of police services to the community at national, provincial, area, and local levels

- Improving transparency in the service and accountability of the service to the community
- Promoting joint problem identification and problem solving by the service and the community

These forums and boards are the real interface between the police and public. The main aim is to develop the police/public partnership in a joint effort to combat crime. However, to accomplish this, South Africa's community policing forums need to play a bigger role in the fight against crime in the country, including helping to monitor the performance of local police stations. The role of the country's community policing forums and boards needs to be broadened to include the justice and correctional service systems. The government has also recognized that a framework needs to be put in place to provide more resources to community policing forums and to enable said forums to help assess police performance.

Independent Police Investigative Directorate

The constitution calls for an independent complaints directorate but it was mandated in the Police Act, Act 68 of 1995. This meant that the same Minister would exercise control over the police service as well as the agency tasked to investigate police misconduct. This was corrected when the IPID was established under its own enabling legislation, the Independent Police Investigative Directorate Act, 2011. The objects of the IPID Act are (a) to give effect to the provision of the constitution establishing and assigning functions to the directorate on national and provincial level; (b) to ensure independent oversight of the SAPS and municipal police services; (c) to align provincial strategic objectives with that of the national office to enhance the functioning of the directorate; (d) to provide for independent and impartial investigation of identified criminal offences allegedly committed by members of the SAPS and municipal police services; (e) to make disciplinary recommendations in respect of the members of the SAPS and municipal police services resulting from investigations conducted by the directorate; (f) to provide for close cooperation between the directorate and the secretariat; and (g) to enhance accountability and transparency by the SAPS and municipal police services in accordance with the principles of the constitution.

According to the act, the IPID must investigate the following (specified) matters:

- Any deaths in police custody;
- Deaths as a result of police actions;
- Any complaint relating to the discharge of an official firearm by any police officer;

- Rape by a police officer, whether the police officer is on or off duty;
- Rape of any person while that person is in police custody;
- Any complaint of torture or assault against a police officer in the execution of his or her duties;
- Corruption matters within the police initiated by the Executive Director on his or her own, or after the receipt of a complaint from a member of the public, or referred to the Directorate by the Minister, an MEC, or the Secretary, as the case may be; and
- Any other matter referred to it as a result of a decision by the Executive Director, or if so requested by the Minister, an MEC or the Secretary of Police as the case may be.

Republic of South Africa (2011b)

Civil Society and the Media

Apart from informal oversight through the media, there are also other formal structures although they are not dedicated to police oversight. These include the Public Protector, the South African Human Rights Commission, and the Public Service Commission. Consequently, formally and informally, there is a plethora of oversight structures and a vigilant media and civil society. The involvement of civil society in the major corruption issues in the SAPS is a good example. But, despite these, corruption remains an ever present problem in the South African police and society generally also.

Police Leadership Issues

A proverb states that a fish rots from its head. In the case of the SAPS, this is indeed a fact to be considered when looking at the increasing number of respondents who consider the police as corrupt as evidenced from the different surveys that have been conducted. Corruption Watch (2012), for example, quotes a report from the Human Sciences Research Council that found 66% of the public held the view that the police are corrupt. Due to the evidence and the adverse publicity about police corruption, this perception can be justified (see, e.g., Abreu 2013a). Nonetheless, the police challenged the survey methodology and complained that the sample of respondents was too small (Abreu 2013b).

However, a policing expert was quoted as saying to "also take into consideration the annual police statistic reports from 2010, 2011 and 2012 [which] showed an increase of 120% of corruption against its members. It is therefore not hard to believe that most South Africans feel police are corrupt" (Abreu 2013b, p. 1). Public perceptions about police corruption have also been measured in a study by Roelofse et al. (2014). That study compared public perceptions about corruption in South Africa and Serbia. An overwhelming proportion (91%) of respondents in South Africa stated that the police are corrupt. Although the survey had a small sample, the trend of an increasing negative perception about the police being corrupt is clearly evident in the study. This is up from the findings reported in a 2013 survey that found that 83% of the South African public believe the SAPS is corrupt (*News24* 2013a).

Underlining these perceptions about police corruption in South Africa are the leadership woes. In recent years, two politically appointed National Commissioners of the SAPS have been dismissed. One was found guilty of corruption and sentenced to 15 years imprisonment. He appealed against his sentence but the appeal court dismissed his application. His sentence stems from benefits he received from a convicted drug dealer (Porteous 2011). He was released on medical parole after the medical parole board decided in July 2012 as *City Press* (2013, p. 1) reported "[he] had end-stage renal disease for which he was receiving dialysis. End-stage renal disease means the person has irreversible kidney damage and they end up on dialysis for life." He was subsequently spotted shopping by a newspaper reporter (*City Press* 2013). His successor was also relieved of his duties due to investigations of irregular practices in attempts to rent a new building to serve as police headquarters. He subsequently was appointed as a Deputy Minister.

At the time of writing, the incumbent National Commissioner of Police was the first woman to be appointed to lead the SAPS. Her leadership has been challenged by particularly the official government opposition after she made an appointment of a Gauteng provincial police commissioner. Monama (2013) wrote that the appointment was withdrawn a few hours later when it was realized that the appointee was facing charges of driving under the influence and defeating the ends of justice. According to reports, the appointee said that he did not stop when signalled by a patrol unit as he feared that the uniformed person was a bogus officer. A breathalyzer test later revealed that he had a blood/alcohol content of over three times the legal limit (*News24* 2013b). The South African Institute for Race Relations and the South African Police Union issued statements that they were of the opinion that candidates for such appointments should be subject to thorough background checks and security screening (Monama 2013). Subsequently, the SAPS did put procedures in place to avoid a recurrence of such evident errors.

However, although the continued buzz around the National Police Commissioner is not subsiding, some have found her stance against corruption as very firm. At a police colloquium held on November 2014, she stated, "we must make sure that there is no room for corruption within the

SAPS at all levels and particularly at leadership level" (Author Notes). In personal conversations with the commissioner, this author found her sincere and committed to stamp out corruption. In this connection, Zwane (2014) reported that 19 police officers who apparently colluded with illicit cigarette dealers were suspended without pay in Limpopo, South Africa's northern most province. According to Zwane (2014, p. 1), the National Commissioner said about this incident, "It is never easy to arrest one of your own but it is necessary because our business is fighting crime." However, it remains clear that there is a massive capacity problem in dealing with reported police corruption cases. Consequently, there are large numbers of cases to be attended to. Some serious allegations of police corruption have been made against members of the SAPS that warrant closer scrutiny.

Crime Intelligence Unit

The national Crime Intelligence Unit has also been plagued by allegations of corruption, fraud, and mismanagement. For example, one head of the unit was suspended on allegations of murder and corruption. Newham (2012) indicated that the then acting National Police Commissioner was unhappy with the political interference allegedly from the Minister of Police who had ordered a halt to all internal disciplinary and criminal investigations into the allegations against the head of the unit as well as his reinstatement. A nongovernmental organization Freedom Under Law took the matter to the courts for a review of the decision to lift the suspension and to withdraw charges against the head of the unit. Pursuant to that, the head of the unit was resuspended.

SAPA (2012) made interesting observations, following information leaked to it by senior police officers, on the political skulduggery to appoint a person to the powerful position of the head of intelligence because it enables the elite to decide whose communications can be monitored. Evans (2015a), for example, reported that the previously suspended, and reinstated by the courts (at the time of writing), head of the Directorate for Priority Crimes Investigation (the Hawks) had angered police management by requesting that dockets dealing with fraud cases involving politicians be handed over to him for investigation by the Hawks. So the saga continues and agencies fighting police corruption, and corruption generally, are paralyzed by a continued shuffle in senior management.

Conclusion

Corruption Watch downgrades South Africa's rating virtually every year, and public opinion about police corruption continues to indicate that increasing numbers of South Africans perceive the police to be corrupt. Evidence of corruption, protectionism, and impunity often emerges. On the bright side, there are indications that the National Police Commissioner, at the time of writing, is taking a stand against police corruption. However, the sacking, suspension, and reshuffling of top officials in the police may also be indicative of further protectionism of the politically powerful individuals in the police and in the government. Nonetheless, the National Commissioner of Police should be given a fair chance to introduce her strategies, and only time will tell if schizophrenia is a perceived diagnosis or a true malady of the South African Police's fight against corruption.

Among other things, the police code of conduct that was established in 1997 is being reemphasized and aimed at entrenching a culture of human rights and integrity (SAPS nd, 2014). The code, *inter alia*, specifically addresses corruption. Part of the code states that the SAPS will undertake to:

- Uphold and protect the fundamental rights of every person
- Act impartially, courteously, honestly, respectfully, transparently, and in an accountable manner
- Exercise the powers conferred upon us in a responsible and controlled manner
- Work actively toward preventing any form of corruption and to bring the perpetrators thereof to justice

Clearly, the intention is to create an accountable and transparent police service in South Africa with a commitment to eradicate corruption and fraud. In that regard, an Anti-Corruption Working Group (ACWG) has been established with the responsibility of coordinating strategy and policy development and implementation and monitoring in all cluster departments. According to SAPS (2014), this ACWG is responding to a number of predetermined project-related anticorruption outputs that include

- The development, implementation, and monitoring of an anticorruption framework and revised strategy
- An integrated stakeholder value management and communication approach for the service
- Development of service policy and procedures to structure anticorruption requirements and responsibilities
- The establishment of a dedicated integrity management and investigation capability
- The enhancement of the service's discipline management capability
- The effective and efficient management of members with criminal convictions

In addition, the leadership of the SAPS has recognized that the service has a responsibility not only to actively detect corruption and fraud involving its members but also to provide members and the public with mechanisms to report allegations of corruption and fraud involving members of the service (SAPS 2014). However, detection and reporting of corruption and fraud involving members from both internal and external sources remains a challenge, and the primary reporting mechanism is the National Anti-Corruption Hotline of the Office of the Public Service Commission (OPSC). The SAPS has established close working relations with the OPSC to streamline the receipt of reports on allegations, fast-track the investigation of these allegations by the service, and coordinate feedback to the OPSC (SAPS 2014).

Furthermore, SAPS (2014) also points out that the service has several internal assurance providers who detect corruption and fraud during their assurance activities. Allegations of corrupt and fraudulent activities by members are also reported from internal and external sources to various other structures inside and outside the SAPS, including the presidential hotline, the SAPS crime stoppers line, the SAPS service delivery complaints line, and management at all levels. These allegations are managed similarly to those detected by internal assurance providers.

However, as IRR (2015) also observes, while the police are taking the lead in dealing with corruption and other forms of misconduct and criminality in their ranks, their efforts still fall far short of what is required to stamp out the corruption problem in the SAPS. Consequently, it is with very good reason that members of the public often do not trust the police. This, in turn, raises the question of the extent to which political decision making and influence play a role in weakening policing in South Africa and thereby allowing police corruption and other forms of criminality to thrive. The SAPS, like all other police services, will therefore only be effective if it can work free from political interference and if it can rely on full political support in its efforts to implement policies to combat police corruption and other police misconduct and criminal activities.

References

Abreu, V. 2013a. 1 448 cops have criminal records, audit shows. http://www.iol.co.za/news/crime-courts/1-448-cops-have-criminal-records-audit-shows-1.1554163#.VLldgCvF-So (accessed December 9, 2014).

Abreu, V. 2013b. Cops question methodology of damning report. http://www.iol.co.za/news/crime-courts/cops-question-methodology-of-damning-report-1.1547404#.VLqrRkfF-So (accessed January 12, 2015).

City Press. 2013. Shopping Jackie Selebi makes 'mockery of SA's justice system'. http://www.citypress.co.za/news/shopping-jackie-selebi-makes-mockery-sas-justice-system/ (accessed January 12, 2015).

Conklin, J. E. 1992. *Criminology*, 4th edn. New York: Macmillan.

Corruption Watch. 2012. SA sees SAPS as most corrupt within the state—Survey. http://www.corruptionwatch.org.za/content/sa-sees-saps-most-corrupt-within-state-survey (accessed January 15, 2015).

De Vos, P. 2010. On corruption in South Africa. http://constitutionallyspeaking. co.za/on-corruption-in-south-africa/ (accessed October 19, 2010).

De Vos, P. 2014. Spy tapes: Still no reason to drop charges. http://constitutionally speaking.co.za/category/npa/ (accessed January 13, 2015).

Evans, S. 2015a. Hawks continue to dive into a web of conspiracies. http://mg.co. za/article/2015-01-06-hawks-continue-to-dive-into-a-web-of-conspiracies (accessed January 9, 2015).

Faull, A. 2007. Corruption and the South African Police Service: A review and its implications. http://www.issafrica.org/uploads/Paper150pdf.pdf (accessed January 19, 2015).

Gottfredson, M. R. and T. Hirschi. 1990. *A General Theory on Crime*. Palo Alto, CA: Stanford University Press.

Hope, K. R. and B. C. Chikulo (eds.). 2000. *Corruption and Development in Africa: Lessons from Country Case-Studies*. London, U.K.: Palgrave Macmillan.

IRR (South African Institute of Race Relations). 2011. *Broken Blue Line: The Involvement of the South African Police Force in Serious and Violent Crime in South Africa*. Johannesburg, South Africa: IRR.

IRR (South African Institute of Race Relations). 2015. *Broken Blue Line 2: The Involvement of the South African Police Service in Serious and Violent Crime in South Africa*. Johannesburg, South Africa: IRR.

Katz, R. S. 1999. Building the foundation for a side-by-side explanatory model: A general theory of crime, the age-graded life course theory, and attachment theory. http://westerncriminology.org/documents/WCR/v01n2/Katz/Katz. html (accessed January 19, 2015).

Monama, T. 2013. Phiyega ignores calls to step down. http://www.iol.co.za/news/ crime-courts/phiyega-ignores-calls-to-step-down-1.1575477#.VLrCOkfF-So (accessed December 9, 2014).

Newburn, T. 1999. *Understanding and Preventing Police Corruption: Lessons from the Literature*. Police Research Series Paper 110. London, U.K.: Home Office.

Newham, G. 2012. South Africa: Cele and Mdluli's suspension. http://www.issafrica. org/publications/publication-archives/cpra-daily-briefing/south-africa-cele-and-mdluliandapos;s-suspension (accessed January 15, 2015).

Newham, G. and A. Faull. 2011. Protector or predator? Tackling police corruption in South Africa. http://www.issafrica.org/uploads/Mono182Web.pdf (accessed January 19, 2015).

News24. 2013a. 83% believe SAPS is corrupt—Survey. http://www.news24.com/ SouthAfrica/News/83-believe-SAPS-is-corrupt-survey-20130710 (accessed January 8, 2015).

News24. 2013b. Bethuel Mondli Zuma appears in court. http://www.news24. com/SouthAfrica/News/Bethuel-Mondli-Zuma-appears-in-court-20130910 (accessed January 12, 2015).

Porteous, C. 2011. Appeal dismissed: Selebi must begin sentence in 48 hours. http:// www.thesouthafrican.com/appeal-dismissed-selebi-must-begin-sentence-in-48-hours/ (accessed January 7, 2015).

Rademeyer, J. and K. Wilkinson. 2013. South Africa's criminal cops: Is the rot far worse than we have been told? http://africacheck.org/reports/south-africas-criminal-cops-is-the-rot-far-worse-than-we-have-been-told/ (accessed January 10, 2015).

Republic of South Africa. 1995. *South African Police Service Act 68 of 1995*. Cape Town, South Africa Republic of South Africa.

Republic of South Africa. 2011a. *No. 2 of 2011: Civilian Secretariat for Police Service Act, 2011*. Cape Town, South Africa: Republic of South Africa.

Republic of South Africa. 2011b. *No. 1 of 2011: Independent Police Investigative Directorate Act, 2011*. Cape Town, South Africa: Republic of South Africa.

Roelofse, C. J. 2012. Theoretical reflections on police behaviour: An expansion of reciprocal moral dualism. *Acta Criminologica*, Special Edition No. 2 of 2012: 135–154.

Roelofse, C. J., B. Simonovic, and P. J. Potgieter. 2014. A comparative study of corruption and government efforts to combat it across borders: The case for South Africa and Serbia. *Internal Security* 6(2): 7–28.

SAPA (South African Press Association). 2012. Mdluli 'looted crime unit', says secret report. http://mg.co.za/article/2012-03-18-mdluli-looted-crime-unit-says-secret-report (accessed January 7, 2015).

SAPA (South African Press Association). 2014. SA's corruption index rating worrying: CW. http://www.timeslive.co.za/local/article13396250.ece (accessed January 13, 2015).

SAPS (South African Police Service). nd. Code of conduct. http://www.saps.gov.za/about/conduct.php (accessed January 14, 2015).

SAPS (South African Police Service). 2014. *Annual Report: 2013/14 Financial Year*. http://www.saps.gov.za/about/stratframework/annual_report/2013_2014/ar2014_03_partc.pdf (accessed January 18, 2015).

Sturt, G. 2013. The police personality. http://homepage.ntlworld.com/gary.sturt/crime/police%20personality.htm (accessed February 28, 2013).

TI (Transparency International). 2008. *Corruption Perceptions Index 2008*. Berlin, Germany: TI.

TI (Transparency International). 2014. *Corruption Perceptions Index 2014*. Berlin, Germany: TI.

Twersky-Glasner, A. 2005. Police personality: What is it and why are they like that? *Journal of Police and Criminal Psychology* 20(1): 56–67.

Versluis, J.-M. 2015. Minister in hof gestraf oor bevel geminag is (Translated from Afrikaans—Minister sentenced due to contempt of court). http://www.netwerk24.com/nuus/2015-01-08-minister-in-hof-gestraf-oor-bevel-geminag-is?redirect_from=dieburger (accessed May 20, 2015).

Welch, K. 1998. Two major theories of Hirschi. http://www.criminology.fsu.edu/crimtheory/hirschi.htm (accessed May 13, 2010).

Zwane, N. 2014. Limpopo police officers suspended without pay. http://www.thenewage.co.za/146680-1008-53-Limpopo_police_officers_suspended_without_pay (accessed January 8, 2014).

Cameroon
Police Corruption and the Police Reforms Imperative

7

POLYCARP NGUFOR FORKUM

Contents

General Information on the Cameroon Police.. 126
Nature and Extent of Police Corruption in Cameroon 126
    Extortion of Money at Police Checkpoints 127
    Arbitrary Arrests and Detention 127
    Torture as a Tool of Extortion 128
    Sexual Assault Associated with Extortion.. 128
    Payment to Register a Case 129
    Transportation and Other Logistics "Fees".. 129
    Police Extortion and Other Abuses in the Informal Sector 130
    Police Corruption and the Rule of Law... 130
    High-Level Embezzlement of Police Funds 131
    Corrupt System of Monetary "Returns" 132
    Police Protection for Sale... 133
    Selection and Vetting of Entrants (Recruitment) 133
    Appointment and Tenure of Office for Senior Leadership..................... 134
Police Reforms in Cameroon... 134
    Improvement of the Conditions and Welfare of the Police.................... 135
    Initiatives at the Level of Democratic Policing....................................... 135
    Community Engagement and the Role of the Civil Society Groups 136
    Oversight Bodies.. 136
    Creation of New Institutional Structures 137
    Parallel Reforms... 137
    Zero Tolerance for Corruption and Police Brutality............................. 138
Conclusion 138
References.. 139

The police have extra powers meant to assist them to undertake their duties as watchers of the city (Reiner 2012). Most often, there is the miscarriage of justice and corruption perpetrated by this corps with its resultant consequences. This chapter provides a critical analysis of the nature and extent of police corruption and misconduct in Cameroon and examines and analyzes the police reforms that have either been embarked upon or that are imperative to control and mitigate the deleterious effects of this malpractice and misconduct among the police corps. Before delving into the discussion, it is necessary to define the concepts of "police" and "policing" as applied in this chapter. Police corruption is well defined and analyzed in Chapter 1 of this volume.

Police will be used to refer to the employees of the General Delegation for National Security (to be hence forth referred to as the GDNS) and the Gendarmerie (Pondi 1988; Mbarga Mbarga 1999). According to Newburn and Neyroud (2008, p. 217), policing involves organized order maintenance, peace keeping, rule of law enforcement, crime investigation and prevention, and other forms of investigation and associated information brokering, which may involve the conscious exercise of coercive power.

General Information on the Cameroon Police

The Republic of Cameroon is a multilingual country comprising some 250 indigenous languages corresponding to an estimated 250 ethnic groups. There exists one *lingua franca* (Cameroon Pidgin English) and two official languages (English and French). These official languages are the heritage of Franco–British rule in the country between the end of the First World War and independence in 1960. Under the 1996 Constitution, Cameroon is a unitary, decentralized, and democratic state with a semipresidential regime.

Administratively, the country is divided into 10 regions, 58 divisions, and 349 subdivisions. For these historical reasons, the Cameroon Police Force is the product of both the West Cameroon Police Force, fashioned after British policing, and the police of "La Republique du Cameroun" fashioned after French policing (Pondi 1988). To this can be added the gendarmes who are responsible for policing rural agglomerations. The police (the GDNS) is a force attached to the presidency of the republic with the head of state as its supreme commander. Some of these presidential powers are delegated to the Delegate General for National Security, a civilian ranking having the prerogatives of a cabinet minister. The Cameroon police has a total size of about 18,000 for a population of approximately 23 million giving a police to population ratio of 78 per 100,000 people.

Nature and Extent of Police Corruption in Cameroon

While acknowledging that the various practices of corruption by the police in the areas of recruitment and training, public security, judicial police, and general intelligence discussed in earlier works remain valid (see, e.g., Forkum 2012), we will in the following sections detail the most common and debilitating forms of police corruption in Cameroon, notably bribery, extortion, and related human rights abuses committed largely by rank-and-file police officers and the embezzlement of public funds, enforcement of a system of "returns," and abuse of office by senior police officials that drive many of these abuses. This state of affairs has given the Cameroonian police a very bad image and is frequently captured in media headlines.

Extortion of Money at Police Checkpoints

The most common venue for police extortion in Cameroon occurs at police roadblocks and checkpoints. On a daily basis throughout Cameroon, drivers of taxis, minibuses, and motorcycles are subjected to routine extortion under threats of arrest, detention, and physical injury after being obliged to stop at official or semiofficial police roadblocks. These checkpoints, ostensibly put in place to combat rampant and rising crime, have in practice become a lucrative criminal venture for the police. One driver plowing the Douala–Kousseri road that the author interviewed back in 2010 estimated that the police collected approximately U.S. $4.5 million in illegal "tolls" from some 70 police checkpoints along the highway. The amount paid to, or taken by, the police ranges from U.S. $0.5 to $50. Commercial minibus drivers often pay a fixed amount—ranging from U.S. $1 to $2, depending on the location—to the first police officer they encounter at the roadblock and then are usually waived through without incident thereafter.

Civil society leaders claim that police checkpoints seem to do very little to reduce crime and improve security, primarily because members of criminal gangs often pay off corrupt police officers who appear more intent on extorting money from drivers than combating crimes. In what appears to be an admission that these checkpoints do little to serve security objectives, the minister of police officially disbanded roadblocks in 2012 and replaced them with temporary "nipping points" or sporadic "stop-and-check" operations. Despite this change in nomenclature, it is still the case that, whether "nipping points," checkpoints, or stop and search, whether permanent or temporary, the fact is that at the end of the day, the police still extort.

Arbitrary Arrests and Detention

Numerous police officers, legal professionals, and civil society leaders have characterized the problem of unlawful detention of citizens by police officers with the apparent motivation to extort money as a widespread and growing problem throughout Cameroon (Itoe 1992; Chenghe 1993; Penda 2003). This is in violation of the principles governing detention. The police at times use specific incidents of crime and the high levels of crime, in general, as a pretext to randomly arrest and detain individuals and groups of citizens. Mass arrests and detention ("raiding") is commonly called *Kaléé Kaléé*. What is curious is that although the police operate under the pretext of a crackdown on crime, often following a particular incident of armed robbery or burglary, the victims of this form of police extortion are rarely questioned or interrogated about their alleged involvement in a crime.

Despite the pervasiveness of these abuses, the police leadership has failed to put in place effective measures to prevent this practice and rarely holds offending police officers accountable. The relevant law provides for the possibility of redress for victims of arbitrary detention but the procedure is too lengthy and too costly for the average citizen, and there are no safeguards to prevent the police perpetrator of the arbitrary detention to influence the outcome of the procedure. As a result of police malfeasance, those who wish to pursue justice are denied that right. Similarly, those who should be held accountable for their crimes—notably those with enough resources to pay their way out—routinely escape accountability and could pose a security threat to others.

Torture as a Tool of Extortion

Several United Nations reports have found that torture and ill-treatment are widely practiced by the police and are an intrinsic part of the functioning of the police in Cameroon. Numerous victims of extortion by the police have described having been threatened with or subjected to torture as a means of extracting money from them (Itoe 1992). Family members of other persons held in police custody described being coerced by police officers who threatened to torture or kill the family member being detained. The police in turn profit from their brutal reputation as fearful family members will pay large sums of money to free their loved ones. Allegations of how police tortured and threatened to kill suspects unless huge sums, of up to approximately U.S. $1000, are paid abound. Despite international and domestic law prohibiting the use of torture, the Cameroonian police routinely use torture and other cruel, inhuman, and degrading treatment and are rarely held accountable for it. We found that corruption in the police corps has both directly and indirectly contributed to the use of police torture in Cameroon, and there have now been many documented cases of this practice.

Sexual Assault Associated with Extortion

The police sometimes use the threat of rape and other forms of sexual assault as a means to extort money from women stopped at checkpoints, accosted by the police in public places, or detained in police custody. In some cases, women are told they have the "option" of providing sex in lieu of payment. In a number of cases, police officers carry out their threats and subject their victims to rape and other forms of sexual assault, particularly when women who had been detained refuse to pay all or part of the demanded sum. Although human rights groups have documented numerous cases of sexual assault, the police officers who commit these crimes are rarely held accountable.

Sex workers may be particularly vulnerable because the police can detain them under the pretext of cracking down on prostitution, which is illegal in Cameroon. The police's actions appear to have little to do with enforcing the law, however, since sex workers are rarely charged with prostitution offenses. The sex workers interviewed by the author described frequent police raids in which officers arrive in police vans and round up women standing in the streets at night. The police often subject the women to harassment or physical abuse, forcing them into the vans and transporting them to nearby police stations. There, they routinely demand sums of approximately U.S. $13–$33, as well as sex. Women who are unable to pay the police say they are often forced, under threat of being remanded to prison custody, to have sex to secure their freedom. Others are physically assaulted and raped by police officers.

Payment to Register a Case

Payment to register cases with the Cameroon police is widely recognized, including by the police themselves, as a common and unlawful practice. Despite the police leadership's public condemnation of this practice, many police stations require complainants to pay a "registration fee" ranging from U.S. $10 to $50 for desk officers to register a complaint or file a case. This then becomes a disincentive to reporting.

Transportation and Other Logistics "Fees"

Victims of crimes are also often asked to transport the police to the scene of the crime or to pay for such transport. Police officers seek to justify these fees by referencing their poor logistical support. Police officers will always express dismay at their inability to respond to the complaints of victims because of lack of fuel or a lack of a working vehicle. However, transportation fees can also be another cover for corruption. Demands for transport come in a number of different forms. Police may ask the victim to pay for fuel for a working police vehicle. If vehicles are not available, the police may ask the victim to pay for their transport by commercial motor bike or taxi cab. Sometimes, officers ask for the money outright; other officers have victims ride alongside them and pay the taxi fee upon arrival at the accident scene. That these fees are often bribes becomes clear when officers ask for cash that exceeds—often by substantial amounts—the usual taxi fare to the accident scene. Money is, thus, paid at the stage of lodging the complaint, money for logistics to work on the case, and money to the investigation department to send cases to court. These requests for the victims to fund criminal investigations are so entrenched that if there is noncompliance by the complainant, the case can be turned against him or her.

Police Extortion and Other Abuses in the Informal Sector

The informal sector remains the main provider of employment in Cameroon, with more than 90% of the overall labor force (World Bank 2012) and more than three-fourths are considered vulnerably employed. Yet, it is these low-income workers and their families who are most vulnerable to police extortion and its attendant abuses, including arbitrary arrest and detention, assaults on the person, and mistreatment in custody. The resultant loss of income, as well as the inability of street vendors and drivers to earn an income, creates immeasurable hardships for their families.

Street vendors always fall victim because under the pretext of enforcing vague laws, the police steal or "lose" goods confiscated from vendors during raids or require that vendors taken into custody pay "fees" to be released from jail. While seizure of street vendor goods occurs across the country, it is most pervasive in Yaoundé and Douala. A number of police officers interviewed confirmed that harassment was used as a money-making scheme. Several of these officers said they participate in *njangis* (savings clubs), in which they would pool the daily money they had made from extorting taxi and motorcycle drivers and others.

The Minister of Police has publicly requested that citizens report incidents of corruption and other excesses directly to him by dialing the 500 hotline. Such actions, which have shown no discernible effect, may give some public airing to an issue, but are no replacement for comprehensive government action to discipline and punish police officers engaged in illegal activities.

Police Corruption and the Rule of Law

Criminal suspects with money can simply bribe the police to avoid arrest, detention, and prosecution. For their part, high-level police officials have sold off for their own personal enrichment nearly one-fourth of the police force to provide protection for Cameroon's wealthy elite. This corrupt practice by senior police officials has left the vast majority of Cameroonians without adequate security and has further undermined their right to equal protection under the law.

Many Cameroonians distrust the police's ability to properly investigate crimes or protect them from violence which, in turn and like most of Africa, encourages popular support for vigilante groups and mob violence in a bid to justify police failure. The public maintains a profound distrust in the police who are perceived as ineffective, corrupt, and often complicit in crime.

While abuses by the rank and file, discussed earlier, are the most observable manifestations of police corruption, two other key dynamics—large-scale embezzlement by mostly senior officers and the corrupt system of returns—underlie and indeed drive many of these abuses. To these two can also be added the outright sale of police protection and corruption both in recruitment as well as in appointments to posts of responsibility (all master-minded by the senior officials).

High-Level Embezzlement of Police Funds

A number of mutually reinforcing factors conspire to fuel the rampant levels of corruption within the Cameroon Police corps. The combination of inadequate funding for the police force, embezzlement, and misman-agement of existing funds leaves appallingly little to run essential police operations.

Several high-level police officials have over the years been credibly impli-cated in but never convicted of the theft of police funds destined to cover basic police operations. Basic office materials are never bought but the money allocated is squandered. Cash sent to motivate junior officers during special operations or national day festivities never reach them. In most of these cases, however, the government and the police leadership have failed to properly investigate, prosecute, or discipline implicated officers, much less take tangi-ble steps to prevent future cases of embezzlement of police funds. Apparently, dismissal from a duty post seems enough punishment in Cameroon. This is unlike in neighboring Nigeria where there have been at least sporadic cases of investigation and punishment such as that of the former Inspector General Tafa Balogun, as well as in Uganda where there has been a judicial commis-sion of inquiry into corruption in the Uganda Police Force. In Cameroon, no such investigation has ever taken place, and there seems to be no likelihood of such in the near future.

The embezzlement of vast amounts of public funds destined for the Cameroon police force indirectly impacts the enjoyment of human rights protection in Cameroon by limiting the capacity of the police to conduct criminal investigations and provide protection from violent and other forms of crime. Left with limited investigatory capacity, the Cameroonian police routinely resort to extortion in part to fund basic police services and the torturing of criminal suspects as their primary tool for collecting evidence.

Other police officials have noted that the operational deficiencies experienced by the rank and file in police stations throughout Cameroon were less a result of high-level embezzlement and more due to insufficient resources to meet policing needs. Despite large budget increases to the police, these officers said that the budget was still insufficient to adequately support police operations on the ground. These budgets are also usually augmented by vast sums of money from the presidency and local governments as well as from private sector donations and trust funds. If properly allocated, these combined revenue sources could provide adequate resources for essential police services in Cameroon. But the police administration has failed to disclose in any transparent manner the sources and amounts of revenue received from each or the use of these funds. It appears that much of these resources are siphoned off or mismanaged. This wall of silence is justified by claiming "security reasons." But, the police in a democratic society must make it possible to be audited without infringing on security constraints.

Apart from salaries that take up approximately 73% of the police budget, the usual lack of fuel or stationery at police stations can only be explained either by the fact that the allocation is inadequate or by mismanagement. While we are not in a position to determine the appropriate funding levels or estimate the proportional impact from the theft of police funds by senior-level police officials, it is clear that the negative implications of this deficit is significantly worsened by embezzlement of funds on the part of senior police officials. These facts are corroborated by civil society leaders, high court judges, and both serving and retired police officers at all levels of the chain of command.

Corrupt System of Monetary "Returns"

Police officers of all ranks describe the existence of a scheme of "returns" throughout the police hierarchy, by which superiors demand that their subordinates pay informal sums from the money made from bribes and extortion. Sometimes, these amounts influence the process of placement and transfers to posts by the assigning officer. In many cases, superior officers set monetary "targets" for their subordinates and remove from their posts those who fail to meet those targets. The returns then move up the chain of command as officers who take returns from their subordinates in turn pay their superiors for the same reasons.

Several police officers and civil society leaders in Cameroon identify the system of returns as a key dynamic underlying, and indeed driving, the extortion and related abuses perpetrated by Cameroonian police officers at all levels. We interviewed 15 police officers, including 3 in senior posts, as well as a former senior police official who either personally paid returns or confirmed the existence of the system of returns in the Cameroon Police Force.

They characterized the problem as widespread, pervasive, and deeply embedded into the practices of the force. These unanimously believe rightly or wrongly that the return goes right to the top of the chain of command. However, the senior police leadership, for the most part, denies the existence of the corrupt system of returns in the Cameroon police. Whether due to the difficulty of establishing such cases or to the leadership willfully turning a blind eye to these corrupt practices, the police have failed to hold accountable senior officers who demand or accept returns from their subordinates.

Police Protection for Sale

A good proportion of police officers are assigned by their superior officers to undertake private businesses as security guards and personal orderlies. While the services of these officers have been illegally sold off to provide protection for Cameroon's elite, the vast majority of ordinary Cameroonians who cannot afford to buy police protection are left with inadequate security. This widespread practice results in a significant financial benefit for senior police officials who personally take in money from private individuals and businesses to assign rank-and-file officers to private posts and then gain further by extracting "returns" from these same lower-ranking officers. Even police escorts are outrightly paid for. This outsourcing at times is for other gratuities like promotions. This is the case, for example, of the huge number of police officers guarding the extended family of the country's president.

Selection and Vetting of Entrants (Recruitment)

The power of selection of police recruits rests with the president of the republic who delegates these powers to the minister in charge of the police. The training center does not participate in the selection process but simply receives the recruits and trains them. Corruption in the Cameroon police often starts during the process of recruitment, which is marred by corruption, tribalism, and nepotism. The payment of bribes by recruits sets a precedent for corruption. Some of those who bribe to enter the police force borrowed at exorbitant interest rates and are forced to corrupt themselves in order to pay back this money. By the time they finish paying this off, corruption must have become their habit and of course becomes hard to terminate.

After recruitment, the training stage is not corruption free either. Training of superintendents and assistant superintendents is done by the National Advanced Police School in Yaoundé, which has a regional character, for it receives recruits not only from Cameroon but also from Congo, Chad, Equatorial Guinea, Togo, and Gabon. The Police Training College trains constables and inspectors. In either school, bribing of trainers is rampant for such reasons as allowing trainees to shy away from some of the harsh physical exercises, to cover up absenteeism, and to pass exams. During exams, for example, recruits contribute money to bribe invigilators and exam graders, and it is even alleged that part of this money goes right up to the commander of the school. With the increase in the hourly pay of part-time instructors, it is hoped that this may control corruption in the school and result in the hiring of more qualified trainers.

Appointment and Tenure of Office for Senior Leadership

The president of the republic as supreme commander of the police recruits, promotes, sanctions, and appoints the police to posts of responsibility. Once new recruits enter the police force, they often have to bribe their superiors to be assigned to lucrative posts—assignments where police officers have ample opportunities to demand bribes and extort money from the public—or to be considered for promotion. A post is considered to be lucrative either as a function of the particular assignment—for example, manning a roadblock or directing traffic—or due to their geographic locations, such as commercial centers or regions of the country where the police are more likely to come into contact with wealthy individuals, business people, or market traders. For instance, police officers of the Mobile Wing Yaoundé will prefer the Douala road since it is much more lucrative as it links the commercial capital of Douala to Yaoundé. So at all levels, there is this issue of post buying and continuous payments to remain there. A former Cameroon police participant of a UN mission explains that to be deployed for a United Nations mission or an African Union mission, you need to pay a bribe of U.S. $2000 and $1000 to the respective commissioners in charge of these missions. Even while in the mission, you have to, from time to time, contribute money coordinated by the contingent commander and send it to the respective commissioner at home.

Police Reforms in Cameroon

This chapter posits that genuine police reform in Cameroon can be traced from the signing of a series of Presidential Decrees in November 2012. The reforms particularly concern the improvement of the conditions and welfare of the police, training and capacity building, creation of new police stations and services, termination of routine road controls, institution of the call hotline 500, zero tolerance for corruption and police brutality, and numerous initiatives at the level of democratic policing such as community policing, gender balance and mainstreaming, and community engagement and the role of civil society organizations.

Improvement of the Conditions and Welfare of the Police

Through a series of decrees of 2012, the lives and work of the police were to be drastically improved. Those decrees included the following:

- The reduction of the number of years of longevity to qualify for promotion to a higher grade.
- Institution of an allowance for uniforms of approximately U.S. $10 for all grades.
- An increase in risk allowance by 5%.
- Freedom to resign from the force.
- An increase in the retirement age for employees of the rank of constable, inspector, assistant superintendent, and superintendents of police. There is equally the possibility for an employee who attains the age limit for retirement to be offered extension of service by the president, being maintained on a contract basis, being maintained as a consultant, or being raised to an honorary rank.
- Bonus for those who on retirement have children above age 21.
- Special bonus is equally allocated for each 5 years of continuous service.

Initiatives at the Level of Democratic Policing

As Chapter 1 portrays, police organizations tend to be change averse. This is what Reiner (2012) refers to as police conservatism. The Cameroon police force is no exception. These, notwithstanding, changes have either taken place or are expected to take place, especially with respect to community policing, gender balance and mainstreaming, controlling sexual exploitation and abuse, use of oversight bodies, and the role of the civil society.

Community policing has been an in-house word in Cameroon for the past 10 years. Without necessarily defining the term, it has come to be understood as building a friendlier and available police force vis-à-vis the population (Sadate 1996). Hence, the creation of the "Equipes Special d' Intervention Rapides" (special rapid intervention teams) as well as police posts at road junctions and some neighborhoods goes a long way to making the police more available.

At the level of gender balance and mainstreaming, the proportion of women in the Cameroon police is estimated at less than 10%. Sex is one of the prohibited grounds for discrimination. However, women in the Cameroon police find themselves discriminated against at recruitment and appointments. An affirmative action can help salvage this situation. In appointments, depending on the person doing it, some fragile effort is made to place women in some strategic positions. But there is no law obliging the powers to do so. This needs to be institutionalized into law. Also, sexual exploitation and abuse is rife in the work place. Female officers offer sex to have and maintain lucrative posts as well as promotions, while their male counterparts use money or other practices. It is unfortunate that the series of decrees of 2012 were all silent on gender.

Community Engagement and the Role of the Civil Society Groups

Civil society is almost nonexistent in Cameroon as far as occupation of public space is concerned. To date, there is no civil society organization in Cameroon that engages the police. However, there are cases of media reports on police excesses, failures, and successes. This author appeals for a more vibrant civil society organization to engage with the police such as the CLEEN Foundation in Nigeria, the African Policing Civilian Oversight Forum in South Africa, the Usalama Reforms Forum in Kenya, and the Commonwealth Human Rights Initiative in India. They may also want to visit the Dutch branch of Amnesty International to learn more on how to engage with the police.

Oversight Bodies

In Cameroon, police excesses and misconduct are under the jurisdiction of the Special Division for Service Control (Police of Police). This has been criticized by the United Nations Committee against Torture, which prefers a neutral civilian body. In its 44th session in May 2010, under consideration of reports submitted by state parties under article 19 of the Convention, the committee had this to say:

> While noting the establishment in 2005 of a Special Police Oversight Division, the so-called 'Police des Polices', attached to the Department for National Security, the Committee remains concerned about this institution's lack of independence and objectivity. It is concerned that inquiries into allegations of unlawful acts, including torture or cruel, inhuman or degrading treatment, committed by the police, are carried out by police officials of the Special Police Oversight Division. In this regard, the Committee is concerned that only a few complaints against police officials are admitted, give rise to prompt, impartial and exhaustive investigations, and lead to prosecutions and convictions.
>
> UNCAT (2010, p. 7)

They consequently called on the state party, Cameroon, to "establish a body that is independent of the police and ensure that allegations of torture and other cruel, inhuman or degrading treatment or punishment are the subject of prompt, impartial, thorough and effective investigations" (UNCAT 2010, p. 7). We are still waiting for this body to be created, more than 10 years after.

Creation of New Institutional Structures

The year 2012 witnessed the creation of a Police Reference Hospital, a management council for National Security, and an Academy of National Security of Cameroon. However, these new structures are yet to become operational. Also, 6 central public security police stations, 97 public security police stations, 78 police posts, 9 divisional central intelligence police stations, 100 intelligence police posts, and 45 border police posts were created. The newly created services had to wait until January 2014 for officials to be appointed to man them. At the time of writing more than 90% of the new units are yet to have sites and personnel. Worst still, some of the posts have not been situated in the map of Cameroon due to the high involvement of politicians in the decisions. For the appointments proper, it abounds with the appointment of dead officers, the appointment of some officers to more than two posts in far off towns, and the nonappointment of some officers that are due appointment. For this reform to have meaning, it is urgent that these appointment errors be corrected and the services equipped with material and personnel.

Parallel Reforms

As Osse (2006, p. 22) puts it:

> Too often human rights strategies seeking to address problems that involve the police ignore the fact that the police are part of a broader security and justice system for which they cannot be held fully responsible. Similarly, sometimes human rights strategies do not fully understand the complexities of the interplay between State, public and police that requires the police to have some degree of autonomy (within boundaries) and to decide on how to respond to law and order situations.

This calls for an input on parallel relevant reforms. The justice sector is benefiting from the logistics support from the European Union. A new Criminal Procedure Code (Law No 2005/2007 of July 27, 2005) has been enacted that highlights much of the common law system. It has been described "both as evolutionary and revolutionary, a fruit of a scholarly and subtle dosage of the traditions of common law and Romano - Germanic laws" (Ndifiembeu 2006, p. 28). It, for example, insists on the presumption of innocence and fair and effective trial within a reasonable time, to name but a few. These parallel reforms can also improve on police efficiency.

Zero Tolerance for Corruption and Police Brutality

The disciplinary council is now financed for speedy trials. The trend of the decisions of the disciplinary council shows zero tolerance for corrupt officials. The most glaring example is the dismissal for corruption in 2012 of the third in command to the then Inspector-General.

The police minister also published an official statement denouncing police brutality and explained the effect such deviant actions have on the image of the police in the country within an era of democracy. This statement is now exhibited in all police stations.

Conclusion

In Cameroon, members of government and politicians abuse the police for their own agendas; recruitment is politicized; and oversight bodies are partisan. The police force is generally understaffed; communications and transport infrastructures are inadequate, impacting on the quality of police work; and evidence handling and forensic capacities are inadequate. Moreover, recruits are not well educated on intake, and training does not address all elements required, while human rights violations persist. Community policing is frustrated by a lack of trust in the police and public perception of the police is largely negative. Poor pay and conditions of service lead officers to take bribes and efforts to address corruption are inadequate and inconsistent. At the same time, oversight remains limited or insufficiently independent.

As this chapter demonstrates, police corruption takes many forms in Cameroon. It is a recurring and tenacious element in policing and can be highly pernicious. Its ramifications go beyond the police organization. It cannot be looked at as isolated incidents because it is engrained and systemic. It requires holistic reforms. The first step in tackling police corruption is to acknowledge that the evidence graphically illustrates that policing and corruption are inseparable (Punch 2009). It is also important to acknowledge that corruption is found in all sectors of the society. As such, the proposed recommendations on measures to fight police corruption in Cameroon such as parliamentary oversight; prosecution (special anti-corruption courts); external accountability; education on ethics, integrity, and governance; depoliticization of the police; asset declaration; and increase in pay and improvement of working conditions, as discussed in earlier works (see, e.g., Forkum 2012), remain valid. However, considering the prime duty of the police and the place they occupy within the framework of the State, it is incumbent on Cameroonians to insist on a policy reforms process where combating corruption in the police is prioritized.

References

Chenghe, T. T. 1993. Human rights and judicial police powers of search, interrogation and detention in the Anglophone Provinces of Cameroon. Yaoundé, Cameroon: Unpublished dissertation.

Forkum, P. N. 2012. *Police Corruption in Cameroon and Uganda: A Comparative Analysis*. Saarbrucken, Germany: Lambert Akademic Publishing.

Itoe, M. T. 1992. Police powers and human rights abuses in the Bamenda urban area. Yaoundé, Cameroon: Unpublished dissertation.

Mbarga Mbarga, V.-H. 1999. The frontier police and its socio-professional context. Yaoundé, Cameroon: CEPER.

Ndifiembeu, B. N. 2006. *A Handbook on the Criminal Procedure Code of the Republic of Cameroon*. Yaoundé, Cameroon: Author.

Newburn, T. and P. Neyroud (eds.). 2008. *Dictionary of Policing*. Devon, U.K.: Willan Publishing.

Osse, A. 2006. *Understanding Policing: A Resource for Human Rights Activists*. Amsterdam, the Netherlands: Amnesty International.

Penda, S. A. 2003. The protection of the rights of the accused in criminal trials: A case of Anglophone Cameroon. Yaoundé, Cameroon: Unpublished dissertation.

Pondi, P. 1988. *La Police au Cameroun (Naissance et évolution)*. Yaoundé, Cameroon: Edition CLE.

Punch, M. 2009. *Police Corruption: Exploring Police Deviance and Crime*. London, U.K.: Routledge.

Reiner, R. 2012. *The Politics of the Police*. Oxford, U.K.: Oxford University Press.

Sadate, S. 1996. *Le Policier et son Public dans une Société Démocratique*. Yaoundé, Cameroon: CEPER.

UNCAT (United Nations Committee Against Torture). 2010. *Consideration of Reports Submitted by States Parties Under Article 19 of the Convention: Concluding Observations of the Committee Against Torture: Cameroon*. New York: United Nations.

World Bank. 2012. *Unlocking the Labor Force: An Economic Update on Cameroon: With a Focus on Employment*. Yaoundé, Cameroon: World Bank Cameroon County Office.

Developing Societies Case Studies: Asia-Pacific

Hong Kong
Police Corruption
and Reforms

8

DENNIS LAI HANG HUI

Contents

Police Corruption: Brief Conceptual Overview 144
Overview of the Key Incidences of Police Corruption in Hong Kong
(2002–2015) 144
Evolving Institutional Mechanism for Control of Police Corruption in
Hong Kong 148
Conclusions: Factors Influencing the Prospect of Police Corruption in
Hong Kong 152
References 154

Hong Kong has been celebrated as one of the societies in the world with very little corruption. Remarkably, the Hong Kong Police Force (HKPF) has been able to transform itself from a corruption-ridden organization to a highly professional one. Nonetheless, there are still many reports of corruption cases within the HKPF. This chapter identifies the key features of police corruption in Hong Kong and attempts to provide an overview and analysis of the institutional structure for combating said police corruption. It extends existing theoretical analyses to develop an institutional explanation in accounting for the scale and features of police corruption in Hong Kong.

The work follows Huntington's idea of institutionalism looking at the extent to which the political institutions of a society can "curb the excesses of personal and parochial desires" (Huntington 1968, p. 24). It follows that reducing police corruption also involves a scaling down of the norms thought appropriate for the behavior of public officials (Huntington 1968). The argument is extended into the understanding of the institutional mechanism for controlling police corruption in Hong Kong and the role of the Independent Commission Against Corruption (ICAC) in that regard. The chapter concludes by looking at the factors that affect the scale of police corruption in Hong Kong.

Police Corruption: Brief Conceptual Overview

Police corruption is a very elastic concept. It "takes diverse forms and can alter over time" (Punch 2009, p. 31). Police corruption involves a wide range of activities such as abuses of official position for personal gains, violations of laws and professional codes of policing practice, and deviations from normative standards (Punch 2000, 2009). While police corruption may be connected to a certain *noble* or *approved* cause (Newburn 1999) and does not necessarily give rise to victimhood (Punch 2009), it compromises the institutional integrity of a policing system and undermines its legitimacy. From the sociological–criminological perspective, police corruption reveals the dysfunctionality of a policing system in minimizing opportunities for deviance. Factors such as police culture, organizational knowledge, and the police–criminal nexus carry implications for the likelihood and scale of police corruption. From the criminal justice perspective, police corruption relates to procedural justice, public interest and institutional oversight, and the issues that articulate the importance of police accountability.

Police corruption occurs at two levels: "operationally on the street or back in the office behind the scenes" (Neild 2007, p. 2). Scholars have developed different typologies in order to better conceptualize police corruption as discussed in Chapter 1. The best known typology has been developed by Roebuck and Barker (1974) and was later enriched by Punch (1985). They basically identified the following nine types of police corruption, namely, (1) corruption of authority, (2) kickbacks, (3) opportunistic theft, (4) shakedowns or extortion, (5) protection of illegal activities, (6) the fix, (7) direct criminal activities, (8) internal payoffs, and (9) flaking or padding. Meanwhile, Neild (2007) developed another classification focusing on the nature of police corruption. Essentially, police corruption can be classified into four types, namely, (a) petty individual corruption, (b) bureaucratic corruption, (c) criminal corruption, and (d) political corruption (Neild 2007). These types of police corruption are linked to different reasons and require different strategies of detection and investigation.

Overview of the Key Incidences of Police Corruption in Hong Kong (2002–2015)

In this section, a select sample of the key cases related to police corruption in Hong Kong is highlighted covering the period 2002–2015. For 2002, the following cases were reported:

- A police officer was found to have stolen a lighter, approximately U.S. $257, a silver bracelet, a golden necklace, and a silver ring from a suspect. The officer was given a 6-month jail sentence.

- An officer with the rank of senior police constable committed forgery by producing counterfeit documents to his seniors to demonstrate his good financial status. He was sentenced by the court to perform 200 h of community service.
- A police officer was charged with violating the Prevention of Bribery Ordinance (POBO) by involving himself in an unauthorized loan, in the amount of approximately U.S. $3500, and for using a dishonored check for repaying the money. He was released because of insufficient evidence.
- Two police sergeants and ten constables were charged by the ICAC for obstructing justice in an investigation related to a 2001 incident involving arranging for four civilian suspects to be scapegoats in a gambling raid.
- A police officer was charged with fraud as she failed to fully disclose her financial status when applying for an approximately U.S. $22,000 loan. The court issued her a 240 h community service sentence.
- A detective police constable received a bribe of approximately U.S. $645 from a suspect who was involved in blackmail and had also declared himself to be a member of a triad society. The officer was given a 3-month sentence (adjusted to be an 8-month sentence after a review).
- A police officer was charged with perverting the course of justice in relation to a car accident involving a public celebrity. The officer was given a 6-month sentence (*Apple Daily* 2002a,b,c,d; Chow 2002; Lewis 2002).

In 2003, some of the police corruption cases that were reported are the following:

- A senior police constable filed an application for a judicial review by the High Court to overturn the decision by the Force Discipline Adjudication Unit relating to his connection to the triad society in Macao. He was subsequently ordered to take early retirement. The court dismissed his application and opined that the decision by the police is legitimate as it is the duty of the police to uphold the highest level of integrity.
- A Senior Superintendent of Police and a senior inspector, a station sergeant, and three civilians were arrested in connection with an alleged sex-for-tip-offs case. The court found the senior superintendent guilty of misconduct and handed out a 3-year sentence. The judge in the case noted that "it is the clearest case of 'keeping sweet' corruption, where advantages are given to someone in authority, without asking for a *quid pro quo* at the time the advantage is given,

but building a store of goodwill to provide a basis for future corrupt demands."

- A police constable was charged with abusing his position. The officer was found to have helped himself to fish balls and dumplings from a hawker's food stall and on one occasion spitting chicken in the hawker's face and punching the hawker's wife in the stomach.
- A Chief Inspector of Police was found to be connected to a charge of obtaining unauthorized access to a computer with a view to dishonest gain for himself (*Apple Daily* 2003; Chan 2003; Chow 2003; *Hong Kong Economic Times* 2003).

For the period 2004–2005, the following were some of the police corruption cases that were reported:

- A police sergeant was found to be guilty of accepting a bribe of approximately U.S. $5200 in exchange for tipping off a pimp. The sergeant was given a 3-year jail sentence.
- A Chief Inspector of Police was found guilty of money laundering in the amount of approximately U.S. $1.4 million from suspected illegal bookmaking proceeds. He was given a 3.5-year jail sentence.
- A senior detective constable was accused of accepting a bribe of an amount of approximately U.S. $1300 from a man in exchange for not prosecuting him for a suspected deception offence (Hui 2005; Shamdasani 2005; Wong 2005).

In 2006, the following police corruption cases were reported:

- A Chief Inspector of Police was found guilty of inciting his friend to mislead the ICAC by giving false information over an unauthorized loan.
- A police sergeant was charged by the ICAC for swindling a woman.
- An antitriad constable was charged with perverting the course of public justice when he instructed a suspect to conceal the identity of the mastermind in a criminal case.
- A Senior Inspector of Police was found to have illegally accessed information relating to two police informers. He was also found to be in possession of methamphetamine.
- A police officer was found to having illegally accessed information of deceased persons and used the information to facilitate the funeral business of his relatives (*Apple Daily* 2006a,b; SCMP 2006a,b; Tsui 2006).

For the period 2007–2008, the following police corruption cases were made public:

- A senior police constable was found guilty of illegal soccer book-making and money laundering of over U.S. $232,000. He was found to have turned his disciplined services quarters into a center of soccer bookmaking.
- An indebted senior police constable was found to have stolen bail money and exhibits and was given a 20-month prison sentence.
- Four police officers were found to be in possession of ketamine and suspected to have committed the indictable offence of living on the earnings of prostitution of others.
- A senior police constable was charged with forging signatures on a witness statement (*Apple Daily* 2007, 2008; *Ming Pao Daily News* 2007).

In 2009, the following police corruption case was reported:

- A police officer was found guilty of raping a teenager and molesting a 21-year-old woman and two others in a police station. The officer was also charged with perverting the course of justice by offering bribes to a victim. He was given a 12-year jail sentence (Tsui 2009).

For the period 2012–2013, the reported police corruption cases were the following:

- Three police officers were found to have accepted protection payments from the operators of two massage parlors and a gambling den.
- A police district commander was convicted in the Eastern Magistrates Court for receiving U.S. $645 in gifts and discounts from a restaurant in exchange for turning a blind eye to its liquor license violations (SCMP 2012a; Luk 2013).

For the 2014–2015 period, at the time of writing, the following police corruption cases were reported:

- A police constable was penalized for failing to comply with the POBO that required him to declare all of his properties, expenditures, and liabilities.
- A police station constable was found to have solicited and accepted advantages from his subordinates.

- A police constable was found to have disclosed confidential information to another police constable and was given a 15-month sentence.
- A police sergeant and two others were suspected of having received bribes and operating an illegal gambling den.
- A police constable was found guilty of indecent assault at a police station (ICAC 2014a,b,c; *The Sun 2014*; SCMP 2015).

Based on the foregoing incidences, several features of police corruption can be identified. First, most of the irregularities have been connected to petty individual corruption and, to a lesser extent, criminal corruption. The more common one is the protection of illegal economic activities. As such, the police–criminal nexus has not been very strong with only occasional collusions between the triad society and the police in isolated cases, nor have there been signs about the possible reemergence of *syndicated corruption*. Second, police corruption has not been bounded by rank as both junior and senior police officers have been found to have been involved in different forms of police corruption. It also appears that the police officers involved in many corruption cases have abused their positions in accessing certain privileged information. Third, in some cases, the police have sought to benefit themselves through perverting the course of justice. Such offences are of particular importance in the context of Hong Kong given that its legal system is built on the legal principle of due process. It therefore follows that any such incidences can undermine the credibility of the criminal justice system.

Evolving Institutional Mechanism for Control of Police Corruption in Hong Kong

The institutional mechanism for control of police corruption in Hong Kong has evolved substantially since the colonial era. Before the establishment of the ICAC, police corruption had been alarmingly rampant. Problems such as *tea money* and *black money* became part of the everyday life in the 1960s and 1970s. Bribery became a lucrative business and the police from all ranks could make a good fortune out of their extensive involvement in different corrupt undertakings. The extensive collusion between the police and the criminals in every realm of the society then jeopardized the orderliness of the colonial regime and resulted in the growth of many underground activities, such as prostitution, gambling, and illegal drug dealings. Institutional attempts had been made by the colonial government to arrest the situation, such as the establishment of the Advisory Committee on Corruption in 1956, the Target Committee on Corruption by the Commissioner of Police in 1960, and the Anti-Corruption Office in 1971 in dealing with cases of bribery and corruption (Blair-Kerr 1973). Yet, these agencies did not live up to their expectations. Nor had the POBO been able to exercise its deterrent power. No less important was the prevalence of *syndicated* corruption that involved the extensive collusion between the police and the triad societies in perpetuating their rent-seeking behaviors.

The public discontent with the worrying scale of police corruption reached its apex when Chief Superintendent Peter Godber was able to escape from the colony after he had been ordered to explain his excessive wealth in 1973. Shortly after the Godber incident, Sir Alastair Blair-Kerr was commissioned by the colonial authority to look into the matter. He concluded that the unsatisfactory state of affairs should be properly dealt with by the establishment of a new anticorruption agency independent from the police (Blair-Kerr 1973). While anticipating the potential resistance to his recommendation, he suggested that the gravity of the situation seemed to justify an institutional overhaul. The call for an independent agency for anticorruption was then given a powerful boost when Sir Murray MacLehose, the then governor of Hong Kong, affirmed his commitment to establish an independent body that could garner public support and confidence. Despite the opposition and political tug-of-war that emerged, the ICAC was established in 1974.

From the institutional perspective, the establishment of the ICAC was essential not only in holding the police accountable for their misdeeds but also for enhancing the institutional capacity of the colonial state in maintaining the political order of Hong Kong. As the colonial economy witnessed dramatic growth, it became imperative for the colonial state to develop institutional mechanisms in order to forestall the opportunities for making use of unfair and predatory practices that could undermine the development of a *laissez-faire* mode of colonial capitalism. What became very important was how the colonial authority perceived corruption as no longer a criminal issue as such, but an issue of political security (Hong Kong Legislative Council 1974). Consequently, one needs to recognize and appreciate that the ICAC had in reality become an institutional agency in expanding the disciplinary power of the colonial state without overrelying on the HKPF alone.

Since its inauguration, the ICAC has displayed a high degree of institutional continuity and integrity. It has done so, among other reasons, to ensure its organizational autonomy and coherence. Consequently, here, the actual operation of the ICAC needs careful scrutiny. According to the ICAC Ordinance (Chapter 204), the ICAC is vested with a wide range of law enforcement powers in relation to corruption. Currently, the ICAC adopts a three-pronged approach to its anticorruption campaign, namely, law enforcement, prevention, and education. Their statutory duties are as follows: On the front of law enforcement, the Operations Department shall (1) receive and consider allegations of corrupt practices; (2) investigate any alleged or suspected offences under the ICAC Ordinance, the POBO, and the Elections (Corrupt and Illegal Conduct) Ordinance; (3) investigate any alleged offences of blackmail committed by a prescribed officer through misuse of office; and (4) investigate any conduct of a prescribed officer, which is connected with or conducive to corrupt practices. On the front of prevention, the Corruption Prevention Department shall (1) examine the practices and procedures of government departments and public bodies and secure revision of any that may be conducive to corruption and (2) advise upon request of private organizations or individuals on how to prevent corruption. On the front of education, the Community Relations Department shall (1) educate the public against the evils of corruption and (2) enlist public support in combating corruption (ICAC 2014c). This organizational structure has not witnessed substantial changes since it was put in place.

Meanwhile, hand in hand with the establishment of the ICAC has been the organizational reforms of the HKPF for ensuring its accountability. Essentially, in the course of the reforms of the HKPF since the 1970s, there has been increasing attention paid toward the issue of police integrity and the development of institutional mechanisms for combating police corruption. Several legal and regulatory instruments have been developed to ensure the proper ethical discharge of police duties. The first is the Police (Discipline) Regulation, which was promulgated in 1977. According to the regulation, any inspector or junior police officer may face disciplinary measures if he or she pleads and/or is found to be guilty of the offences as specified in the regulation (Regulation 3).

In addition, the Police General Orders provide specific provisions to prevent police corruption (HKPF n.d.a). For example, Chapter 6 specifies that a police officer shall not directly or indirectly solicit or receive any gratuity, present, subscription, or testimonial, either in his or her official or private capacity, unless in accordance with the general permission given under the Acceptance of Advantages (Chief Executive's Permission) Notice 2010. In addition, it is specified that a police officer shall not place himself or herself under financial obligation to any person or organization unless otherwise specified. Chapter 6 also provides that a police officer should avoid connecting themselves to money lenders and acting on behalf of commercial financial institutions. The HKPF is also subject to jurisdictional control by the POBO and the common law offence of misconduct (HKPF n.d.b).

Other preventive measures have also been put in place to ensure the highest degree of professionalism. First, the existing procedures for recruitment are now based on a high degree of transparency. Candidates have to undergo a robust set of selection procedures involving assessment of general knowledge, language proficiency, cognitive ability, and integrity checks. This set of selection procedures has been developed to ensure that only the most suitable candidates are selected. Second, integrity management has been incorporated into the organizational structure of the HKPF. Over the past few years, the HKPF has been developing programs to instill a sense of integrity among all ranks of police officers. Through the Strategy for Integrity Management, four approaches have been specified on which the HKPF relies for promoting the best ethical practices. These approaches include education and culture building, governance and control, enforcement and deterrence, as well as rehabilitation and support (HKPF 2010). To further enhance the effectiveness of the strategy, ethics and integrity education has been jointly implemented by the Service Quality Wing, the Personnel Wing, and the Police College of the HKPF (Hong Kong Legislative Council Panel on Security 2010). A behavioral guideline has also been developed by the HKPF outlining "the parameters of behavior expected of them both on and off duty" (HKPF 2010, p. 4).

In a sense, combating police corruption in Hong Kong demands a certain level of interaction between the police and the ICAC. In order to maximize the institutional capacity for combating police corruption, a Corruption Prevention Group was formed in 1981, which comprises senior officers from the police and the ICAC's Corruption Prevention Department (Lee 2003; Manion 2004). Other briefings for regional and district commanders are arranged on a regular basis (Hong Kong Legislative Council Panel on Security 2004). At the operational level, an Operational Liaison Group has been set up for directorate officers of the police and the ICAC to meet regularly on operational matters of mutual interest (Lee 2003). In 2009, a Force Committee on Integrity Management was established. It is manned by senior officers from both the HKPF and the ICAC for identifying issues relating to the promotion of honesty and integrity of the HKPF (Hong Kong Legislative Council Panel on Security 2010). Meanwhile, the Internal Investigations Office (IIO) became the operational interface between the HKPF and the ICAC. "Through the IIO, the Operations Department conducts referral of cases and obtains information and necessary assistance in facilitating ICAC investigations and operations. Except in urgent operational situations, the IIO is invariably informed in advance of action to be taken against police officers, e.g. arrest and the reason for the arrest" (Hong Kong Legislative Council Panel on Security 2004, pp. 2–3).

Yet, the relationship between the HKPF and the ICAC was ruptured by different incidents. For example, as early as in 1977, the HKPF organized a large-scale protest outside the headquarters of the ICAC to express their grievances. This episode of police mutiny ended when the then colonial Governor Murray MacLehose announced his plan to pardon cases of police corruption (Lam 2014). Another crisis of the relationship between the police and the ICAC occurred in 2002 when a senior superintendent was publicly identified and put on notice of suspicion for soliciting sex services in exchange for tip-offs about vice raids. On the one hand, the HKPF expressed their concern about the publicizing of the identity of the suspected officer and said that the ICAC should have been more circumspect (SCMP 2002). The ICAC, meanwhile, alleged that they had approached the HKPF before administering any raids. It was not until the intervention by the then Hong Kong Chief Executive that the tension subsided. In 2010, the HKPF organized a raid of the ICAC's new headquarters when two ICAC graft busters were suspected of having coached witnesses to provide false evidence (SCMP 2012b). This, obviously, resulted in discontent among the staff of the ICAC.

Conclusions: Factors Influencing the Prospect of Police Corruption in Hong Kong

This chapter has argued that the existing institutional framework for controlling police corruption remains very effective in eliminating opportunities for the police to engage in corrupt behaviors. There are several factors that could account for the low level of police corruption in Hong Kong. First is the institutional integrity of the internal and external control mechanisms. As has been argued earlier, the multipronged approach toward police anticorruption in Hong Kong has created an institutional structure that discourages rent-seeking behaviors by the police. In addition, the extensive linkage between the HKPF and the ICAC has enhanced the institutional capacity of the Hong Kong government in responding to different forms of police corruption. Second, the development of a values-based framework within the HKPF has facilitated the creation of a corruption-free organizational setup. In particular, the emphasis placed on professionalism, integrity, and honesty is considered important in establishing a service-oriented police culture (Wong 2012).

Third, the high degree of fairness and predictability in determining the pay and benefits of the HKPF personnel has definitely been one of the factors in discouraging police corruption. Currently, the salary structure of the HKPF is determined and reviewed by the Hong Kong Standing Committee on Disciplined Services Salaries and Conditions of Service. When reviewing the structure of salaries for the HKPF, the committee shall take into consideration a basket of factors. The relevant factors include the special nature of the police force, the changing sociopolitical environment in Hong Kong, the changing need for border security, changes in crime trends, changes in public order events, the responsibility of secondary duties, and customer orientation and service quality (Hong Kong Standing Committee on Disciplined Services Salaries and Conditions of Service 2008). The principle governing the rationale used by the committee in reviewing the salary structure of the HKPF was laid down in 1988 as follows:

> Accepting the special position of the police, however, we still have to regard policemen as members of the public service discharging public functions and as members of society with needs and wants which have much in common

with those of other members of the society. In free communities under the rule of law the police function cannot be successfully performed without the moral and material support of the great mass of society, and to separate the police too far from the rest of the public service and from society at large would not be in the long-term interests either of them or of the community they serve. We do not believe that that is what police representatives want; we believe they wish to be fairly remunerated for the unique task which they perform.

Hong Kong Government (1988, para 4.7)

On the other hand, several possible challenges that affect the nature and scale of police corruption in Hong Kong can be identified. Among them is the changing political dynamics in Hong Kong and the emerging challenge in preventing political corruption. With the growing uncertainty of political development in Hong Kong, how the HKPF maintains its political neutrality has become an emerging concern of the public. This is especially the case since the emergence of the Occupy Central Movement in 2014 when there were clashes between the police and the public of different scales. These events have resulted in the deterioration of the police–public relationship, giving rise to a growing sense of "us versus them" mentality (Williams 2002). Such tendencies may frustrate the collaborative basis between the public and the police for combating police corruption.

Next, the dominance of the paramilitary tradition of the HKPF (Jiao et al. 2005) may mean that public accountability may not be a primary concern in developing anticorruption programs. Indeed, the existing conceptualization of police governance in Hong Kong remains a highly legalistic one, focusing on the behaviors that contravene the prevailing laws, regulations, and codes of practice. While this kind of rational–legal strategy of combating corruption is indispensable, how public interest is located in the development of the anticorruption regime is an issue that deserves attention. This is particularly important when Hong Kong has yet to adopt the principle of civilian oversight into practice. This could limit the prospect for developing a more accountable form of police governance.

Finally, the rise of anticorruption campaigns in mainland China may create new momentum for Hong Kong in curbing police corruption. While Hong Kong is being governed under the "One Country, Two Systems" formula, its political and administrative practices have been increasingly informed by the changing political climate in China. Although it would be premature to argue that there will be a growing convergence between mainland China and Hong Kong in their policing practices (see Lo 2012), it is likely that the new wave of anticorruption campaigns in China would lend support to the Hong Kong government and strengthen its political will to combat police corruption.

References

Apple Daily. 2002a. Jing zhang she feifa jiedai dan piao (Police Constable involved in illegal borrowing), April 5:A16.

Apple Daily. 2002b. Qian zhai jing tu yong jia wenjian bi chufen (Indebted police producing counterfeit document), February 9:A14.

Apple Daily. 2002c. Jing yuan tou yifan caiwu pan jian bannian (Police sentenced to jail after stealing belongings of a suspect), January 29:A18.

Apple Daily. 2002d. Yi jieshou 14K huilu jing yuan bei bu (The police caught for accepting bribes from a triad society), November 1:A16.

Apple Daily. 2003. Ducha she bu chengshi yong jing diannao (Inspector involved in dishonest use of police computer), November 13:A16.

Apple Daily. 2006a. Gaoji ducha bei kong lanyong jingfang diannao (Police Senior Inspector accused of the misuse of computer), July 5:A14.

Apple Daily. 2006b. Yi zhu yuefu bin yi ye qu sizhe ziliao jing she shan ru jingfang diannao shoushen (Police assisting relatives by passing privileged information), July 12:A16.

Apple Daily. 2007. Lian shu sou wanzi siren huisuo ju si nannu jing yuan bei kong kao CoCo wei sheng (4 police caught for living on earnings of prostitution in Wan Chai), October 4:A10.

Apple Daily. 2008. Jilu budui sushe bian waiwei dou zhong an zu tan yuan she shou bo lan kai shen (Police caught for turning disciplined services quarters into a gambling centre), January 22:A20.

Blair-Kerr, A. 1973. *Second Report of the Commission of Inquiry under Sir Alastair Blair-Kerr*. Hong Kong, China: Hong Kong Government Printer.

Chan, C. 2003. Constable stole hawker's food, court told. http://www.scmp.com/article/411870/constable-stole-hawkers-food-court-told (accessed February 1, 2015).

Chow, M. 2002. Nicholas Tse escapes threat of jail sentence. http://www.scmp.com/article/399596/nicholas-tse-escapes-threat-jail-sentence (accessed February 1, 2015).

Chow, M. 2003. Senior HK policeman guilty of vice charges. http://www.scmp.com/article/436319/senior-hk-policeman-guilty-vice-charges (accessed February 1, 2015).

HKPF (Hong Kong Police Force). n.d.a. Police General Orders. http://www.police.gov.hk/ppp_en/11_useful_info/pgo.html (accessed January 10, 2015).

HKPF (Hong Kong Police Force). n.d.b. Ethics and integrity in the Hong Kong Police Force. http://www.police.gov.hk/info/doc/ethics&IntegrityPaper.pdf (accessed January 26, 2015).

HKPF (Hong Kong Police Force). 2010. Legislative Council Panel on Security: Integrity Management and Behavioral Guidelines of the Hong Kong Police Force. http://www.legco.gov.hk/yr09-10/english/panels/se/papers/se0601cb2-1633-7-e.pdf (accessed February 1, 2015).

Hong Kong Economic Times. 2003. Gaoji ducha she hei gezhi qiu fu he bai (Senior Inspector seeking judicial review after being dismissed), January 21:A25.

Hong Kong Government. 1988. *Review Committee on Disciplined Services Pay and Conditions of Service Final Report* (Rennie's Report). Hong Kong, China: Government Printer.

Hong Kong Legislative Council. 1974. *Official Report of Proceedings: Thursday, 31st October.* Hong Kong, China: Legislative Council.

Hong Kong Legislative Council Panel on Security. 2004. Operational Liaison between the Police and the ICAC. http://www.legco.gov.hk/yr03-04/english/panels/se/papers/se0119cb2-955-4e.pdf (accessed February 1, 2015).

Hong Kong Legislative Council Panel on Security. 2010. Background brief prepared by the Legislative Council Secretariat for the meeting on 1 June 2010: Integrity management and behavioral guidelines of the Hong Kong Police Force. http://www.legco.gov.hk/yr09-10/english/panels/se/papers/se0601cb2-1633-8-e.pdf (accessed February 1, 2015).

Hong Kong Standing Committee on Disciplined Services Salaries and Conditions of Service. 2008. *Report on the Grade Structure Review of the Disciplined Services November 2008.* Hong Kong, China: Government Printer.

Hui, P. 2005. Sergeant who took bribes from pimp jailed for 3 years. http://www.scmp.com/article/500259/sergeant-who-took-bribes-pimp-jailed-3-years (accessed February 1, 2015).

Huntington, S. P. 1968. *Political Order in Changing Societies.* New Haven, CT: Yale University Press.

ICAC (Independent Commission Against Corruption). 2014a. Policeman penalized for failure to comply with POBO notice. *Press Release,* January 20. http://www.icac.org.hk/en/pr/index_uid_1514.html (accessed January 2, 2015).

ICAC (Independent Commission Against Corruption). 2014b. Policeman gets 15 months for misconduct over leakage of confidential information. *Press Release,* September 16. http://www.icac.org.hk/en/pr/index_uid_1612.html (accessed February 1, 2015).

ICAC (Independent Commission Against Corruption). 2014c. Organizational structure. http://www.icac.org.hk/en/about_icac/os/index.html (accessed January 30, 2015).

Jiao, A., R. W. K. Lau, and P. Lui. 2005. An institutional analysis of organizational change: The case of the Hong Kong Police. *International Criminal Justice Review* 15(1): 38–57.

Lam, L. 2014. Forty years since its creation, how the ICAC cleaned up corruption in Hong Kong. http://www.scmp.com/news/hong-kong/article/1428093/forty-years-its-creation-how-icac-cleaned-corruption-hong-kong?page=all (accessed January 25, 2015).

Lee, A. S. K. 2003. Corruption in the police: How do you clean it up? http://www.icac.org.hk/en/acr/sa/cp/index.html (accessed January 20, 2015).

Lewis, T. 2002. ICAC charges 12 officers over 'staged' gambling raids. *South China Morning Post.* http://www.scmp.com/article/389145/icac-charges-12-officers-over-staged-gambling-raids (accessed February 1, 2015).

Lo, S. S.-H. 2012. The changing context and content of policing in China and Hong Kong: Policy transfer and modernization. *Policing and Society: An International Journal of Research and Policy* 22(2): 185–203.

Luk, E. 2013. ICAC heat set for cop guilty of meals scam. http://www.thestandard.com.hk/news_detail.asp?pp_cat=30&art_id=134003&sid=39709289&con_type=1 (accessed February 1, 2015).

Manion, M. 2004. *Corruption by Design: Building Clean Government in Mainland China and Hong Kong.* Cambridge, MA: Harvard University Press.

Ming Pao Daily News. 2007. Jianshouzidao she kuan 28 wan lan du jing tou bao jin qiu 20 yue (Indebted police given to a 20-month sentence for involving in a 280-thousand-debt), February 14:A16.

Neild, R. 2007. *USAID Program Brief: Anticorruption and Police Integrity.* Washington, DC: USAID.

Newburn, T. 1999. *Understanding and Preventing Police Corruption: Lessons from the Literature.* Police Research Series Paper 110. London, U.K.: Home Office.

Punch, M. 1985. *Conduct Unbecoming: The Social Construction of Police Deviance and Control.* London, U.K.: Tavistock.

Punch, M. 2000. Police corruption and its prevention. *European Journal on Criminal Policy and Research* 8(3): 301–324.

Punch, M. 2009. *Police Corruption: Deviance, Accountability and Reform in Policing.* Cullompton, England: Willan Publishing.

Roebuck, J. B. and T. Barker. 1974. A typology of police corruption. *Social Problems* 21(3): 423–437.

SCMP (*South China Morning Post*). 2002. ICAC head kowtowing to police, August 18:1.

SCMP (*South China Morning Post*). 2006a. Cigarette blamed as blaze kills elderly woman, March 15:4.

SCMP (*South China Morning Post*). 2006b. Sergeant charged with duping woman, April 20:4.

SCMP (*South China Morning Post*). 2012a. City digest, July 31:1.

SCMP (*South China Morning Post*). 2012b. Conviction ends ICAC officers' stellar run, May 1:2.

SCMP (*South China Morning Post*). 2015. Officer groped woman in police station toilet, January 17:1.

Shamdasani, R. 2005. Officer was running betting operation, court told. http://www.scmp.com/article/505696/officer-was-running-betting-operation-court-told (accessed February 1, 2015).

The Sun. 2014. Jing zhang she jie xiashu qian bei bu (Police caught for soliciting money from his subordinates), March 3:A11.

Tsui, Y. 2006. Officer told triad to lie, court hears. http://www.scmp.com/node/567310 (accessed February 1, 2015).

Tsui, Y. 2009. Ex-officer jailed 12 years for police station rape. http://www.scmp.com/article/692890/ex-officer-jailed-12-years-police-station-rape (accessed February 1, 2015).

Williams, H. 2002. Core factors of police corruption across the world. *Forum on Crime and Society* 2(1): 85–99.

Wong, K. 2012. *Policing in Hong Kong.* Burlington, VT: Ashgate.

Wong, M. 2005. Detective accused of accepting $10,000 bribe. http://www.scmp.com/article/505525/detective-accused-accepting-10000-bribe (accessed February 1, 2015).

India
Nature of Police
Corruption and
Its Remedies

9

ARVIND VERMA

Contents

Nature of Police Corruption in India.. 158
    Common Corrupt Practices.. 159
Reasons for Indian Police Corruption...161
Democracy and Corruption.. 163
Efforts to Control Police Corruption... 165
Judicial Activism... 169
What More Needs to Be Done? 171
Conclusion 175
References..176

Police departments around the world are generally perceived to be corrupt. Even the Scandinavian police organizations are known to have deviant officers who misuse their authority for personal gain. This is not surprising. Given the immense power the police exercise and the limited supervision they face, police officers do give in to their temptations and indulge in corrupt practices. As commonly experienced, and as discussed in Chapter 1, there are a large number of ways in which corrupt police officers act for personal gain. From minor bribes and free coffee, which the Knapp Commission characterized as *grass eaters*, to becoming *meat eaters* who pass information to the mob and sell seized drugs, police deviance knows no limit (Armstrong 2012). Police departments around the world range from *bad apples* to *rotten barrel* and those affiliated from organized pervasive corruption.

As the strong arm of the state, the police enforce the laws and protect the political regime from internal threats. Corruption in nondemocratic societies is thus easy to understand. If the regime is illegitimate, as in dictatorships, then the police become an appendage to the shenanigans of the ruling elite. In democratic societies, where people enjoy freedom of speech and various liberties and choose their own government through transparent elections, police corruption is much more difficult to explain. While the democratic polity determines the deviance seen in the bureaucracy and administrative system, it seems apparent that police officers indulge in corrupt practices because the system creates a good number of opportunities and the checks and balances that could hold them accountable are weak or toothless.

This chapter examines the nature of police corruption in India and argues that the democratic polity explains why it exists, why it is unable to control it, and finally how democracy in India is generating new mechanisms to combat corrupt practices. We describe the nature and extent of corruption and then the nature of democracy to explain the relationship. We present a large variety of attempts to deal with corruption and finally look into ways in which the citizens themselves are beginning to contest corruption utilizing the democratic space available to them. Lessons for other societies are also discussed.

Nature of Police Corruption in India

The police in India are perceived to be an extremely corrupt organization (Verma 1999). Citizens are reluctant to approach the police even in cases of victimization as they are apprehensive of extortion by the officers. Bribe taking is common among police personnel, and for even routine services, there are demands for money. For example, in everyday experiences, citizens have to bribe the police officers to register complaints of crime victimization, to pay for avoiding traffic tickets, and to expedite investigations and take action against antisocial elements. Police officers routinely extort a *hafta tax* (weekly sums) from street vendors and even established businesses to avoid harassment. These officers also commonly avail themselves of goods and services from restaurants, shops, and transport agencies without paying for them. Khaki—the uniform color worn by the police—is now a symbol of corruption and extortion.

In many ways, the police system resembles a pervasively organized corrupt organization (Sherman 1978). Corruption is widespread among all the police departments, and police personnel cooperate and act together to extort from citizens and businesses. The "khaki" code of silence (Skolnick 2002) is strong, and there are few instances where police officers have voluntarily reported their fellow colleagues for corrupt practices or even unlawful acts. Most often, they shield each another and destroy evidence to protect fellow colleagues. The vigilance department (which functions as the Internal Affairs Unit), composed of police personnel on deputation, is notoriously slow and incapable of trapping corrupt officers. Even supervisors are reluctant to act against personnel for demanding bribes or extorting from the citizens. Only the top police leadership of the Indian Police Service (IPS)—officers that enjoy high status—is able to assert some control and discipline the subordinate ranks. However, it is now accepted that the IPS has also become notoriously corrupt within its higher echelons. Consequently, from the lowest constables to the highest-ranking Director General of Police, they are known to be corrupt and extortionist.

Common Corrupt Practices

Police officers indulge in corruption in a number of ways. The junior most rank of constables who form the bulk of police personnel extorts bribes from plying vehicles and from small shopkeepers and street vendors and collects payments on behalf of the police station officers. All the businesses and vendors regularly pay a fixed amount of money to the local police station depending upon the nature and profitability of their operations. Patrolling constables go out and collect money from vendors, shop owners, and drivers plying their vehicles on the streets. The collections are then shared among all the personnel serving in the concerned police station and many times with distant supervisors also. Almost all commercial vehicles also similarly pay a levy to the local police for carrying out their business. Additionally, police officers extort from the citizens to register their victimization complaint and to visit their homes to investigate crimes. Money is also extorted from victims to arrest offenders and to ensure that prosecution occurs smoothly.

Since the police leadership controls the transfer and posting of subordinate officers, this power is misused to share part of the collections made at the police station levels. Superintendents of police and other senior-ranked officers post their confidants at the police stations through whom they make their money. Recalcitrant subordinates are sent away to difficult posts to force them to be part of the organized corruption racket. Apart from transfers and postings, police leaders also have the power of performance evaluation and promotion of the subordinate ranks. Such powers are also similarly utilized to expand organized corrupt practices within the organization. Another peculiar form of organized corrupt practice also exists among the office staffs who cooperate with the field staff in falsifying records to misuse public funds. Police organizations have large budgets and every year spend a great deal of public funds to make a variety of purchases that range from vehicles, computers, communications equipment, guns, office stationery, to uniforms. These expenditures run into millions of dollars annually. Accountants and office staffs handling the purchase and supply of these items indulge in petty corruption and take cuts from the vendors. Furthermore, in sanctioning money for field offices, and even for allowances, the staff takes a cut from the police officers on the understanding that the latter inflated the invoices.

This has now become a rather peculiar form of corruption within the IPS. Since officials know about the corrupt practices of their fellow officers, they squeeze their share by blocking or expediting the concerned decisions. For instance, when a license is being given by one office, the related account office where the contract is to be routed or from which the no-objection certificate is required, all wrest their share of the bribe from the front official. In the State of Bihar, at the police headquarters, several officials were charged for extorting money from field police offices that were allotted funds for various projects. The understanding was that these field officers will be siphoning the funds allotted for the projects and hence must share with headquarters-based officers who were making the allotments. This corruption appears to run across the country where central and state governments and public sector officials pay percentages of funds allotted for development to departments controlling the funds and the required paperwork.

Moreover, the political leadership that has power over the police leadership also participates in the corrupt system. Political leaders control the police and use this power to ensure that their personal businesses, companies, and interests are safeguarded. The parliamentary system of government and the electoral politics have led to the consolidation of political party machines that seek out money to run the political system. Elections are a costly affair requiring millions of dollars to contest (Pocha 2014). Reaching out to the 1.2 billion citizens in a large diverse country with multiple languages, diverse cultures, and poor infrastructure requires massive funds. The political leadership is constantly searching for supporters, donors, and the means to run their large political apparatus. This invariably leads to political corruption and misuse of public resources. The police, as the strong arm of the state, play a significant role in the mechanisms of the political machine. Arm-twisting potential donors and threatening the opponents of a ruling party are roles that the police play for that ruling party. All of this destroys the neutral and independent functioning of the police organization. The police, acting at the behest of the ruling elite, would not act against the shenanigans of the powerful and connected. Thus, the nexus ranging from political leaders all the way down to the patrol constable makes the system rotten and brazenly corrupt.

Of course, police are not the only public department that is corrupt in the country. Corruption pervades almost all government departments, and the politicians are perceived to be self-serving. Moreover, corruption is not a new phenomenon in modern India. Political corruption has been a fact of life for thousands of years, and there are ancient books that vividly describe the practices of 2000 years ago (Kumar 2012). In modern times, doing business in the country is now impossible without participating in corruption. The situation has deteriorated to the extent that public officials routinely extort even when the citizen is not approaching the government. The *hafta tax* collection by the police—a practice of collecting weekly bribes from vendors and businesses for them to continue operating in the area governed by the local police—is simply one face of this extortion. Bribes have to be paid to provide food to those locked up on false charges or even to obtain basic birth, death, and school leaving certificates. Officials extort bribes from those seeking treatment at a government-run hospital, buying subsidized food from public distribution shops, boarding a reserved compartment of a train, or even praying without getting into a queue at a temple controlled by the government.

The subordinate bureaucratic officials extort and extract from the citizens by misusing their authority and discretion in their basic service functions. The police patrol officer, the municipal office inspector, the clerks working in registry offices, and those processing passport applications are the common faces of extortionist government officials. They are detested and feared for the coercion occurs openly and without seemingly any supervision over their activities. The other form of corruption is mutually beneficial. The trader or the businessperson is willing to grease the palms of government officers who have the power to grant licenses and permission to run their enterprise. In most cases, these officers exercise discretion over allotment of scarce resources controlled by the state. The sale of frequencies for telecom services or coal blocks or mineral resources all involve transactions where the beneficiaries are willing to pay bribes to get such concessions from the government.

Reasons for Indian Police Corruption

The reasons for corruption within the Indian police are many but generally related to the colonial model of policing and the lack of accountability in the Indian political and policing system. The police in India were organized in 1861 as a colonial force to facilitate the Raj at a low cost to the British rulers. Poorly paid and ill-trained, this body of men constituted the Indian police that were given extraordinary discretionary judgments and immense powers to deal with the native population. The police were designed to strike terror in the hearts of the people so that they could not pose any challenge to the British rule. Unfortunately, a police system deliberately designed to subjugate the people and promote colonial interests was nevertheless continued after the country gained independence. The reasons could be traced back to the time of independence when the departing British partitioned the country into India and Pakistan. This partition was traumatic, badly managed, and led to a massive transfer of population. It is believed that more than 5 million people were uprooted as Hindus and Sikhs and fled from what is now Pakistan, while a large number of Muslims too fled to Pakistan and Bangladesh.

Moreover, this population shift was catalyzed by massive riots that targeted vulnerable minority communities in each country. The large-scale killings prompted the government of India to retain the administrative structure established by the British, and ever since, it has been in place with only minor changes. Even though India adopted a democratic system of governance and the constitution laid down extensive rights for the citizens, the police system remained in place without any modifications. In fact, the Police Act of 1861 is still in force, operating with minor changes; and the police organizational structure, recruitment, training, and ethos remain the same. The founding fathers believed that with independence, the police personnel would serve the people, but without any fundamental changes, policing in India continues as before.

In such a situation, even though the Indian police are largely unarmed, the power of arrest and search and seizure given in the law is sufficient to harass any citizen. The police have the power to detain anyone under suspicion for 24 h, and as part of the investigation procedures, police officers can search any premise on grounds of expediency without obtaining a warrant from the judiciary. The frequent use of force by police officers in dealing with citizens was a natural way to rule the country by the British, and unfortunately this still prevails today. There is little forensic assistance in investigation, and most suspects are tortured to extract confessions. The so-called third-degree method of inflicting extreme brutality upon suspects has become an accepted form of investigation procedures. Moreover, the Indian police are also known to kill suspects in staged encounters (Belur 2010). Police forces in Mumbai, for example, combated the organized crime syndicates by simply eliminating people suspected of working with the mafia groups.

Similarly, the police of the states of Uttar Pradesh and Madhya Pradesh combated dacoity (robbery by a gang) in the notorious Chambal valley by killing a large number of suspects. Today, the police combat left wing extremists in Central India pretty much in a similar fashion by killing their members. Terrorism in the State of Punjab in the 1980s and 1990s was similarly fought brutally by *encountering* a large number of suspect militants. Consequently, police have acquired a perception of immunity in using force, and this forms a factor in extorting money from the citizens. The people fear the police officers and would avoid getting involved with them at any cost.

Moreover, the system is designed with no local accountability for public officials. The Indian police system is organized at the state level and functions under one command led by the Director General of Police. Since the states are big (some have populations greater than 200 million), the police organizations are also large and generally unmanageable. The State of Uttar Pradesh has a population of 204.2 million as per the 2011 census, and 296,000 personnel serve as one police unit—the largest civil police force anywhere in the world. Such a centralized large police service creates problems of not only management but also supervision. Since there is no system of local accountability, the citizens have to approach a distantly placed superintendent to seek any redressing of their complaints. Most local officers therefore function with little apprehension of reprimand from their supervisors. Furthermore, the system of internal vigilance is also slow and cumbersome and that hinders action against delinquent police officers. The net result is that police corruption remains pervasive and unchecked.

Poor management of the police department is another significant reason for pervasive organized corruption. The record keeping system is still manually maintained and has become unwieldy. It is impossible to retrieve information quickly and develop systems for performance appraisal. It is difficult to compile even the work done by a particular officer let alone compare it with other officers. There is no central repository of a criminal database, and it takes days to determine if a suspect is involved in other crimes. Poor record keeping provides avenues for police officers to indulge in corrupt practices. False cases can be hoisted against common people not accepting the demands of the officers. Redressal of complaints is hampered by poor records and makes it difficult for supervisors to inquire into such citizen complaints.

An insightful perspective is to explain police corruption in India as a form of economic *rent*. This perspective suggests that an official having something unique or special in his/her possession is likely to charge more than the normal price for its use to earn economic or monopoly profits. This would suggest that bribery and extortion involving police personnel occur because the officers exercise discretion in law enforcement and order maintenance. As described earlier, Indian police officers' unchecked discretion in exercising options and the lack of accountability create a situation of monopoly for the officers. The immense power of arrest, search, and seizure empowers the police officers to threaten the hapless citizen and thus exploit these powers. In such a situation, the officers can extract a huge economic rent for his or her services and decisions. Officers can choose, for instance, to stop someone for speeding or the violation of one of hundreds of minor laws and threaten imposing a fine or let go of the violator at a price.

Democracy and Corruption

The foregoing discussion however needs to be understood in the context of the democratic system of the country. For almost a decade after independence, India faced extraordinary challenges to its stability. Creating a country comprised of more than 1.2 billion people who speak more than 25 distinct languages in more than 5000 dialects, whose diversity in customs, culture, dress, food, and even religious beliefs surpasses that of all of the Americas, is a daunting challenge anywhere in the world. To compound the immense poverty, the complete bankruptcy and poor infrastructure left behind by the British added to the challenges facing national leaders. Immediately after independence, India also had to face a war from Pakistan that tried to wrest the Muslim majority Kashmir region, and the northeastern tribes of Naga and Mizo and hundreds of other minor groups also tried to break away from the country. The Chinese captured Tibet and then attacked India in 1962 that inflicted a major defeat on the army. All of these factors contributed to create a strong political and administrative center and dissuade decentralized administration. Thus, Indian democracy evolved into a system where major decisions were/are made from distant national and state capitals. All government officials serve in large centralized bureaucracies with little accountability to the local people.

While the founders were leaders of uncontested integrity and probity, the postindependence politicians found public office to be a good source of personal gain. Within 20 years of independence, the new breed of political leaders had made corruption synonymous with state power and showed no hesitation in using elected offices for personal benefit. Election campaigns began to see the influx of massive unaccounted for money to bribe voters and influence the process. Initially, politicians used goons to chase the opponents and capture the polling booths. Soon, the goons themselves jumped into the fray, and a curious phenomenon dubbed "criminalization of politics" entered the Indian lexicon (Verma 2005). The system was blatantly managed to ensure that police would not act against those in power, and soon partnerships developed between the corrupt politicians, police officers, business people, and organized crime syndicates. Even today, the number of elected representatives in the current parliament facing criminal charges reached more than 100 (ADR 2014). Corruption within the police organization is thus directly related to the prevailing democratic process of the country.

Even though regular elections see changes in government, India has been functioning like an illiberal democracy (Zakaria 1997) where the system of police accountability is compounded by a number of factors in the country. First, at the time of writing, there is still no Citizen Accountability Bureau, Ombudsman, or body that can directly hold the police accountable to the citizens. Acts have been passed by the parliament that will establish an ombudsman type of institution at the national and state levels, but it is still in formative stages. Currently, the system provides accountability through the elected representative in the form of the Home Minister and standing committees of the parliament and state assemblies. However, these are far too distant for ordinary citizens to approach and find redress of their grievances.

The Superintendent of Police (SP) who heads the district police does provide direct accountability. The SP has the power to initiate internal inquiries into any citizen complaint and to take action against any delinquent subordinate officer. But most police managers well understand the futility of departmental procedures for dealing with the problems of citizen complaints against police personnel. The procedure of departmental inquiry into complaints against police officials is generally inherently defective in India

(Verma 1995). Most inquiries are conducted by police supervisors who share bonds with fellow officers and bias against citizen complainants. The formality of procedures also compounds the problem. Delaying tactics employed by offending officers, frequent transfers of conducting or supervising officers, and excessive workloads of normal policing further affect early resolution of these citizen complaints. Besides, an inquiry by police supervisors is inherently deemed prejudiced and lacking objectivity. Citizens therefore remain dissatisfied and aggrieved by internal mechanisms of holding police officers accountable.

Efforts to Control Police Corruption

Corruption within the police and other public bodies is a serious concern in any democratic society and India is no exception. Despite obvious limitations in governance and administrative problems, there are some systems being put in place to make public officials accountable. India has opted for a parliamentary system of government based upon a constitution that empowers every citizen to vote for a government of his or her choice. There is no other example of enfranchising millions of illiterate, poor, and exploited people in such a manner that provides a government by, of, and for the people. India's democratic institutions have performed reasonably well, and the country has maintained its democratic ethos for more than 67 years now. While problems of governance remain, the system has developed some checks and balances to ensure probity in public offices and integrity in its functions. Even though the police have gained notoriety for not following the due process, misuse of force, and indifference to citizen complaints, various mechanisms for holding police accountable to the people have been developed. These help prevent corrupt practices and deter officers from indulging in corruption. We describe a few key such mechanisms below.

According to the List II (State List) Seventh Schedule of the Constitution of India, public order and the police in India are a state (provincial government) subject. The respective state governments administer the recruitment, training, and functions of police officers. However, members of the IPS, an elite cadre recruited by the Union Public Service Commission, hold all of the senior ranks in various police organizations. The IPS is deemed to be an "all India service," and its members are allotted to different states where they hold all the senior leadership positions. While they remain under the control of the state government during this deputation, the Ministry of Home Affairs under the union government regulates their service. Through this arrangement, the central government exerts some indirect control over the police organization of every state to provide uniformity and checks and balances within the large police system.

The central government has further taken a large number of measures to prevent, stop, and target corruption in the police service. A good number of service rules have evolved to structure police officers' conduct and functions. Systems of checks and balances have been developed within the IPS to control exercise of discretion and ensure that police officers abide by administrative rules. There are elaborate rules that guide how officers must interact with the citizens. All such transactions also must be recorded and senior officers closely supervise officers' functions. The Indian police enjoy extensive powers of arrest, search, and seizure, but this is now being tightly controlled by judicial oversight. The police cannot detain a violator for more than 24 h and must produce the detainee in front of a judicial magistrate. The notoriety for making frivolous arrests and/or to browbeat and extort money from the hapless citizens has also been recently curtailed. The government has brought in an amendment where this power has been restricted. Now the police officers may arrest, but they are required to release the accused on bail if the offense for which the arrest is made carries a punishment of less than 7 years. Every arrest is closely scrutinized and does help control the misuse of the power of the police.

In India, police officers selected to the prestigious IPS—through a tough nationwide examination system—are given all the leadership positions and enjoy extraordinary status in the organization and even in the country (Verma 2011). Even though the black sheep and *bad apples* have emerged in this cadre, the service still enjoys a high reputation and now makes efforts to control the deviance of subordinate officers. IPS officers oppose political directives, shield honest officers, and administer police services professionally. IPS officers directly lead all police units, and they provide strict supervision and checks upon the shenanigans of corrupt officers. They also control criminal investigations and meet citizens directly. Thus, the IPS officers play a major role in controlling corruption within their ranks and ensuring that citizen grievances are quickly addressed.

As a formal method, the government has created the Vigilance Department in every state as a unit to probe complaints of corrupt practices against the police. Senior and experienced IPS officers head these vigilance departments and function behind the scenes to examine corruption and take action against the guilty. According to the data from the National Crime Records Bureau (2014), in 2012, some 1989 cases were registered against police officers in the country. Based upon inquiries, 3896 officers were sent up for departmental action and 799 were recommended for trial and to face prosecution. The Central Bureau of Investigation (CBI) is the apex body—similar in structure and functions to the Federal Bureau of Investigation in the United States—designed to combat corruption in public services. The CBI usually focuses upon senior police officers and organized corruption in the police service. The CBI has successfully investigated and prosecuted a large number of senior police officers and helped ensure probity in the police system.

The Central Vigilance Commission (CVC) as an independent body for the prevention of corruption in government units has also been established. In a case ruling, the Supreme Court of India intervened in the functioning of anticorruption agencies and directed that statutory status be conferred upon this commission. Following this judicial directive, the CVC Act of 2003 was promulgated for the creation of the CVC to inquire into offenses alleged to have been committed under the Prevention of Corruption Act, 1988. The act also empowered the CVC to exercise superintendence over the CBI to review the process of prosecution against police officers (CVC 2014).

Since police corruption is invariably related to the violation of rights of the citizens, another body that exercises supervision over police functions is the National Human Rights Commission (NHRC). This was established on October 12, 1993, and its statute is contained in the Protection of Human Rights Act (PHRA), 1993 as amended through the Protection of Human Rights (Amendment) Act, 2006. The chairperson of the commission can only be an individual who has served as the chief justice of the Supreme Court of India to provide great authority to the commission and considerations of human rights in the country. The commission has been actively involved in matters relating to civil and political rights, including the protection of human rights in areas affected by terrorism and militancy, and custodial violence and torture alleged against police officers. The Investigation Division of the commission carries out spot investigations all over the country on behalf of the NHRC. Furthermore, it facilitates the collection of facts from all parts of the country relating to varied complaints made to the commission, in scrutinizing reports received from the police and other investigation agencies, and in looking into reports of custodial violence or other misdemeanors. In addition, the division analyzes the intimations and reports from the state authorities regarding deaths in police and judicial custody as well as deaths in police encounters. While inquiring into complaints under the PHRA, the commission has all the powers of a civil court trying a suit under the Code of Civil Procedure, 1908 (NHRC 2011). The NHRC considers extortion of citizens by the police to be a violation of the human rights of the citizens and acts expeditiously against the officers.

An extraordinary initiative has been the passage of the Right to Information (RTI) Act, 2005 in the country. The Central Information Commission (CIC) has been established to implement the provisions of this Act. Its 2012 annual report (CIC 2014, p. 1) states:

The Right to Information Act, 2005 since its inception has rightly been acknowledged as the path breaking law. It has both enabled as well as empowered citizens of the country to learn and be aware about the functioning of the processes and procedures of governance hitherto shrouded in the culture of secrecy. It has also heralded a new era of transparency and accountability in the functioning of the Public [police] Authorities; and thereby in the entire process of governance.

The RTI Act, 2005 grants every citizen the right to seek information, subject to provisions of the act, from every public authority about the various tasks and activities those public authorities perform. It prescribes two approaches to achieving these twin objectives: an appellate mechanism for adjudication and review of functioning of police authorities and penal provisions to check and contain intentional and willful nondisclosure of information. There is also in place an elaborate code of disclosure of information comprising of streamlining record maintenance including in digital mode for proactive disclosure and effective dissemination among the citizenry. The act also empowers the CIC to obtain reports from every public authority, including the police, on specific issues to enable it (the CIC) to analyze and discern the status and emerging pattern about the implementation of the act. According to the CIC (2014), in the year 2012, the Delhi police received 34,384 citizen requests for information. The act stipulates a specific officer within each public office, including the police service, to be designated as the information officer who is responsible for providing the desired information to the citizenry.

The RTI Act has been an extraordinary success in the country. It has exposed corruption in police offices and provided relief to a large number of citizens. One unfortunate method to assess its impact is to note that a number of *RTI activists*, citizens who filed for information against malpractices in government offices, were murdered for their pursuits (CUTS International 2010). As a result, the Public Interest Disclosure (Protection of Informers) Bill, 2010 was introduced in the parliament on August 26, 2010, and another bill, the Whistleblowers' Protection Bill, 2011, was signed into law in May 2014. The latter legislation aims to protect a person who exposes alleged wrongdoing in public offices, projects, and functions. In particular, the law provides protection to those who expose corruption, cheating, fraud, and even mismanagement in public bodies. The law is likely to expose corrupt practices within the police service and help in the taking of action against delinquent police officers. The CVC has been specially empowered by this new whistleblower law to receive complaints, assess public disclosure requests, and safeguard the complainants. The CVC can also restore the positions lost by whistleblowers if it is determined that the said whistleblowers suffered retaliation from their employers and/or superiors (CVC 2014).

The Comptroller and Auditor-General (CAG) is another position mandated by the Constitution of India to promote "accountability, transparency and good governance through high quality auditing and accounting and provide independent assurance to the Legislature, the Executive and the Public, that public funds are being used efficiently and for the intended purposes" (CAG n.d.a). The functioning of the CAG ensures that organized pervasive corruption within the police service related to misuse of public funds in procurement, expenditure, and other expenses is kept in check. The CAG asserts that its core values such as independence, objectivity, integrity, reliability, and transparency form the benchmarks for assessing its performance (CAG n.d.b). In a country beset by corruption scandals of growing magnitude, the CAG has provided some checks against the blatant political shenanigans. For example, the CAG undertook the audit of the modernization of the police under the auspices of the Home Ministry. In its scathing report (CAG 2005), it commented upon the neglect of police control rooms, misuse of funds, and neglect of adequate infrastructure. In an unusual evaluation, the CAG conducted a check of records relating to the reporting time of crimes/accidents in randomly selected police stations. The CAG found fault with police performance in dealing with heinous crimes such as murder, looting, dacoity, threat to life and property, and accidents. The CAG criticized the government and the police authorities stating that at both the beginning and the end of the review period it witnessed no improvement in performance as a result of the modernization scheme. Auditing the modernization scheme implementation in the State of Uttar Pradesh, for example, the CAG found it to be deficient. The report states:

> Despite availability of sufficient funds, there was shortfall of 75 per cent in construction of houses and 77 per cent in non-residential buildings against their respective targets. There was no fresh addition to the existing fleet to enhance the mobility of the police as envisaged. City control rooms remained ill equipped; as a result improvement in response time of police was not achieved. Outdated weapons to the extent of eighty per cent were still in use by the police force. There was no augmentation in capacity of training and FSLs. There was also no progress in office automation and little progress in computerization of PSs (CAG 2005, p. 63).

Clearly, the CAG remains a bulwark against corrupt practices of police managers running the administration of the IPS.

Judicial Activism

In a democracy, the powers of the executive are kept under check primarily by an independent media and the judicial system. Despite attempts by several Indian governments, these two institutions have remained relatively free and critical of the government. The Supreme Court of India in particular has been extremely vigilant in addressing citizen complaints against the police and public officials. Article 32(1) of the constitution empowers a citizen to directly approach the Supreme Court for enforcement of the fundamental rights guaranteed under Part III Articles 14–32 of the document. The Supreme Court and the high courts are authorized to take cognizance of any such complaint and issue orders as a writ. It is this provision that was creatively utilized for extended judicial action that is now called the Public Interest Litigation (PIL) system. Bhagwati (1987, p. 20) asserted: "The judiciary has to play a vital and important role not only in preventing and remedying abuse and misuse of power but also in eliminating exploitation and injustice. For this purposes it is necessary to make procedural innovations in order to meet the challenges posed by this new role of an active and committed judiciary."

Since the 1970s, the Indian courts have begun this unique form of judicial activism that has addressed human rights abuses and held the police accountable. In order to enable citizens to approach the courts, the judges began accepting even a letter written by some aggrieved or concerned citizen to initiate judicial intervention into cases. This form of PIL has developed into a powerful procedure to rectify administrative, economic, and political problems that concerned the citizens and were not handled by public officials. Police officers, abusing their power for corrupt practices, violating citizen rights, and not following due process, have all been reprimanded and taken to task through simple letters written to the judges. As a result, a large number of reforms described earlier came about after the intervention of the courts. For example, the Supreme Court helped make the CBI gain some form of autonomy. This helped in the investigation of charges against corrupt politicians and senior officials and the successful prosecution of a number of them in recent years. The Supreme Court entertained the petitions from concerned citizens about getting information on government transactions. This intervention finally led to the passage of the RTI Act that helped exposed corruption in the police and other public offices. The Whistle Blower Protection Act and the establishment of an independent ombudsman have all been forced upon the reluctant political leaders by the judiciary.

Democracy also allows the citizens to exercise freedom of speech, assembly, and right to protest as provided in the constitution. This has been continuously utilized to force governments to pay heed to complaints against policies and processes that affect the people. In fact, many Indian governments were voted out of office by public agitation against their corruption. The issue of corruption in public offices, particularly in the police service, reached a crescendo in 2012 when a movement led by Anna Hazare (one of India's well-acclaimed social activists) staged spectacular protests in Delhi and other parts of the country. Hundreds of thousands of citizens protested and demanded the establishment of an independent ombudsman type of institution to probe allegations of corruption in government departments. The shenanigans of the law minister to dictate to the CBI and dilute its criminal investigations further enraged the country. Against this background, the demand to have an independent ombudsman to ensure integrity in public office caught the imagination of the citizens that came out in large numbers to support Anna Hazare and his demand for combating corruption. These vociferous citizen demands finally led to the passage of an Ombudsman Act in 2014 that provides for the establishment of an ombudsman body for the union and for the states to inquire into allegations of corruption against public functionaries including police officers. This is a new institution and, at the time of writing, is yet to begin functioning in the country. Hence, it is not possible to examine and comment upon its effectiveness in combating corruption within the police services.

Nevertheless, having an office of the ombudsman provides the promise of effective action against corruption in the police service. As an independent, neutral, confidential, and informal practitioner, the ombudsman will be able to curb corruption and other malpractices in police administration by offering options for dealing with citizen concerns; fostering appropriate, efficient redress of grievances; and even working for appropriate systems change. Such an office can work as a bridge between citizens and the state agents to emphasize the issues of fairness, safety, equity, justice, and welfare. The ombudsman, in practice, is deemed to be a neutral institution that mainly seeks to foster a fair process, rather than delivering a specific outcome. It is therefore conceivable that the ombudsman in India may work competently and honorably offering informal dispute resolution options rather than seeking to punish someone. Thus, the ombudsman's office will be effective if it focuses upon listening, coaching, intervening, mediating, and facilitating generic approaches to the problem of corruption and extortion indulged in by police officers.

What More Needs to Be Done?

As discussed earlier, the bane of police corruption in India flows from the democratic polity where the politicization of policing has made it extremely difficult to control the said police corruption. However, the democratic space has encouraged multiple and diverse voices to emerge that have questioned the bottlenecks in the system to deal with police corruption. Citizen movements and activists have shown that a determined approach implemented through specialized and empowered investigative agencies can be effective in combating police corruption. This is borne out by the experiences of Singapore and Hong Kong, two Asian nations where police corruption was endemic and now almost unknown. The lessons from these two countries suggest that anticorruption agencies and measures cannot be effective unless there is political will to back the efforts (Quah 1995).

Politicians provide the resources and authority to go after the corrupt, but to be effective, the agencies must be independent in their functions. The citizens must perceive any anticorruption crusade to be professional and impartial before they accept the results as credible. This implies that people in high places and well connected must be seen to be facing the scrutiny of the police investigators just as anyone else. Moreover, the police can only function honestly if competent and professional leaders are at the helm of their organization. The lesson from Singapore and Hong Kong is that the selection of top leaders of anticorruption units, including police internal anticorruption units, must be carefully and transparently done where only merit counts and nothing else. Investigators serving in these units must also be those with impeccable integrity and professional training to bring credibility and legitimacy into the system.

It is also clear from examples of these two and other societies that the system must have strong checks and balances. This will come by participation of civil society and nongovernmental organizations in public management decisions, public access to information about the performance of public officials, and transparency in public functions. Furthermore, corrupt practices such as bribery, embezzlement, money laundering, and obstruction of justice need to be investigated quickly and effectively. Asset recovery of proceeds from corrupt practices is another important factor in dealing with corrupt police officers. Important and recent legislations like the establishment of the office of the ombudsman, the Protection of Whistleblowers Act, and the RTI Act appear to suggest that the government of India is finally beginning to take strong steps against corruption in public offices.

Citizen movements have also forced the government to take several steps to bring transparency in official functions. The delivery of government information and services via the Internet and the use of information and communications technology to execute the functions and to manage them effectively, which is generally referred as e-governance, are being introduced as a major tool to combat corruption. IT-enabled e-government can improve the transparency of the bureaucratic process and therefore promote accountability. An interesting attempt to apply IT services in promoting transparency and involving the citizens is the information on the website of the CVC. This includes the list of nominated officers from different departments who are entrusted with the responsibility of taking the complaints and the corruption statistics of various departments. One very important aspect of the World Wide Web is that it allows for the publishing and dissemination of the list of corrupt senior officers who have been charged with corruption and/or punished for the same. A public survey into the effectiveness of this experiment revealed that 83% of respondents believed that naming charged officers would have a deterrent effect (Pathak and Prasad 2005, p. 12).

A creative solution is the concept of competitive bureaucracy to deal with the problem of corruption (Shleifer and Vishny 1993). In a comparative study of Russia and India, Drugov (2007) examined the impact of competition among bureaucrats on their power to misuse discretionary judgments. In India, the driving license is given from a single office, and hence the officers exercise complete control over the process. In Russia, such a license can be obtained from any police office situated in the district. The choice of going to more than one office to obtain a license induces competition among various officials, and this reduces the extortion that prevails when operating through a single office. The Indian case is described as a *monopoly* regime where the license must be obtained from a prespecified police office; hence, this office has a monopoly power over the applicants in that district. The Russian case is akin to a competition regime. Any applicant can request the license from any bureaucrat; therefore, bureaucrats must compete for the applicants. This concept is worth experimenting with in India where citizens are given the option of filing a criminal case at any police station and not restricting the jurisdiction of the investigators to a particular region. Thus, any police officer will have the power to investigate any crime in his/her district of operation. Open competition among the police investigators and the choice given to citizens will reduce bribery and obstacles in registration of cases. This will also give incentive to the officers to act professionally in order to attract citizen complainants in larger numbers.

The above is also based on the author's experience of handling delinquent subordinate police officers. In a particular police station, I was then serving as the SP of the district police and did not specify who would serve as the station house officer (SHO) of a notorious police station. Everyone serving in that police station was informed that they would be evaluated after a month to determine who was fit to be appointed as the SHO. This became an incentive for the officers to do well and serve the citizens in order to attain the coveted position. For a month, the citizens were surprised to receive helpful and professional attention. The officers courted the citizens and would do their best to quickly address their grievances and complaints. For that month, the number of crimes solved increased significantly, and most importantly, the citizens happily informed me (the SP) about the safety, security, and service they experienced.

The recent establishment of kiosks in Bangalore to provide for online registration of complaints is another example of this method. The Bangalore Police have established a remote registration system to ensure better access to the citizens and combat corruption in the registration of complaints. The IT company Cisco helped design and install a kiosk at a popular shopping mall where people can go and file a complaint about criminal victimization.

The system involves a remote first information report (FIR) filing system that uses Cisco's telepresence technology and remote expert government service system. The kiosk is equipped with high-definition video and high-quality audio, a touch screen, and a virtual keyboard to connect the complainant to a designated police officer in the control room. The complainant is virtually transported to the control room where the FIR is registered after incorporating digital signatures as required by the law. The citizen is able to review the complaint with an experienced officer to ensure that the FIR is free of errors. Once the document is prepared, the citizen also gets a free copy as an instant acknowledgment. The system also permits the citizen to submit his or her own complaint by digitally signing, scanning, printing, and submitting it online. The kiosk is also equipped to provide other services such as police verification certificates and to take reports of lost items. This system has attained an unusual popularity among the residents of Bangalore and more such kiosks are being installed. Most importantly, it has introduced competition among various police stations and will likely reduce corruption in crime registration.

Though not widely known, over the past 10 years, there has also been a grassroots, bottom-up eruption against corruption. Indians can, and are fighting to, curb corruption in their communities and countries. They are organizing and strategically using nonviolent actions such as civil disobedience; petitions; vigils; marches; sit ins; RTI; demanding transparency; monitoring and auditing of authorities, budgets, spending, and services; social networking and blogging; coordinated low-risk mass actions; creation of parallel or independent institutions; social and economic empowerment initiatives; street theater; songs; humor; and public pledges (New Tactics in Human Rights 2010).

Entrepreneur Shaffi Mather has launched an unusual citizen initiative. He argues that "bribes and corruption have both a demand and a supply side, with the supply side being mostly of greedy corporate unethical businesses and hapless common man. And the demand side being mostly politicians, bureaucrats and those who have discretionary power vested with them" (Mather 2009, p. 1). This is a promising and innovative approach that is emerging in the country. A group of concerned citizens are also developing a service that will contest asking for a bribe and/or other corrupt practices. A team of legal experts has set up BribeBusters in Kerala as a business processing outsourcing (BPO)-like social venture to help citizens and institutions fight bribery. An individual when forced to pay a bribe can hire BribeBusters to combat the official. BribeBusters uses the RTI Act to request public information about the transaction and thus help prevent bribery. Being market driven, and based upon a token fee, this service aims to use existing tools like the RTI Act, hidden cameras, surveillance, and peer pressure to ensue fulfillment of citizen grievances without paying a bribe. This group is planning to set up standard processes that will be available through a call center–based franchise system to serve anyone confronted with a bribe. So far, BribeBusters has handled about 100 cases successfully, mainly in its home State of Kerala. Interestingly, in many cases, the perpetrator simply backed off after BribeBusters made the first contact. At this stage, the cases are smaller ones, ranging from getting a passport renewed to registering a new company. Over the next several years, BribeBusters will go national as a fee-based BPO to stop payment of bribes and prevent corruption. This appears to be the ultimate weapon to combat all types of corruption in the country.

Another remarkable online social media group has recently emerged that is bringing attention to and information about corrupt police personnel. This website is called "I-paid-a-bribe" (www.ipaidabribe.com) and provides some interesting information about this issue. According to this website, Indian citizens filed a staggering 6333 reports against police officers demanding bribes, which is the highest among all government departments. In the State of Karnataka, where this NGO is based, more than 2224 complaints were filed with this website in which the citizens allegedly paid bribes. Interestingly, this website also invites citizens to inform about honest officers and instances where no bribe was demanded or accepted in public duty. This is acting as a very strong mechanism to control corruption within the police service.

Conclusion

Policing by nature is coercive and the police personnel represent the strong arm of the society. The police are not only endowed with extensive legal powers but also have historically exercised unquestioned authority over the citizenry. Power corrupts and absolute power corrupts absolutely. This dictum sums the reasons why police corruption exists extensively. In India, the lack of local accountability and the illiberal nature of the democratic polity have created the circumstances where police officers function with few checks and scrutiny. Poor supervision and administrative problems of pursuing charges against the personnel have only encouraged corrupt practices.

The political system has also been corrupted with the advent of criminals and swindlers getting into elected offices. While these situations have led to the perception of India being a corrupt society, the democratic polity has nevertheless been creating spaces for citizens to hold rulers accountable. The independent media and, in particular, the judiciary have developed creative mechanisms to force accountability on the politicians. As Indian democracy matures, and as the middle class grows in number and demand, better administrative means are going to be implemented to control corruption in the police and other public bodies. The simultaneous growth of professionalism within the police system, e-governance, and greater transparency are further catalyzing processes to deal with deviant behavior. In the coming days, corrupt police officers are going to face their nemesis.

References

ADR (Association for Democratic Reform). 2014. Lok Sabha elections 2014: Analysis of criminal background, financial, education, gender and other details of candidates. *Press Release*, May 9. New Delhi: ADR.

Armstrong, M. 2012. *They Wished They were Honest: The Knapp Commission and New York City Police Corruption*. New York: Columbia University Press.

Belur, J. 2010. *Permission to Shoot? Police Use of Deadly Force in Democracies*. Heidelberg, Germany: Springer.

Bhagwati, P. N. 1987. Social action litigation. In *The Role of the Judiciary in Plural Societies*, eds. N. Tiruchelvam and R. Coomaraswamy, London, U.K.: Frances Printers.

CAG (Comptroller and Auditor General). n.d.a. Mission. http://www.saiindia.gov.in/english/index.html (accessed February 1, 2015).

CAG (Comptroller and Auditor General). n.d.b. Core values. http://www.saiindia.gov.in/english/index.html (accessed February 1, 2015).

CAG (Comptroller and Auditor General). 2005. *Home Ministry Police Audit Report (Civil) for the Year Ended 31 March, 2005*. CAG, Delhi, India.

CIC (Central Information Commission). 2014. *Annual Report 2012*. New Delhi, India: Government of India Press.

CUTS International. 2010. Analyzing the right to information Act in India. http://www.cuts-international.org/cart/pdf/Analysing_the_Right_to_Information_Act_in_India.pdf (accessed September 16, 2014).

CVC (Central Vigilance Commission). 2014. *Annual Report 2013*. New Delhi, India: Government of India Press.

Drugov, M. 2007. *Competition in Bureaucracy and Corruption*. http://www.economics.ox.ac.uk/materials/working_papers/paper369.pdf (accessed February 1, 2015).

Kumar, T. 2012. *Corruption in Administration: Evaluating the Kautilyan Antecedents*. http://idsa.in/issuebrief/CorruptioninAdministrationEvaluatingtheKautilyan Antecedents_TarunKumar_121012 (accessed February 1, 2015).

Mather, S. 2009. A new way to fight corruption. https://www.ted.com/talks/shaffi_mather_a_new_way_to_fight_corruption/transcript?language=en (accessed January 23, 2015).

National Crime Records Bureau. 2014. *Crime in India 2012*. Faridabad, India: Government of India Press.

New Tactics in Human Rights. 2010. Empowering citizens to fight corruption. https://www.newtactics.org/empowering-citizens-fight-corruption/empowering-citizens-fight-corruption (accessed February 1, 2015).

NHRC (National Human Rights Commission). 2011. *Annual Report 2010–11*. New Delhi, India: NHRC.

Pathak, R. D. and R. S. Prasad. 2005. Role of e-governance in tackling corruption and achieving societal harmony: Indian experience. *Paper presented at the Workshop on Innovations in Governance and Public Service to Achieve a Harmonious Society*, Beijing, Germany, December 5–7.

Pocha, J. S. 2014. How money subverts Indian elections. *The Huffington Post,* July 9.

Quah, J. S. T. 1995. Controlling corruption in city states. *Crime, Law & Social Change* 22(4): 391–414.

Sherman, L. 1978. *Scandal and Reform: Controlling Police Corruption.* Berkeley, CA: University of California Press.

Shleifer, A. and R. Vishny. 1993. Corruption. *Quarterly Journal of Economics* 108(3): 599–617.

Skolnick, J. 2002. Corruption and the blue code of silence. *Police Practice and Research: An International Journal* 3(1): 7–19.

Verma, A. 1995. Police accountability: Beyond the question of control. *Indian Police Journal* 42(1): 28–40.

Verma, A. 1999. Cultural roots of police corruption in India. *Policing: An International Journal of Police Strategies & Management* 22(3): 264–278.

Verma, A. 2005. *Indian Police: A Critical Evaluation.* Delhi, India: Regency Publications.

Verma, A. 2011. *The New Khaki: The Evolving Nature of Policing in India.* Boca Raton, FL: CRC Press, Taylor & Francis (Special Indian Edition).

Zakaria, F. 1997. The rise of illiberal democracies. *Foreign Affairs* 76(6): 22–43.

Royal Solomon Islands Rainbows across the Mountains—The Issue of Police Corruption

10

GARTH DEN HEYER

Contents

Police Reform in Postconflict Countries 180
Police and the Concept of Systems Failure 181
Corruption in the Solomon Islands 182
Perception of Corruption in Solomon Islands 183
Post 2003: The Ramsi Era 184
    Regional Assistance Mission to the Solomon Islands 184
    Major Issues with the RSIPF 185
    RSIPF Anticorruption Investigative Capability 186
Reforming the RSIPF 187
    Civilian Oversight 189
    Professional Standards 189
    Implementation of RSIPF Reforms 190
    Establishment of an Anti-Corruption Agency 190
    Challenges of Reform 191
Conclusion 191
References 192

In 2007, Sam Alasia, a Solomon Islands national, published an article where he recounted a story of when he was a young boy on Malaita Island in the early 1960s that whenever a rainbow appeared in the sky, he was always reminded by the elderly not to point his fingers at it (Alasia 2007). Alasia was told that his fingers would get burnt or cooked. This created a tradition of fear, and no one dared point at rainbows whenever they appeared. However, according to Alasia (2007), we are reminded in the Bible that the rainbow is God's promise to us that he will not destroy the earth again. This chapter asks whether the Royal Solomon Islands Police Force (RSIPF) are that rainbow across the mountains and whether they are capable of ensuring that they will not be party to another ethnic conflict in the Solomon Islands.

The major actor in the process of instituting state stability in a postconflict nation is the police. The police are the key component that connects the public to the nation's democratic framework, ensuring that sustainable development, democracy, peace, and security take place (den Heyer 2010a). Within this framework, the police must understand that their role in stabilizing a postconflict nation must be consistent with democratic policing and democratic development (Pino and Wiatrowski 2006). Police reform may be viewed as an important *point of entry* for security sector development and a prerequisite for the establishment of democratic accountability (Griffiths et al. 2005).

How do postconflict countries begin to redevelop when the police were part of the conflict, or when a country suffers from various forms of corruption and there is no capability to undertake the investigation of serious corruption allegations, especially when the allegations involve senior officials or parliamentarians? This is the case in Solomon Islands.

Given the obstacles that police reform programs in postconflict countries must face, it becomes apparent that there are several factors to consider which may influence the success of any proposed police reform. Outlining these factors in relation to the RSIPF is the focus of this chapter. The greater political history and environment in Solomon Islands, the problems of the RSIPF, and the dynamics of the islands that they regulate will be discussed. This discussion is an attempt to identify the *forces for change* in Solomon Islands policing, and in particular, how change in the RSIPF is articulated within a police reform program. The chapter will identify a number of drivers for reforming the RSIPF, especially in the context of corruption. In this respect, this study analyzes the policy changes needed in relation to the RSIPF and for the investigation of corruption in Solomon Islands and what is required to underpin a program of police reform.

Police Reform in Postconflict Countries

When considering reforms for the police in developing or postconflict countries, there are a number of points and limitations that need to be contemplated. First, owing to the total devastation of a nation's infrastructure and the collapse of government agencies, the environment creates an opportunity for the most dramatic restructuring programs to be developed (Varenik 2003). Second, police reforms in postconflict nations tend to be based on the desire to create a new professional police (Varenik 2003), force, or service with formal independence from the military. Third, police reforms require a wider government criminal justice sector reform (Das and Marenin 2000). Reforming the criminal justice sector is a major challenge in police reforms. The reforms must be comprehensive and include all of the agencies within a sector, not just the police. Another major consideration when contemplating police reforms in any country is that it must take place within a comprehensive public sector–wide reform program. The criminal justice sector is seamless and reform cannot focus on one justice sector agency to the exclusion of others (Bayley 2006).

A limiting factor that must be considered in police reforms in a postconflict country is that of corruption. If corruption is widespread and "if there is no culture of accountability or transparency in public or private organizations, it is unlikely that there will be meaningful police reform" (Casey 2009, p. 61). To be able to address corruption, it is essential that the country first has a noncorrupt and accountable police and criminal justice sector (Casey 2009).

Police reforms in postconflict nations include a range of contextual drivers (Savage 2007). These contextual drivers cover areas such as police governance and accountability, the police organization and police management, policing styles and policing models, policing structures and policing agencies, the police role and police community relations, and police training and conditions of employment. However, a number of these contextual drivers operate on a global rather than a national level and, as a result, provide the components relevant for the development of postmodern or late modern societies (Savage 2007). These components place pressure on the organizations and institutions (such as the police) in developing societies to operate in specific ways and to take particular forms, which usually involve adopting western methods and processes.

Police and the Concept of Systems Failure

The police in postconflict nations are often perceived as either being involved in the conflict, taking one side or the other in the conflict, or as suffering from a form of systems failure. A systems failure can have an important formative influence on policing and police organizations and can be defined as a negative series of events that can take many forms. Identifying the elements that contribute to a systems failure within the preexisting organizational arrangements can assist in driving institutional change and transformation (Savage 2007).

However, systems failure can also be viewed positively as it may provide the opportunity to review alternative methods of delivering police services and by supporting new agendas for change (Savage 2007). The analysis of a systems failure may be instrumental in creating an incremental change program that can form a foundation to change organizational culture, opinions, and actions and to set in motion a longer-term process of establishing a more open and democratic police organization.

Corruption in the Solomon Islands

Corruption in Solomon Islands ranges from low-level nepotism among kin-ship groups and wantoks in areas such as the appointment of a fellow wantok and the bribery of low-level government officials to "systematic and elaborate schemes of payoffs and kickbacks involving large resource extraction projects" (Roughan 2004, p. 4). According to Roughan (2004, p. 4), corruption in the Solomon Islands now "occupies a unique position in the country, being both a cause of serious problems and an effect of deeper ones."

The years following independence in 1978 brought to the forefront a number of national governance issues in the islands. First, creeping institutional and government corruption, poor governance, and the unsustainable exploitation of natural resources—particularly the native forests and fishing—by foreign firms (Watson 2005) all became prevalent following independence. Second, the unsuitability of the Westminster constitutional system that centralized resources and governance in the capital Honiara rather than in the provinces was also problematic. These problems have been exacerbated by wantok politicians competing for government resources (Watson 2005).

These structural issues were further aggravated by the population drift to the national capital, Honiara, throughout the 1980s and 1990s, causing social problems, such as increasing the scarcity of housing and unemployment. These problems led to a heightening of tensions between various ethnic groups (McDevitt 2006), in particular between the inhabitants of Guadalcanal and Malaita over issues such as land, internal migration, and compensation claims.

The conflict between the two groups was largely unopposed by a police force that was affected by corruption and that was instrumental in exacerbating the situation. Alliances were formed with opposing groups based on wantok loyalties and, in some cases, providing arms and ammunition to militants directly from the RSIPF armory (McDevitt 2006). The depth of the involvement of the RSIPF in the conflict was further accentuated by their participation in a *de facto* coup in June 2000.

At the village level, people found themselves without even the most basic of services. The normal social welfare responsibilities of a national government, particularly in the areas of health and education, were almost entirely reliant on aid funds from the international donor community and church groups (McDevitt 2006).

These problems, although mainly attributable to the weakness in governance, were also directly related to the weakness in law and order and gave Solomon Islands all the appearances of being a troubled nation in a steady state of decline or, as McDevitt (2006) described, as even a failing state.

The civil service, the RSIPF, the legislature and executive, and parts of the private sector have been complicit in increasing systemic and structural corruption in Solomon Islands (Roughan 2004). There has also been decreasing professionalism and integrity in the public service that has made it increasingly susceptible to political interference and, over time, has resulted in a decline in the independence of the public service. Running in parallel to the loss of independence has been an erosion of oversight agencies, "both as part of the trend across the public service as well as because of targeted resourcing pressures. This situation has been normalized through public ignorance, as well as a lack of institutional leadership within the agencies" (Roughan 2004, p. 36).

Perception of Corruption in Solomon Islands

As there has been very little research or investigation of corruption in Solomon Islands, perceptions as to the level of corruption are based on what Roughan (2004, p. 9) call *common knowledge*, or "the 'off-the-record' word of informed insiders, snippets of official documentation, and the occasional intimation or allegation in the media by rival politicians or community leaders." As Roughan (2004) identifies, while these methods of gathering information may be far from satisfactory and probably unreliable, these sources do however form the basis for estimating the level and consequence of corruption in Solomon Islands.

Most Solomon Islanders view corruption as being a political or a high-level problem. This is a result of media focus on incidents of high-level corruption involving senior government department officials and politicians in fraudulent schemes, excessive illegal natural resource extraction, or the prejudiced exercise of executive powers (Roughan 2004).

Roughan (2011) surveyed the inhabitants of the Solomon Islands to ascertain a "better understanding of notions of and demands for official, public, governmental accountability within the Solomon Islands population, both urban and rural" (Roughan 2011, p. 2). More than 95% of the survey participants recognized the term corruption, but 15% of participants "had an inaccurate understanding of it or professed ignorance thereof" (Roughan 2011, p. 5). However, 92% of participants recognized the term "responsibility."

Survey participants were given three examples of nonperformance of government employees—a teacher, a nurse, and a police officer. In the nurse example, 60% of the survey participants blamed the nurse for their nonperformance and 40% blamed the government or the health system. In the teacher and police officer examples, half of the participants blamed the government employee and half blamed the government or the institution.

When the participants were asked whether or not they would contact the police officer's supervisor, 100% said that they would (Roughan 2011).

The survey revealed that there appears to be an unwillingness of members of the public to visit culpability of nonperformance on government institution frontline workers. These views on accountability differ significantly from those codified in the Solomon Islands governance institutions (Roughan 2011) and form comprehensive perceptions and tolerances as to what is an acceptable level of corruption in government institutions.

Post 2003: The Ramsi Era

Regional Assistance Mission to the Solomon Islands

It was widely perceived by both the Solomon Islands Government and the countries of the South Pacific Forum that the public sector in the Solomon Islands did not function owing to the long-running conflict, and given the new security era following the tragic events of 9/11, the country was in need of reform (Kabutaulaka 2005). As a result, the first components of the Regional Assistance Mission to Solomon Islands (RAMSI) arrived in Honiara in July 2003.

RAMSI was based on a three-phase plan (Glenn 2007). The objectives of the commencement or the first phase was to restore stability by disarming the combatants, reestablishing law and order, capturing militant leaders and criminals, and strengthening the RSIPF (Glenn 2007). The consolidation or the second phase would focus on institutional reform but would also concentrate on eliminating government agency corruption. The final phase would highlight Solomon Islands sustainability and self-reliance (Glenn 2007).

The difference with the Solomon Islands Mission was that it was a police-led intervention mission. This meant that the nature of the Mission was law enforcement focused and that the Mission was to provide the platform for improving security for Solomon Islanders and for developing government institutions. Greener (2009, p. 128) observed that the police-led mission "indicates that the mission will have different objectives and will rely on different methods to achieve those objectives."

From the outset, RAMSI systematically pursued corrupt and criminal individuals and Members of Parliament (Moore 2007). The RAMSI Participating Police Force (PPF) quickly implemented a number of steps to instill public trust, respect, and confidence and to demonstrate that no one was above the law. Initially, more than 160 RSIPF officers were arrested and charged, including two deputy commissioners, and approximately 25% of the force was dismissed (Goldsmith and Dinnen 2007), including the entire 400 officer paramilitary division and all of the special constables.

RAMSI then strengthened the justice system by improving court facilities and supporting the public prosecutors and public solicitor's offices with the appointment of expatriate magistrates and lawyers (Moore 2007).

The view held by Solomon Islanders was that the PPF and RSIPF would investigate the corrupt activities of senior public servants and politicians (Wainwright 2005). The establishment of the PPF–RSIPF Joint Corruption Targeting Task Force did initially have a number of successes, with the arrests of senior public servants and politicians, including the former Prime Minister and the former Minister of Health (Wainwright 2005). However, the investigation and the prosecution of these offenders have proved to be delicate and complicated.

While the RSIPF has not brought as many of the alleged offenders to justice as first envisaged, the public appear to hold a reasonable level of confidence in the police. In the annual People's Surveys, the 2013 survey showed that approximately 40% of participants were satisfied with the help of the RSIPF, with 70% saying that they were treated with respect and 64% believing that the RSIPF had improved in some or most ways in the past 5 years (ANUedge 2013).

Major Issues with the RSIPF

At the time that the Solomon Islands were granted independence, the RSIPF was widely regarded as an efficient and highly effective police force and a model for the newly emerging island states of the South Pacific. However, from the beginning of the tensions in 1998 until the involvement of RAMSI in 2003, there had been a progressive decline in the effectiveness, capability, and professional skills of the RSIPF. The force's knowledge and expertise across the range of police disciplines had eroded to the point where the organization was no longer able to effectively fulfill its law and order responsibilities (den Heyer 2010b).

The RSIPF was severely compromised and its infrastructure extensively weakened during, and by, the conflict (Roughan 2004; Dinnen et al. 2006). A large number of senior and other police officers were complicit or actively involved in a wide range of "illegal and criminal activities both during the conflict and after the signing of the 2000 Townsville Peace Agreement" (Roughan 2004, p. 22). The capacity of the organization to respond to an emergency or to lawlessness was extremely limited and the skills of the majority of officers were low, with most officers "incapable of undertaking routine criminal investigations, or of apprehending suspects" (Dinnen et al. 2006, p. 89).

At the arrival of the PPF, the organizational structure of the RSIPF had deteriorated to the degree that there were no policies covering the process of promotion, and rosters and payroll records were out of date, making it impossible to know the actual numbers of officers and their location; procurement, budgets, and expense controls were nonexistent, as were communications and organizational infrastructure; and there was no internal or external oversight capability (Dinnen et al. 2006; den Heyer 2010a,b). RSIPF promotions were based on political or kin-based (wantok) connections, causing the organization to be excessively top heavy, with the majority of these senior officers not knowing their role or their responsibilities (Dinnen et al. 2006). This also meant that a large number of senior officers did not merit being in the role that they were in and that they were often overwhelmed by the demands of the role and the concepts of modern policing. This created a deficit in organizational leadership (den Heyer 2010a).

The power of kinship loyalty and an individual's commitment to wantoks in the RSIPF and the wider Solomon Islands government institutions restricts the capability of the organization and poses major problems with police investigations and prosecutions, especially when gathering information from a particular ethnic or community group (Dinnen et al., 2006). These problems are exacerbated by the limited sense of public service in Solomon Islands.

The growing level of police corruption weakened the capability of the RSIPF (Dinnen et al. 2006). The low level of pay, the politicization of the senior ranks, and the continual turnover in police officers at the executive level also contributed to the detriment of the RSIPF (den Heyer 2010a). The police commissioner, for example, is replaced with every change of national government, which offers little in the way of organizational stability.

RSIPF Anticorruption Investigative Capability

Prior to 2003, corruption cases were treated the same as any other criminal case and were investigated by the RSIPF's Criminal Investigation Department (CID) as there was no specialist corruption investigative agency or department (Roughan 2004). The corruption investigation activities of the CID prior to 2003 were limited by the capability of the department and the skills of individual officers and to the extent to which specific cases were brought to their attention (Roughan 2004). Corruption charges brought against an RSIPF member during this period could be brought to prosecution through one of two methods: "through a charge of official misconduct, or breach of the Leadership Code, or through the criminal charges or breaches of the Penal Code" (Roughan 2004, p. 22).

Since late 2003, three principal anticorruption capabilities within the RSIPF have been established: the Corruption Squad (formally the Corruption Targeting Team), the Fraud Squad, and Professional Standards and Internal Investigations Section (PSII). The investigation of corruption external to the RSIPF is the responsibility of the Corruption Squad, while the responsibility of the PSII is to investigate internal RSIPF matters, breaches, and actions of staff members. The Fraud Squad primarily investigates fraud offenses within the Laws of Solomon Islands Penal Code Chapter 26.

The Corruption Squad was established in 2004, with RAMSI's assistance, to specifically investigate corrupt public officials, but now also investigates any allegation of corruption (Barcham and Lambrides n.d). The squad comprises five RSIPF officers and five PPF advisors and is managed by an RSIPF inspector.

However, none of the RSIPF members of the squad have received any specific anticorruption training and, as a result, rely heavily on the PPF advisors. Second, the squad is understaffed. At the time of the Barcham and Lambrides research, the squad was undertaking 27 investigations, with a further 34 waiting to be started, a number of which were politically sensitive. Third, if the PPF were to withdraw its resources, the sustainability of the squad would be in question. Fourth, the RSIPF has inadequate powers to investigate and deal with corruption, which has resulted in an inability to be proactive in detecting corruption (Barcham and Lambrides nd), and they are not in a position to be able to implement anticorruption marketing campaigns.

The final issue is the absence of a framework for sharing investigative information between the squad, the Leadership Code Commission (LCC) that investigates the official misconduct of government employees, and the Internal Revenue Department. As a result of this weakness, investigations are often lacking adequate information to complete a strong brief of evidence that assists with a prosecution.

Reforming the RSIPF

The activities of police occur in a specific context, of which they themselves have been shaped by and, to some extent, which they shape in return (Marenin 2005). A nation's cultural, political, and economic history will have an influencing effect on the type and the form of the reform undertaken, "both in what is possible and can be sustained over time" (Marenin 2005, p. 40) and what elements of the reform will not be accepted or successful. As a result of the police being part of the wider government system, their reform must be supportive and sustainable and cannot be undertaken in isolation from other government agencies.

While the policy and academic communities have sought to define *police reform*, there has been little fundamental theory developed in relation to reforming police organizations or of officers' roles and functions in postconflict nations and even less on how to implement any proposed program of reforms (Call 2003; Pino and Wiatrowski 2006; den Heyer 2012).

The major problem with the literature in comparative political science is that it only provides a framework for political change and does not examine the reform of police institutions (Lum 2009). Most of the literature that examines police reform in postconflict nations discusses the issue in general terms and is characterized by universal perceptions about best practice and lessons learned rather than being based on accepted theory and processes (den Heyer 2010a). This means that the research that does exist provides little empirical knowledge of police and justice institutions in postconflict nations from which propositions might be drawn.

There is also little evidence that police reforms and capacity development efforts have resulted in sustainable outcomes (Griffiths et al. 2006). This is principally because effective reforms are difficult to implement, and institutions take time to be developed to a level where they are capable and confident in their delivery of services to the community. Furthermore, there is little substantiation that specific programs of police reforms that were designed to improve capacity or service effectiveness have produced any measureable effects (den Heyer 2010b).

The absence of relevant research into police reforms in postconflict societies and owing to previous development programs not delivering sustainable outcomes means that there is no universal understanding as to the purpose of the police as an institution, and the definitions that do exist are western-centric and lack credibility in the regions in which they are imposed (Hills 2009). Owing to the absence of best practices of postconflict society police reform models, the following discussion in relation to reforming the RSIPF takes a holistic approach, which takes into account the cultural and development history of Solomon Islands.

There are a number of concepts that comprise any police organizational reform. The first is that in reforming the RSIPF, the symbolic effect that the reform has had on the public's confidence in the organization needs to be appreciated (Griffiths et al. 2005). The second concept is that the police are usually the most visible and immediately present aspect of a government; and the third concept is that the police are in a unique position to provide the foundation for a sense of security and stability and for confidence to be held in the government (Griffiths et al. 2005).

The three concepts provide the context for the identification of four primary areas that impact police institutional building, their service delivery, and, ultimately, the public's confidence in police. The four components that influence police behavior and police organizational development are (1) service delivery philosophy, (2) police culture, (3) the politicization of the police, and (4) the police–public relationship (Jackson and Lyon 2002; den Heyer 2010b, 2012).

The major issues within the context of institutional police building are, as many researchers have pointed out, that policing in general is a difficult task (Crank 1998; Skolnick and Bayley 1986; Walker 1998; Wilson 1989) and that even in western countries, police are often faced with a lack of resources, weak public support, and often criticism from the government (Cole and Gertz 1998; Ron 2000). The following five topics form the discussion pertaining to improving the professionalization of and reducing corruption in policing in Solomon Islands.

Civilian Oversight

Western countries have instituted similar policies and structures in response to acts of police violence and corruption since the 1950s. One approach that has been adopted to counter police corruption has been to establish independent or civilian oversight bodies (OBs). OBs are independent of police, and of government, and their introduction was intended to increase the transparency of the activities conducted by police and to investigate alleged misconduct by police officers.

The goals of OBs are to monitor police activities and to respond to the needs of the community. The functions of the bodies include ensuring that citizen complaints against police behavior are investigated and accurately documented and proceed toward a fair and equitable adjudication. Acting as a measure of police integrity, OBs are crucial to establishing public trust, increasing legitimacy, and serving as mechanisms to respond to community concerns.

Professional Standards

The second component of OBs was the introduction of an internal professional standards framework or code of conduct and the establishment of an internal investigative unit within the RSIPF. Holding individual RSIPF officers responsible for the way in which they perform their duties, as opposed to their effectiveness in doing so, can be strengthened by the prevention of misconduct in two distinguishable ways: first, by evaluating patterns of abuse and recommending corrective legal or administrative action and, second, by deterring indiscipline through the investigation and punishment of individuals who misbehave (Bayley 2006).

The RSIPF established a Professional Standards Unit in early 1998 to investigate allegations of police corruption and allegations of improper official behavior. While this unit was reasonably successful, especially with the assistance of RAMSI advisors, the Police Act (1972) lacked the legislative capability to punish serious offending by RSIPF officers. The Police Act 1972 was replaced with a new act (2014) in March 2014. The new police act and regulations established a code of conduct that provided a more robust accountability framework to ensure that the police service was held more accountable.

Implementation of RSIPF Reforms

There are three areas that form the backdrop of any RSIPF reforms and need to be considered in the implementation of any reforms. The first is that similar to a number of former British colonies, Solomon Islands was ill-prepared for the challenges of independent statehood following the gaining of independence (Dinnen 2007). This meant that Solomon Islands did not have, and is only starting to have, a physical and social infrastructure, skilled personnel, and the government administrative capability to form a collective nation.

The second area to be considered in any police reform is that in the majority of reform programs, attention is typically paid to the highest and the lowest ranks of a police organization. However, the most important level within any organization during the design and implementation of a change management program is middle management (Marenin 2005). Middle managers can hinder the progress of implementation, or they can assist with the implementation of the program. These managers provide the linkage between the practitioners and the executive of an organization, and this is the juncture where information is exchanged between these different levels. This means that without support from mid-level managers, any proposed reform is almost guaranteed to fail (Marenin 2005). The introduction of any reform program must include middle managers.

The third area of consideration is the general level of education. The literacy rate is approximately 22% in Solomon Islands and the illiteracy rate is 38%, with approximately 40% of over 15-year-olds being semiliterate (Ramoni 2000). Such a low level of literacy impacts on education levels, an understanding and acceptability of corruption, and reform of the RSIPF and the wider government system.

Establishment of an Anti-Corruption Agency

The current structure and coordination of Solomon Island government departments does not enable the RSIPF to investigate corruption adequately. One option to increase the capability of the Solomon Islands government to overcome the weakness in reducing corruption is to establish a specific anticorruption agency (ACA). The RSIPF Corruption Squad could be transferred or the officers could be seconded to a new independent agency. The Financial Intelligence Unit and a prosecutor from the Department of Public Prosecutions could also be seconded to the ACA.

The establishment of an ACA could improve the ability of the Solomon Islands agencies to combat corruption by centralizing the technical skills required to investigate and prosecute corruption offenses, increase the capability of individual members of the agency, and decrease the likelihood of political interference. The ACA could also have oversight of investigations of allegations of corruption against the RSIPF. Such an arm's length investigations can only serve to enhance the integrity of the RSIPF.

Challenges of Reform

The first major challenge in the reforms of the RSIPF are the issues of wantokism (giving preference to kin) and kastom (customary ways of behaving) and how these can be accommodated for in a proposed change program. According to Moore (2007, p. 149), as "an acceptable amount of grease makes the Solomons wheels go around," these cultural concepts could be used to an advantage in a change program or to ameliorate problems, but cannot be ignored. The reality is that these concepts are resilient and continue (Moore 2007), and the question is to what level the concepts change from being cultural to being corruption.

The second major challenge in conducting the reforms for the RSIPF is identifying the appropriate reforms model and not relying on the multitude of alternative policing models, systems, styles, and approaches that exist around the world (Savage 2007). Using or adapting policing models from other countries may pose a weakness in the service delivery of the RSIPF as these forms of policing have been shaped by nation-specific history, laws, politics, social structures, and cultures that create variation and difference (Savage 2007).

Conclusion

This chapter has briefly examined corruption within the RSIPF and the institution's role in investigating corruption in Solomon Islands. The major findings of this investigation is that the RSIPF is still in its infancy in undertaking complex corruption investigations and that a number of areas of reform need to be considered to ensure that corruption is combated and policing professionalism is maintained in Solomon Islands.

To ensure that any RSIPF program of reforms is sustainable, the program must recognize that the RSIPF plays a linking role in the criminal justice system and that they provide the framework for developing and implementing justice sector and wider state-building opportunities. This means that to be effective, any proposed police reforms require an integrated and coordinated approach (OECD 2007).

Reforming the RSIPF will require an intimate knowledge of how the organization works, the strategies of management, their connections to the larger criminal justice processes, and the historical practices of the criminal justice system in Solomon Islands (Bayley 2006). Western nations often do not do this well when providing advice and assistance, especially in the area of anticorruption including the prosecution of senior political figures (Goldsmith and Dinnen 2007), and public support for such actions can be tenuous or almost nonexistent as well. Specific loyalties can easily outweigh appeals to pursue and prosecute "corruption when allegedly corrupt leaders have longstanding relationships with their supporters, for whom notions of statehood, citizenship and the rule of law have little historical resonance" (Goldsmith and Dinnen 2007, p. 1106). This means that the reform of the RSIPF can only be undertaken by the following:

1. An understanding of the RSIPF and the place it holds in Solomon Islands. This familiarity with the RSIPF should include consultation with local groups.
2. Connections to local sources for values and public legitimacy.
3. Displaying a degree of flexibility and humility in regard to the objectives to be achieved.
4. Adopting a methodology of practice that is flexible and adaptive to local circumstances, including the ability to defer to local knowledge.
5. Including a project that strengthens the political structures that underpin policing in the reform program.
6. Ensuring that the reform program is not limited to short-term technical aspects of police service delivery but is more comprehensive and includes the wider state sector institutions (Goldsmith and Dinnen 2007).

The methods adopted to reform the RSIPF to lessen corruption cannot be separated from the wider economic and political reforms of Solomon Islands. To reduce corruption in Solomon Islands, the reforms should pursue socioeconomic equalities and promote policies and procedures that improve the position of women and young people. The goals of the reforms for the RSIPF should include sustainable legitimacy, skilled professionalism, and effective accountability (Caparini and Marenin 2003). Professional behavior and individual and organizational accountability support legitimacy. Accountability will strengthen the process of professionalizing the RSIPF, and legitimacy will provide the license for the police to secure a relationship with the public of Solomon Islands. The adoption of these steps should bring the RSIPF closer to the Alasia (2007) vision of a rainbow and their not being a party to threatening the security of Solomon Islands again.

References

Alasia, S. 2007. Rainbows across the mountains: The first post-RAMSI general elections in Solomon Islands, April 2006, and the policies of the second Sogavare Government. *The Journal of Pacific History* 42(2): 165–186.

ANUedge. 2013. *2013 SIG (Solomon Islands Government) RAMSI: People's Survey Report.* http://www.ramsi.org/wp-content/uploads/2014/07/FINAL-Peoples-Survey-2013-1-final-111900c1-79e2-4f41-9801-7f29f6cd2a66-0.pdf (accessed January 23, 2015).

Barcham, M. and S. Lambrides. n.d. Feasibility study for the creation of a Solomon Island anti-corruption agency. http://www.dfat.gov.au/foi/downloads/draft-feasibilty-study-sol-island-anti-corruption-agency.pdf (accessed October 8, 2014).

Bayley, D. 2006. *Changing the Guard: Developing Democratic Police Abroad.* New York, New York: Oxford University Press.

Call, C. 2003. *Challenges in Police Reform: Promoting Effectiveness and Accountability.* New York: International Peace Academy.

Caparini, M. and O. Marenin. 2003. *Transforming the Police in Central and Eastern Europe.* Geneva, Switzerland: Geneva Center for the Democratic Control of Armed Forces.

Casey, J. 2009. *Policing the World: Theory and Practice of International Policing.* Durham, NC: Carolina Academic Press.

Cole, G. and M. Gertz. 1998. *The Criminal Justice System: Politics and Policies.* Belmont, CA: Wadsworth.

Crank, J. 1998. *Understanding Police Culture.* Cincinnati, OH: Anderson Publishing.

Das, D. and O. Marenin. 2000. *Challenges of Policing Democracies: A World Perspective.* Amsterdam, the Netherlands: Gordon and Breach Publishers.

den Heyer, G. 2010a. Evaluating police reform in post conflict nations: A Solomon Islands case study. *International Journal of Comparative and Applied Criminal Justice* 34(1): 213–234.

den Heyer, G. 2010b. Measuring capacity development and reform in the Royal Solomon Islands Police Force. *Policing & Society* 20(3): 298–315.

den Heyer, G. 2012. *The Role of Civilian Police in Peacekeeping: 1999–2007.* Washington, DC: Police Foundation.

Dinnen, S., A. McLeod, and G. Peake. 2006. Police-building in weak states: Australian approaches in Papua New Guinea and Solomon Islands. *Civil Wars* 8(2): 87–108.

Dinnen, S. 2007. A comment on state-building in Solomon Islands. *Journal of Pacific History* 42(2): 255–263.

Glenn, R. 2007. *Counterinsurgency in a Test Tube: Analyzing the Success of the Regional Assistance Mission to Solomon Islands (RAMSI).* Santa Monica, CA: Rand Corporation.

Goldsmith, A. and S. Dinnen. 2007. Transnational police building: Critical lessons from Timor-Leste and Solomon Islands. *Third World Quarterly* 28(6): 1091–1109.

Greener, B. 2009. *The New International Policing.* Basingstoke, Hampshire, U.K.: Macmillan Publishers Limited.

Griffiths, C., Y. Dandurand and V. Chin. 2005. Development assistance and police reform: Programming opportunities and lessons learned. *The Canadian Review of Policing Research.* http://crpr.icaap.org/index.php/crpr/article/viewArticle/32/40 (accessed December 21, 2014).

Hills, A. 2009. *Policing Post-Conflict Cities.* London, U.K.: Zed Books.

Jackson, A. and A. Lyon. 2002. Policing after ethnic conflict: Culture, democratic policing, politics and the public. *Policing: An International Journal of Police Strategies and Management* 25(2): 221–241.

Kabutaulaka, T. 2005. Crowded stage: Actors, actions and issues. In *Securing a Peaceful Pacific*, eds. J. Henderson and G. Watson, pp. 407–422. Christchurch, New Zealand: Canterbury University Press.

Lum, C. 2009. Community policing or zero tolerance? Preferences of police officers from 22 countries in transition. *British Journal of Criminology* 49(6): 788–809.

Marenin, O. 2005. *Restoring Policing Systems in Conflict Nations: Process, Problems, Prospects*. Occasional Paper No. 7. Geneva, Switzerland: Geneva Center for the Democratic Control of Armed Forces.

McDevitt, B. 2006. Operation helpem fren: A personal perspective. *Australian Army Journal* 3(2): 63–80.

Moore, C. 2007. Helpem fren: The Solomon Islands, 2003–2007. *The Journal of Pacific History* 42(2): 141–164.

OECD (Organization for Economic Cooperation and Development). 2007. *DAC Handbook of Security System Reform: Supporting Security and Justice*. Paris, France: OECD Publishing.

Pino, N. and M. Wiatrowski. 2006. *Democratic Policing in Transitional and Developing Countries*. Aldershot, U.K.: Ashgate.

Ramoni, J. 2000. *Education for All: The Year 2000 Assessment*. Honiara, Solomon Islands: Department of Education.

Ron, J. 2000. Savage restraint: Israel, Palestine and the dialectics of legal repression. *Social Problems* 47(4): 445–472.

Roughan, P. 2004. *National Integrity Systems: Transparency International Country Study Report: Solomon Islands 2004*. Victoria, Australia: Transparency International.

Roughan, P. 2011. *Rapid Assessment of Perceptions – Accountability and Corruption in Solomon Islands*. Honiara, Solomon Islands: Islands Knowledge Institute.

Savage, S. 2007. *Police Reform: Forces for Change*. Oxford, NY: Oxford University Press.

Skolnick, J. and D. Bayley. 1986. *The New Blue Line*. Glencoe, IL: The Free Press.

Varenik, R. 2003. *Exploring Roads to Police Reform: Six Recommendations*. Project on Reforming the Administration of Justice in Mexico, USMEX 2003-04 Working Paper Series. La Jolla, CA: Centre for US-Mexican Studies, University of California, San Diego.

Wainwright, E. 2005. Australia's Solomon Islands commitment: How is it progressing? Speech to the *Sydney Institute*, 29 November. https://www.aspi.org.au/__data/assets/pdf_file/0017/17045/EW_RAMSI.pdf (accessed December 21, 2014).

Walker, S. 1998. *Popular Justice: A History of American Criminal Justice*. New York: Oxford University Press.

Watson, G. 2005. Conflict overview. In *Securing a Peaceful Pacific*, eds. J. Henderson and G. Watson, pp. 401–406. Christchurch, New Zealand: Canterbury University Press.

Wilson, J. 1989. *Bureaucracy: What Government Agencies Do and Why They Do It*. New York: Basic Books.

Developing Societies Case Studies: Latin America and Caribbean

IV

Argentina
Revisiting Police Corruption and Police Reforms in a Captive State

11

GUILLERMINA SERI

Contents

Institutional and Historical Coordinates and Reforms of the Police........... 198
Police Corruption, Democracy, and the State 200
Moralizing Corruption and Praising Political Conduction:
Epistemological Obstacles and Concluding Remarks 203
References.. 205

In 2013, Argentines topped Latin Americans in their assessment of each country's rising corruption, only followed by Mexicans and Venezuelans. Indicated in scandals, surveys, and international rankings, Argentina's reputation for corruption has clearly worsened in recent years. Thus, in 2013, for example, 72% of Argentine survey respondents judged corruption to be a very serious problem in the nation, with 58% noting that corruption had risen "a lot"; three in four respondents judged the government's anticorruption measures ineffective; 16% indicating they had bribed a police official in the last 2 years; and most agreed that it is important to have personal contacts to get things done (Associated Press 2013).

Corruption is generally defined as the misuse of public power for private benefit. In the misappropriation of public goods, money, trust, or power for private gain, corrupt behavior includes a variety of forms ranging from bribes to favoritism, kickbacks, extortion, and fraud (Morris and Blake 2010). As noted by Andreas and Martinez (2014), corruption exhibits different facets and modalities according to the institutions that it impacts. Although it takes time for most corruption issues to gain recognition among citizens, awareness of the dreadful consequences of corruption seems to be growing, and in such a way that it ranks third among the main concerns of Latin Americans, after crime (public safety) and unemployment. And the challenges that its illegal and hidden character poses to its study make public perceptions of corruption a generally accepted proxy. Nonetheless, it is one that has consequences in itself due to the fact that high perceptions of corruption tend to undermine economic growth, the legitimacy of and support for the government, and people's faith in democracy (Morris and Blake 2010).

Whereas corruption is a widespread state problem, police officers tend to be the most visible representatives with whom citizens come in closer contact and, at the same time, the former enjoy discretion in the exercise of major state prerogatives including the use of deadly force as discussed in Chapter 1. This is in part the reason why police corruption gains visibility in societies. Echoing the voices and perceptions of Argentine police officers based on field interviews I conducted, this chapter dissects the question of police corruption and police reforms in Argentina as a salient sign of broader corrupt governmental structures and a dangerous facilitator to the slow but steady expansion of the captive state. The latter expression captures the trend by which more and more state apparatuses across Latin America are infiltrated by criminal networks and turned progressively inoperative, into a tool of impunity and lawlessness (WOLA 2007). Parochial, often dismissive, views of the seriousness of corruption among members of the police may be conducive to its tolerance and thus to its further expansion. In the end, corruption occupies a paradoxical place, as one of the main reasons for, but yet a major structural factor blocking, democratic reforms.

Institutional and Historical Coordinates and Reforms of the Police

"The police officer, what he feels is the indignation felt by any citizen because [the police officer] is part of the infrastructure of the State, he forms part of the State, and the discrediting of the police is because of that, because we are [seen as] the State. Which is true. And the sad thing is that the State washes their guilt with the police," explained a Bonaerense (Buenos Aires Provincial Police) officer in La Plata in 2008. Argentina functions with a federal police, 23 provincial police forces, one metropolitan police for the capital city of Buenos Aires, and an airport police. In addition, there are militarized security forces, the Gendarmerie and the Prefecture, which police borders, ports, and airports, and are often assigned the policing of protests and shantytowns. In charge of federal crimes such as drug trafficking, the federal police maintain delegations in all the provinces. Following reforms and reversals, Argentine police forces still keep parallel ranks of officers and subordinate personnel. Compared to a caste division, those in subordinate positions have limited career possibilities and lower salaries than senior officials.

The police forces were organized in Argentina during the nineteenth century to discipline and suppress groups perceived as threats in the elitist republic—mostly the poor and the indigenous populations (Kalmanowiecki 2000; Centeno 2008). Amidst mass immigration and the fast growth of the Argentinean society, the police developed a tradition of repressive and violent treatment of activists and the poor. In the twentieth century, professionalization made the police more effective without necessarily promoting democratic allegiances or leading to less abusive policing, but actually making police relations with politicians increasingly opaque (Bonner 2014). By the mid-twentieth century, police bodies had become "conspicuously immune to any form of accountability and democratic control" as explained by Kalmanowiecki (2000, p. 37). Modeled after the federal police, or at least since then, the provincial police forces traditionally have fallen under the purview of governors.

Police opaqueness increased as President Juan Domingo Perón's 1953 Code of Police Justice gave the police a special legal status that was outside civilian jurisdiction (Andersen 2002), consolidating autonomy and clandestine traditions of spying, torture, the use of paramilitary violence, and corruption. After the overthrow of Perón through a military coup in 1955, military officials were increasingly designated to head police forces. In the years following, the Argentine police underwent militarization along a cold war script of fighting so-called internal enemies. The most sinister outcome of militarization materialized after the March 1976 military coup that installed the dictatorship of *El Proceso* (the process). Many in the police actively participated in thousands of forced disappearances (estimated at 30,000), illegal state repression, and the running of hundreds of clandestine centers of detention or death camps.

After 1983, the new, restored democracy had to struggle with police traditions of corruption and involvement in state terror. After the necessary demilitarization efforts that characterized the 1980s, the need for police reforms came to the public's view in the 1990s, following a number of scandals that exposed high levels of police corruption and abuses—including kidnappings for ransom and murders by the police. As a crisis followed the sinister murder of the photojournalist José Luis Cabezas in January 1997 with Bonaerense police complicity, and as it was revealed that Cabezas was investigating police corruption and links of government officials to drug traffickers (Barili 1998), the governor of the Buenos Aires province, Eduardo Duhalde, embarked on a process of police reforms of what he came to define as a "maldita policía" ("cursed police").

Within a few months, a respected former human rights prosecutor and Minister of Justice, Leon Arslanián, implemented an ambitious plan. Arslanián began by forcing the top hierarchy of the police into retirement while firing more than 4000 police officers with criminal or disciplinary records. Massive dismissals or "purges"—which he implemented at least eight times—were needed, as Arslanián thought, to get rid of criminal networks populating the police. The reform proceeded then to decentralize the police, to institute citizen forums, and to fight corruption seeking to make the police force both efficient and accountable to the citizens. However, precisely as it started to touch the hubs of corruption, the reform was heavily sabotaged by both the police and politicians, and it had to be halted. This police sabotage included the withdrawal of police services leading to sudden increases in crime rates.

Elected president in 2003, Nestor Kirchner, asked for "a thorough purge" of the police in Buenos Aires province. We must stop being hypocritical he said as he observed that members of the police were behind most kidnappings for ransom. In turn, Kirchner's Minister of Justice, Gustavo Béliz, denounced crooked politicians who finance their campaigns with money generated by police corruption (COHA 2004). Like others before, President Nestor Kirchner pledged to reform the police, which he characterized as "oozing with pus."

These were the conditions under which the reform was resumed in 2004. Again under Arslanián's leadership, the reform was once again interrupted. Although going further than other comparable initiatives, the reform of the Bonaerense police showed characteristic traits and limits. As became customary, across Argentine districts, following crime scares and scandals involving abuse and corruption, reforms and new policies were announced from time to time, often to be forgotten or even reversed and usually around the proximity of elections or new scandals.

The last significant police reform shift has been taking place since December 2010, when after the killings of protesters in Parque Indoamericano, in Buenos Aires, President Cristina Fernandez de Kirchner created a national Ministry of Security under Minister Nilda Garré. This was initially a reason for hope given Garré's trajectory as a human rights advocate. However, Garré saw herself progressively displaced from power by the growth of the figure of a military official, Sergio Berni, whose tough on crime rhetoric and rising influence led to a *de facto* power militarization of policing, which became increasingly visible in the growing repression of social protests. In the meantime, Argentina and its police forces continue to sink in surveys and assessments of corruption. And drug trafficking and organized crime have both continued to grow.

Police Corruption, Democracy, and the State

While the Bonaerense police is generally perceived as an institution where work and crime intersect, as a critic put it when describing the film named after the force (Bradshaw 2003), corruption is acknowledged as widespread across all Argentine police forces and appears as one of the main reasons behind different proposals for reform. Lesser, everyday forms of corruption provide those in the police with "small change" to compensate for generally low salaries and allow otherwise unimaginable consumption levels such as buying a house or a new car.

Structural factors lie behind these patterns. Democratization in Argentina overlapped with economic crises, structural adjustment, and the rise of a mass of citizens marginalized from the formal labor market, without legal protections, and often having to make a living out of legally unregulated if not from illegal activities. In fact, many in the police acknowledge that their reason to join the police force was the lack of jobs and alternative economic opportunities. Yet, their police salaries are generally low. In a typical observation, one of my police interviewees described how "the salary paid by the state does not suffice. This causes exhaustion and stress." With poor training and low salaries, especially those among the subordinate personnel frequently have to take additional jobs to make ends meet, most often as private guards or guarding especial events after normal work hours. Not only do these jobs undermine their performance, but they also create opportunities for corruption.

Amidst thin budgetary resources and too meager police salaries, "corruption is the currency… and the state knows it," explained a member of the Bonaerense police. Police chiefs try to prevent corruption cases from being made public, given that "it is bad for the government that such things be seen." But preventing corruption is a different story. In fact, an interviewee from Córdoba explained, "prostitution, gambling, all that is arranged with the police…. There are many places where that corruption is headed by a political personality." It is common knowledge that the police collect funds of illegal origins for local politicians and for political campaigns. "The powers that be play politics and make fortunes through us. The Ministry of Security is a money making machine for big politicians," notes a Bonaerense police officer in La Plata, the provincial capital.

At deeper layers, corruption backfires and undermines police and state effectiveness. Survey respondents identify police corruption as a main source of insecurity, crime, and interpersonal violence in Argentina. "There is a point where corruption kills, you see? This is what I see and what bothers me as a policeman, a person, and a citizen," explains a member of the Bonaerense police. "As a police officer and as a human being, I feel anger," he continues, and shares an experience: "I put my chest in the streets, trusting that you, politician would buy me proper bulletproof vests." But the politician did not do so, the Bonaerense officer states. The vests were useless, as were the alleged bulletproof police cars. Why I asked? Because—the policeman explains—the politician took some of the money.

In the force to which one of my interviewees belongs, every 48 h a police officer gets fired due to corruption, abuse, or use of excessive force with no chance of reinstatement. Between 2007 and 2014, more than 2164 officers were dismissed for those reasons and this was approximately 6% more than in previous years. Just during 2014 there were over 56 full dismissals, the strongest sanction that police officers may be subjected to, as it bans them from reentering the force. These numbers of firings are high and they can be compared to the past "purges" administered by Arslanián.

In 2008, years before the scandal that led to the resignation of the Córdoba provincial police chief on grounds of corruption, an interviewee from Córdoba acknowledged that corruption had "escalated to all police levels" and that it had become "organic and structural, which is the most difficult [type of corruption] to eradicate." In fact, once mafia-type and other criminal groups infiltrate the state apparatus, in particular those state's agencies charged with coercion, as Davis (2009, pp. 221–245) notes, the state's capacity to enforce the rule of law, to protect the people, and to fight corruption finds itself severely limited. At that point, to be effective reforms may call for "restructuring or eliminating entire state agencies." Paradoxically, however, the increasing dominance of corruption networks tends to block the possibility of such reforms.

Decades into democratic life, across Argentine districts, the frequent proximity of the police to episodes of political and street violence, torture, murders, and kidnappings remains salient. The number of cases of drug trafficking, extortion, and kidnappings ran by gangs of federal and Bonaerense police officers is now quite "alarming," the media reports. Every day the federal police finds itself forced to open a new investigation for corrupt and criminal activities of its members. With the number of police officers selling drugs, kidnapping citizens for ransom, and robbing banks, "it is hard to believe that.... police commissioners have been always uninformed of the criminal behavior of their subordinates," a newspaper editorial notes (*La Nacion* 2010).

But police corruption, as Sain (2010, p. 131) notes, enjoys acceptance on the part of politicians. Among police officers and the population at large, corruption tends to be perceived as the result of immoral individual choices instead of what it actually is, "a widely spread and legitimated institutional practice" that sustains illegal mechanisms of collection supported by police and political complicity. Police officers echo this parochial view of police corruption when portraying corruption as immoral individual behavior or as the choice of *bad apples* within their force. Thus, one of my interviewees noted that "If I am a police officer I can go for dinner anywhere – they do not charge me. It is the root of corruption," while another explained corrupt behavior as the choice of "the bad police officer, who moves away from morality and ethics and who stops being a public servant to serve only himself." Also, the fact that members of the police with college degrees do also get involved in corrupt behavior led one of my interviewees from the Mendoza provincial police to wonder "what is the point of having a university degree, if at the end of the day I end up being corrupt – as we have several cases here?"

Instead, Sain (2010) further argues that police corruption results from the institutional decay of the police, of the increasingly precarious conditions of labor under which police agents work, and of the perverse lack of political conduction or democratic controls. Insufficient budgetary allowances, inadequate salaries, the poor living conditions of large numbers of police officers, the lack of means and equipment, inadequate control and accountability mechanisms, patrimonial traditions among the police leadership, and poor education and training are among the factors that contribute to the perpetuation of police corruption. Many police officers receive only a part of their income legally—from their meager police salaries—and the rest *en negro*, as untaxable informal supplements. As the Argentine state denies its police officers the right to unionize on the grounds of maintaining discipline among them, improving their conditions of labor tends to be presented as resulting from political protection or from individual choices ranging from taking additional jobs to taking part in some criminal scheme. This is the reason why those seeking the legalization of police unions argue that unionization could potentially improve their conditions of labor as well as help curb the police mafia and trigger-happy officers who are responsible for hundreds of deaths each year.

Corruption has facilitated the expansion of criminal networks and their progressive embedding in the state apparatus, giving rise to "captive" states— which are the prey of criminal organizations—which see the normal functioning of state institutions undermined, with serious risks to the rule of law, democracy, and human rights. As clandestine, criminal networks infiltrate the state, they proceed to disable accountability mechanisms while resorting to the state's bureaucratic apparatuses and means of violence to facilitate rather than deter criminal activities. Documented across the Latin American region, now also reaching Argentina, state apparatuses are captured by criminal networks in such a way that the state finds itself increasingly unable to maintain order and enforce the law, which in turn favors the further spread of corruption and organized crime (WOLA 2007) in a vicious circle.

Moralizing Corruption and Praising Political Conduction: Epistemological Obstacles and Concluding Remarks

Exploring the root causes of rising criminal violence and corruption across Latin America, Davis (2009, pp. 221–245) remarked on states' severing of ties with their citizens as a result of neoliberal policies. She noted that the abandonment of millions by their states led many to find "alternative 'imagined communities' of loyalties." This took the form of "spatially circumscribed allegiances and networks of social and economic production and reproduction." These communities are formed faster now thanks to informational technologies and social media. When alternative networks such as narco-organizations start providing "new forms of welfare, employment, and meaning," their existence turns equivalent to that of states and threatens to displace state relevance locally, while also resorting to violence to consolidate their territories and loyalties (Davis 2009).

The alternative, violent communities that emerge seem to be quickly expanding in Argentina, accompanying the consolidation of drug trafficking and other criminal activities. In November 2013, for instance, Ricardo Lorenzetti, the head of the Supreme Court, denounced the existence of caravans of heavily armed vehicles entering the country every day through the northern borders (Fontevecchia 2013). Justice Lorenzetti called on his peers in the judiciary as well as all members of government to gather a basic consensus and to cooperate in actions against narco-mafias. The drug trafficking agenda needs to be a priority, he noted (Lorenzetti 2014). Northern Argentina, the city of Rosario, and the governments of the Santa Fe and Córdoba provinces have been seen as already infiltrated by narco-power. Corruption presupposes a chain, as a police officer from Córdoba explains, "I have marijuana from Paraguay and how did it get here?" For the marijuana to make it from Paraguay to Córdoba, "at the center of the republic, it went through a number of places," the officer notes, indicating how corruption exists in the form of networks and chains. If the extension of criminal networks puts us dangerously closer to the horizon of captive states, Argentines still believe that there is a chance to revert the process, as expressed by the 57% of the 2013 Argentine respondents who thought it possible for the state to solve the problem of corruption (Latinobarometro 2013).

As becoming apparent in Argentina, in what some are describing as Mexicanization with the epicenter in the north, the province of Santa Fe and areas within Buenos Aires, corruption has served as a facilitator to the recent rise of drug trafficking and other forms of organized crime that are dramatically transforming the face of the country and altering citizens' everyday life. In this and other ways, Argentina seems representative of broader trends within the region, where trust in the judiciary and the police seem at its lowest, accompanied with a rising perception of impunity and the belief that the police are involved in committing crimes (Zechmeister 2014).

Prevalent among scholars and reformers in Argentina is the idea that a lack of "political control" lies behind police corruption and abuse. Over the last decade, the notion of "asserting political control over the police," as Bonner (2014) puts it, became central in discussions of police reform. Thus, for years now reformers have repeated that the main problem with Argentina's police forces arises from their *desgobierno politico*, or lack of political governance. Police abuse and corruption are seen as the result of police autonomy; hence, *conducción política* (political leadership of the police) in a state that is imagined as a clear pyramid appears as necessary

(Davis 2009). Consequently, the notion that the police need to become an instrument of public security operating under civilian and political leadership became a reformer mantra in Argentina.

In part, as Bonner (2015) explains, notions such as these portray the police as independent from the government and their actions as unrelated to it. This imagined disconnect leads many to see political control as a necessary move linked to progressive police reforms. Yet, Bonner (2015) continues, "an opposing diagnosis holds that the police are in fact under political control and political leaders have little or fluctuating interest in reducing police violence for both political (control of opposition) and economic (corruption) reasons." If Bonner is correct, then the protection of rights and increasing standards of accountability suggest that control of the police by politicians may be far from beneficial.

The extent to which corruption reshapes politics, the question of whether certain forms of political action favor opportunities for corruption, and the specific links between corruption and democracy call for further research. In any case, the expansion of corruption in parallel to the growth of drug cartel activity and organized crime in Argentina invites us to explore the most serious dimensions of corruption and its risks for democracy and state effectiveness. In the meantime, taking into account the extent to which police corruption in Argentina relates to and relies on the protection of politicians, individualized understandings of corruption and also the praising of political conduction of the police as a panacea may be both acting as epistemological obstacles in the path toward regaining the state and its effective policing.

References

Andersen, M. E. 2002. *La policía: Pasado, presente y propuestas para el future.* Buenos Aires, Argentina: Editorial Sudamericana.

Andreas, P. and A. D. Martinez. 2014. The international politics of drugs and illicit trade in the Americas. In *Routledge Handbook of Latin America in the World,* eds. J. I. Dominguez and A. Covarrubias, pp. 376–390. New York: Routledge.

Associated Press. 2013. Argentina leads corruption ranking in A. America. https://es-us.noticias.yahoo.com/argentina-lidera-ranking-corrupci-n-en-latina-145044738.html (accessed February 24, 2015).

Barili, A. 1998. Murder is real. *San Jose Mercury News,* January 13.

Bonner, M. 2014. *Policing Protest in Argentina and Chile.* Boulder, CO: Lynne Rienner Publishers.

Bonner, M. 2015. Rethinking debates on media and police reform in Argentina. *Policing and Society: An International Journal of Research and Policy,* forthcoming. http://www.tandfonline.com/doi/full/10.1080/10439463.2014.993632#. VWHspnnbKTI (accessed February 22, 2015).

Bradshaw, P. 2003. Friday review: Dark side of the force: El Bonaerense 4/5: A searing study of police corruption in Argentina is the latest masterwork to emerge from Latin America. *The Guardian,* September 5.

Centeno, M. A. 2008. Limited war and limited states. In *Irregular Armed Forces and Their Role in Politics and State Formation*, eds. D. E. Davis and A. W. Pereira, pp. 82–95. Cambridge U.K.: Cambridge University Press.

COHA (Council on Hemispheric Affairs). 2004. Argentina's corrupt police force casts cloud over the Kirchner presidency: Some high level politicians tied to police corruption. http://www.coha.org/argentina%E2%80%99s-corrupt-police-force-casts-cloud-over-the-kirchner-presidency-some-high-level-politicians-tied-to-police-corruption/ (accessed February 24, 2015).

Davis, D. 2009. Non-state armed actors, new imagined communities, and shifting patterns of sovereignty and insecurity in the modern world. *Contemporary Security Policy* 30(2): 221–245.

Fontevecchia, J. 2013. Ricardo Lorenzetti: I have not spoken of the law with the President. http://www.perfil.com/politica/Ricardo-Lorenzetti-No-hable-de-la-ley-con-la-Presidenta-20131103-0007.html (accessed February 24, 2015).

Kalmanowiecki, L. 2000. Origins and applications of political policing in Argentina. *Latin American Perspectives* 27(2): 36–56.

La Nacion. 2010. Editorial, September 2.

Latinobarometro. 2013. *Report 2013*. http://www.latinobarometro.org/documentos/LATBD_INFORME_LB_2013.pdf (accessed February 24, 2015).

Lorenzetti, R. 2014. We say to other branches of government that the fight against drug trafficking must be a priority. http://www.infobae.com/2014/03/06/1548238-le-decimos-otros-poderes-del-estado-que-la-lucha-contra-el-narcotrafico-debe-ser-prioritaria (accessed February 24, 2015).

Morris, S. D. and C. H. Blake. 2010. *Corruption and Politics in Latin America*. Boulder, CO: Lynne Rienner Publishers.

Sain, M. F. 2010. Police corruption. *Le Monde Diplomatique*. http://www.eldiplo.org/la-corrupcion-policial (accessed February 24, 2015).

WOLA (Washington Office on Latin America). 2007. *The Captive State: Organized Crime and Human Rights in Latin America*. Washington, DC: WOLA.

Zechmeister, E. J. 2014. The political culture of democracy in the Americas, 2014: Democratic governance across 10 Years of the AmericasBarometer. http://www.vanderbilt.edu/lapop/insights/IO908en.pdf (accessed February 24, 2015).

Trinidad and Tobago
Crime, Police Corruption, and Police Reforms

12

NATHAN W. PINO

Contents

Economic and Political Context 208
Crime in Trinidad and Tobago 210
Policing and Police Corruption 211
Police Reform Efforts in the New Century 214
Current Policing Landscape in T&T 219
Conclusion 221
References 222

Trinidad and the smaller Tobago ("T&T") are small islands that sit between the Caribbean Sea and the North Atlantic Ocean, off the coast of South America just northeast of Venezuela (CIA 2014). At just over 1.2 million, the country's population is comprised of 35% East Indian, 34% African, 15% mixed other, 8% mixed African/East Indian, and 8% other or unspecified (most of whom would be white or of Chinese descent) (CIA 2014). T&T is also religiously diverse, including Protestants (32%), Roman Catholics (22%), Hindus (18%), Muslims (5%), and various others or unspecified (23%) (CIA 2014). The country has enjoyed economic growth thanks to its energy reserves, but inequality remains high.

It is best to understand policing in T&T within the country's postcolonial and Caribbean context, characterized in part by economic underdevelopment, weak governmental and political capacity, and high violent crime rates that stem largely from high young male unemployment and the country's role as a major drug transshipment hub. In spite of numerous evaluations and efforts at reform, the police remain notoriously violent, corrupt, and incompetent, and recent developments leave little hope that systemic and sustainable changes will occur any time soon.

There is scarcity of published studies on police deviance in Caribbean countries, but the small body of academic literature available on the subject consists mostly of historical and philosophical analyses and reports utilizing limited official data: the few empirical studies that can be found focus on police brutality (see Pino and Johnson 2011). This does not mean, however, that the study of police corruption and similar issues in Caribbean countries such as T&T should simply rely on literature and theorizing originating from the global North. The Caribbean is unique in terms of its development trajectory, its processes of urbanization, the importance of tourism in promoting a particular form of social stratification, the role of the Caribbean as a drug transshipment hub, and the recent postcolonial status of Caribbean countries (Bennet and Lynch 1996).

In this chapter, the discussion centers on the economic and political context within which policing in T&T occurs, followed by an overview of the crime problems facing the country. Next, police corruption in the country is documented and then also the various reform efforts attempted. Finally, the chapter ends with recent developments and concluding thoughts regarding the needed role of civil society in any future reform efforts.

Economic and Political Context

T&T is a prime example of an underdeveloped former colony whose workers produced raw material exports for core countries (Isbister 2003). The British used slave labor during colonization to export sugar and molasses to England or the North American colonies. The plantation system did not have any local economic benefits, as plantation agriculture limited industrial growth and stunted modernization (Mandle 1996). After slavery was abolished, the British brought people from India as cheap agricultural laborers, creating ethnic tensions between Africans and East Indians.

Today, U.S. hegemony has brought T&T into the U.S. geopolitical sphere, and the International Monetary Fund (IMF) is part of this incorporation (Conway 1998). The push for foreign investment in oil and gas is part of the enthusiasm for export market niches advocated by neoliberalism (Klak 1998). However, T&T was one of the many nations that fell into a debt crisis in the late 1980s and early 1990s in part due to its dependence on energy exports without diversifying in other areas such as agriculture or manufacturing (Mandle 1996; Payne and Sutton 2001). The government played a large role in the oil-driven economy, but owing to its inability to offset the negative impact of the drop in oil prices, the government reduced its role in the economy further and accepted IMF-style structural adjustment policies (Mandle 1996; Payne and Sutton 2001). The state reduced subsidies and devalued the T&T dollar in the hopes of diversifying the economy. As a result, however, the cost of living went up while wages froze, oil prices continued to drop, unemployment rose, banks loaned less money, and GDP was lowered by almost half (Mandle 1996; Payne and Sutton 2001).

While there was public resistance, it was not enough to keep the government from implementing other IMF-mandated policies, such as reducing social spending on welfare, public housing, education and training, and health services, ending consumption subsidies, and relaxing labor standards for employers (Deere et al. 1990; Mandle 1996; Payne and Sutton 2001). The legacies of slavery and colonialism in terms of limited education meant that there were not enough local individuals in the country with scientific or engineering expertise, leading to technological dependence on the United States and other core countries (Mandle 1996). By the early 1990s, the informal sector grew and crime started to rise swiftly (Deere et al. 1990; Payne and Sutton 2001).

At this point, East Indians and the wealthy in the country sided with the United National Congress (UNC), which was the primary opposition party between 1991 and 1995, while the poor and Africans continued to vote for the People's National Movement (PNM). Today, the current two major political parties are divided largely along these ethnic lines (Deere et al. 1990). After the UNC won the 1995 elections, PNM economic policies mandated by the IMF were continued (Payne and Sutton 2001). Bilateral investment treaties were conducted with the United States, Britain, France, and Canada, mostly in the areas of energy (oil, gas, ammonia, and methanol), iron, and steel. This investment did allow the government to reduce its foreign debt and to start some social programs to improve public services and infrastructure, increase state pensions, and to put in a minimum wage (Payne and Sutton 2001). Unemployment fell to 13.4% in 1998, but due to a lack of diversification, the country is still dependent on the prices of oil, gas, and methanol (Payne and Sutton 2001).

What one observes is that while different parties would take power at various points after independence in 1962, the same economic policies were put in place, and political stability remained fairly intact. Since its independence, T&T has had free and fair elections held on a regular basis in spite of its economic, social, and crime-related problems. However, on three different occasions, there have been extralegal attempts, largely due to economic and social concerns, to dismantle the government (Griffin 1995; Mandle 1996). During the 1970 Black Power Revolt, there was an army mutiny, and a few years later, an urban guerilla movement—the National Union of Freedom Fighters—engaged in an unsuccessful coup attempt (Griffin 1995). A Muslim group called the Jamaat al Muslimeen tried another failed coup attempt in 1990.

Since the mid-1990s, T&T has experienced economic growth, but most people have not improved their quality of life, owing in part to high levels of unemployment and inequality and the very high crime rates that plague the country (Levitt 2005). Women bear the brunt of inequalities more than men. There is a relatively high percentage of female-headed households or households with female primary providers in T&T because of male out-migration and low levels of legal marriage, thanks in part to the legacies of colonialism and slavery (Deere et al. 1990). The relative economic autonomy of women has not resulted in further female participation in government or unions, though women were instrumental in mobilizing against the IMF (Deere et al. 1990).

Crime in Trinidad and Tobago

Since independence, according to the University of the West Indies Criminology Unit, there had been a general increase in homicide from around 50 to 60 murders per year in 1980 to 118 by 2000. Violent acts increased more dramatically after 2000, by roughly 400% (Townsend 2010; Wells and Katz 2008). One reason given for the rise in homicides is the greater availability of illegal guns: while half of all murders involved guns in 2001, three-fourths of murders involved guns by 2007. According to the most recent data (collected from the Trinidad and Tobago Police Service [TTPS]), the number of murders in the country peaked in 2008 at 550, demonstrating a murder rate of 42.3 per 100,000 people (TT Crime Forum nd). The number of murders declined since then: there were 407 murders in 2013 and 386 by the end of November 2014 (TT Crime Forum nd). Many murders are not solved: the murder clearance rate is under 10% (Wells and Katz 2008), partially because citizens do not feel safe reporting crimes, and many believe that some police officers are thought to act as informants for criminal gangs (Deosaran 2002; Parks and Mastrofksi 2008; Pino 2009). According to results from a government-sponsored victimization survey, approximately 25% of residents in T&T have been the victim of a robbery, physical assault (with or without a weapon), or sexual assault over a 1 year period, and the most crime-ridden areas have victimization rates as high as 36% (see Pino 2009). Other areas of T&T have violence rates much lower, below 15%. While violent crime rates have been increasing dramatically in certain areas of T&T, property crime rates show different patterns, at least according to police statistics. Overall property crimes and burglaries peaked between the mid-1980s and mid-1990s, and since then, these rates have declined somewhat.

The drug trade in T&T is also considered a significant contributor to the high rates of violence (Deere et al. 1990; Klein 2004; Townsend 2010). The Caribbean acts as a transshipment hub for drugs from South America on their way to the United States (Deere et al. 1990). The trafficking process is disorganized. There are many small traffickers who lethally compete for drugs to ship abroad. The illegal drug trade in T&T has also been linked to crimes of violence, sex crimes, domestic violence, child abuse, and corruption in law enforcement (Griffith 2000; Nanton 2004). At the same time, the larger drug lords are seemingly above the law. Traffickers infiltrate the highest levels of society and government as well as the police that are thought to be participating in the drug trade, and security forces have been ineffective in intercepting drug shipments (Townsend 2010). It could be, however, that drugs are used as a scapegoat for all of the crime-related problems faced by T&T. According to Klein (2004), the petty users and dealers reportedly do not play as large a role in the crime problem as unemployment and other major social issues.

Policing and Police Corruption

Currently, the police operate at a centralized national level under the TTPS, subdivided into nine divisions (Kurian 2006). Ninety percent of officers in the TTPS are of African descent. Those of African descent were exclusively recruited into the police during the colonial period, and traditional physical entrance requirements favor those of African over East Indian descent. In addition to the national police service, there is an extensive and expanding commercial security sector in T&T, which includes prisoner transport companies, private security for businesses, and gated communities for wealthier residents.

As noted earlier, police corruption and violence are serious concerns in T&T. In fact, citizens fear the police and assume that the police are associated with criminal gangs, and this has reduced citizen cooperation (Parks and Mastrofski 2008). The TTPS face accusations of drug corruption and favoritism, criminal convictions of police officials, and the perception that the police are indifferent and incompetent (Bennet and Moribito 2006). Deosaran (2002) notes that the general public and the media frequently report excessive force, but internal investigations of police misconduct rarely if ever occur in a timely manner, and according to a 1999 report, 18 officers were allowed to continue working for the TTPS after being convicted of serious crimes. The police in turn have developed poor impressions of the public and fail to provide unsolicited police services. The police are antagonistic toward the public and feel demoralized and isolated, leading to a culture of alienation (Bennet and Moribito 2006).

Four reports, presented here in chronological order, identify several problems faced by the TTPS since independence, including police deviance and poor public perceptions of the police. The first three reports were produced by policing experts from the United Kingdom at the request of the T&T government and appear to be available to the public only from the special collections at the University of West Indies library (see Pino 2009). The last report was accessed online.

A 1984 *Report of the Committee on the Restructuring of the Police Service* (CRPS) identified several problems with the TTPS. Within the service, there were poor relations and low morale, including a lack of respect for senior officers among junior officers. The police leadership was seen as weak, thanks to managerial inefficiencies and a lack of communication among senior officers. There were also ineffective disciplinary procedures, unclear and uneven officer workloads, and high supervisor turnover (CRPS 1984).

Regarding public relations, the public viewed the police as repressive, harassing, indifferent, unresponsive, and unsympathetic. Accusations against the police included engaging in arbitrary searches and arrests of minor offenders while ignoring serious crimes and urgent calls for assistance. The police would not engage in foot patrols and would provide the excuse that there were too few vehicles available for officers on duty when citizens complained that police would ignore calls for service. The police were also accused of destroying the homes of squatters and treating suspects harshly and in an uncaring manner. Finally, the police regularly failed to conduct internal investigations of police misconduct (CRPS 1984).

Seven years after the CRPS report, O'Dowd (1991) published a separate *Review of the Trinidad and Tobago Police Service*. He found similar problems within the service such as weak leadership and a lack of internal investigations of misconduct. When internal disciplinary procedures were conducted, they took as long as 5 years, even though most investigations involved minor matters such as showing up to work late. It is no surprise then that there was still a lack of public confidence in the investigation of complaints against the police. Citizens complained of slow or even an absence of police response to their calls for service, and the police were widely accused of impoliteness, discriminatory behavior, and corruption (O'Dowd 1991).

In his report on a Scotland Yard investigation into accusations of police corruption, Graham Seaby (1993) concluded that corruption was endemic and existed at all ranks in the TTPS. As with earlier inquiries, the report identified problems of weak leadership, management, discipline, and accountability within the service, as well as a lack of a sense of community service among officers. Seaby (1993) noted that it was unclear how superficial discipline decisions were made and who made them. The investigation also found recurring incidents of numerous forms of police deviance: requiring citizens to pay for their services, blackmailing suspects (to promise to hide evidence or not arrest), stealing from each other as well as from the canteen, failing to show up for court, embezzling police service funds, assisting each other in corrupt activities, and promoting individuals from within their own groups. The police were accused of shootings and rapes, protecting drug dealers and their activities, and actively engaging in the drug trade (such as transporting cocaine, growing marijuana, and selling drugs). Activities such as embezzlement and drug corruption allowed some senior-ranking members to live beyond their own means. Further, Seaby (1993) determined that officers displayed numerous forms of incompetence and laziness: failing to use scientific investigation techniques and technologies or taking statements from victims and witnesses; developing fatalistic attitudes and acquiescing to the status quo in order to keep their jobs; finding cozy niches in offices instead of going out on patrol; and using knowledge of other officers' corruption as a way to keep their jobs.

A little more recently, Amnesty International (AI) (2006) issued a document on unlawful killings by police and deaths in police custody in T&T, but in many ways, this report demonstrated that policing there had not changed from the 1990s until that point. The report documents excessive use of force, including summary executions, deaths of persons in police custody, and the failure of authorities to properly carry out investigations and sanction officers' conduct. Accusations against the police included officers' involvement in the country's rising violent crime problem, such as allegations of police involvement in kidnappings in 2005: two special reserve officers were arrested for suspected involvement in the abduction of two sons of a prominent businessman. Other witnesses have reported various forms of police harassment (AI 2006).

Problems in investigations into allegations of police abuse include major flaws in both internal and external police complaints mechanisms and a "climate of impunity" that includes lengthy delays in judicial investigations into police shootings (AI 2006, p. 2). Victims are therefore denied rights and access to justice. Several fatal shootings and deaths in custody were reported to AI during 2004 and 2005. A number of these fatal shootings were seen as unprovoked by eyewitnesses but officially attributed to criminal violence and proper defensive responses by officers. Further, official investigations into such cases were not made publicly available, and officers suspected of misconduct were allowed to remain on active duty. The report also identifies and describes eight suspicious fatal shootings and four suspicious deaths in custody occurring in 2003–2005. AI asked police authorities for information on the investigations into these cases but had received none at the time of the writing of the report. However, at times, civil awards are given in cases in which the officers involved were not disciplined or held criminally responsible. In the recent years prior to the publication of the report, AI could identify only two officers convicted of unlawfully killing civilians while on duty. AI complains that the lack of transparency in police investigations of abuses and the lack of data on police excessive use of force makes it difficult for organizations to monitor police conduct (AI 2006).

The colonial legacy of policing and criminal justice in general has continued, with officer training centering on riot suppression and citizens having to solicit police services (Parks and Mastrofski 2008). Prior to the recent reform efforts discussed in the following text, police possessed few usable vehicles and other equipment, police stations were dirty and decrepit, and the TTPS suffered from poor pay as well as inadequate staffing (Parks and Mastrofski 2008). In addition, problems of corruption still persisted, and there was frequent turnover and weak management and supervision, as police leaders wanted to avoid controversy (Mastrofski and Lum 2008; Miller and Hendrix 2007; Parks and Mastrofski 2008). The TTPS also continued to engage in recruitment practices that reflected favoritism, bias, and nepotism (PSC 2004).

Pino and Johnson (2011) found that nongovernmental organization (NGO) and community based organization (CBO) leaders and members, as well as members of the T&T Ministry of National Security and the TTPS, indicated that police deviance was rampant in the TTPS in four broad areas echoed in the aforementioned reports. First, the police do not do enough to prevent crime and protect citizens from victimization. Avoidance of duties, unprofessionalism, and lack of skills and training are among the obstacles in providing adequate services. The second theme involves citizens reporting crimes and suspect mistreatment by police. Reporting citizens, who may be victims, are treated insensitively and fear getting accused of crimes themselves. Further, the police are known to have committed acts of brutality. The result is that citizens are reluctant to report crimes and cooperate with police, despite their desire to have more police protection. Third, police tend to be inconsistent in their treatment of criminals and often respond to less serious crimes harshly and more serious crimes leniently. Fourth, police are thought to engage in corruption and collude with criminals, a reputation that also severely reduces the public's trust and faith in the police and in the government in general (Pino and Johnson 2011).

Police Reform Efforts in the New Century

While T&T was a British colony and its police service still reflects the colonial style in a number of ways, the United States, in part due to its geopolitical interests, is currently influencing policing in T&T. For example, under the rhetoric of the war on drugs and the war on terrorism, the United States and T&T have signed ship rider agreements that allow U.S. law enforcement personnel to engage in hot pursuit and board ships suspected of transporting drugs in T&T's territorial waters (T&T law enforcement agencies are prohibited from engaging in the same kinds of behaviors in U.S. territorial waters) (Griffith 2000). T&T engages in agreements with other entities as well. For example, T&T has signed extradition and mutual legal assistance treaties with various Western countries, while the EU and United States have funded demand reduction programs such as educational campaigns to reduce illicit drug use among the population (Griffith 2000).

These mutual assistance treaties paramilitarize the police further and blur the distinctions between police and military roles. In addition, transnational crime and antiterror frames are used to justify extrajudicial actions that deny civil liberties (McCulloch 2007). T&T has increasingly militarized its police services with aid from foreign countries in other ways as well. For example, in 2004, T&T created the Special Anti-Crime Unit of Trinidad and Tobago (SAUTT), comprised of previous members of the coast guard, TTPS, and the armed forces (Browne 2008). SAUTT is tasked with contending with gang-related homicides, but it is based on the American CIA and trained by the British. This special unit was placed under the authority of the Commissioner of the TTPS in order to contend with concerns regarding the legitimacy and legality of SAUTT (Browne 2008). Yet another state paramilitary group that exists in T&T is the Interagency Task Force, which combines military and police personnel and has been used to sweep through high-crime neighborhoods. However, according to civil society leaders interviewed by Pino (2009), the task force is known to sweep through these neighborhoods utilizing offensive tactics that harass and abuse suspects.

Western aid for policing is not limited to the aforementioned schemes. While Western powers have worked to militarize T&T's security sector further, they have also helped promote policing practices associated with community policing. The government and the police leadership were eagerly committed when the Association of Caribbean Commissioners of Police decided to implement community policing in 1993 (Deosaran 2002). However, poor police capacity and conduct as well as a lack of citizen support were concerns. Police leaders traveled abroad to the United Kingdom and United States to receive training and education on community policing in order to teach other officers back home what they had learned. That being said, by 2002, the support for community policing had dwindled according to one TTPS member, in part because of insufficient recruitment policies, the hiring of officers who were not prepared to perform community-oriented policing tasks, and general police officer resistance (Pino 2009). Many officers were of the view that community policing activities such as interacting and working with the public conflicted with established expectations for police work, viewing community policing as social work or at least not real police work. In essence, the police culture that maintains a separation between the police and the community they serve had not changed adequately (Pino 2009).

Another major attempt at reforming the TTPS started in 2006 with the help of Western consultants. Reforms included consolidating more administrative authority into the hands of the police commissioner, providing the government more opportunities to help direct policy, and by improving civilian oversight (Mastrofski and Lum 2008). These measures modeled reforms implemented in Northern Ireland, but were also designed with input from individuals holding various ranks within the TTPS and the Ministry of National Security (Wilson et al. 2011; Mastrofski and Lum 2008). A Crime Policy Commission composed of experts from both political major parties was to develop bipartisan recommendations for policy change. Improvements in external and independent oversight of the police were to occur through the Police Complaints Authority (PCA) (discussed in more detail below), while policy direction would be directed by the Ministry of National Security as a way to make politicians stakeholders in the process. The police commissioner would have more power to direct hiring, discipline, promotion, and training. Police pay and educational requirements were increased. In addition, officer review procedures were updated, some poor managers were removed, and various attempts were made to make the police more service oriented (Mastrofski and Lum 2008).

As part of these reforms, Parks and Mastrofski (2008) led a subsequent team to create a model station program for the TTPS in 2007. Model stations were based upon Mastrofski's (1999) American community policing model known as *Policing for People* (PFP). PFP is a managerialist service-oriented policing model that views citizens as consumers. Elements of PFP include attentiveness, reliability, responsive service, competence, manners, and fairness (Mastrofski 1999). The reform team created five model stations in high crime, racially varied, and geographically diverse areas: Arouca, Chaguanas, Morvant, San Fernando, and the West End. These stations received structural improvements and extra resources, including vehicles and equipment designed to enhance police capacity and engage in proactive crime management strategies such as identifying crime hot spots. Middle managers had primary responsibility for leadership of the stations. One of three U.S. police field advisors trained additional officers hired for the stations for 80 h (Parks and Mastrofski 2008; Wilson et al. 2011). Officers trained for these model stations were expected to show up to work, engage in foot patrols, spend time with community residents, and manage victim assistance units.

The implementation of the program was not without its difficulties, however. The U.S. field advisors arrived 5 months after the model station program was initiated, and each took a different approach to training officers (Wilson et al. 2011). Some officers would not attend their training sessions or attended only sporadically, and some of those that were trained were soon transferred away from the model stations. In addition, victim assistance staff members were not trained by the end of the first year of model station implementation. Commanders of these stations displayed varying levels of commitment to reform efforts, and high turnover at the command level further hampered program implementation (Wilson et al. 2011). Antiquated recruitment strategies, limited training and frequent transferring of corporals and sergeants, also limited the efficacy of the model station program. As one might expect, in the end, each model station implemented reforms differently by emphasizing certain elements of reform over others. In addition, the police service and special units such as SAUTT maintained aggressive paramilitary tactics during the reform period, occasionally utilizing model stations and their staff for various operations (Wilson et al. 2011).

My research in relation to these more recent reform efforts found that TTPS and Ministry of National Security officials felt that the U.S.-led team to be professional and eager to achieve some laudable goals such as increasing officer education and pay, restructuring the police service, creating model stations, implementing a new customer service orientation to police work, and promoting more proactive strategies to fighting crime (see Pino and Ellison 2012; Pino 2009). Nevertheless, the reforms themselves were perceived as having few positive impacts. Numerous problems included local officer resistance to the proposed changes and no perceived changes in officer behavior. There were not enough systemic changes that might have improved officer training and behavior. In addition, not enough thought was put toward the hiring of foreign consultants or the implementation of reform plans, according to senior police and Ministry of National Security officials. For example, competing teams had to make multiple bids on separate projects spread out over time. This meant that the reform process was put together in a piecemeal, noncomprehensive fashion over time, making it difficult for TTPS officers to carry out the reforms (Pino 2009). Furthermore, the budget for the transformation was underfunded according to one police leader, and officers and resources such as vehicles meant for reform implementation were diverted for other purposes (Pino 2009).

Reforms were also perceived to be inadequate by civil society group members, including leaders of well-established NGOs operating in the most crime-ridden and impoverished parts of the country, for a number of reasons (Pino and Johnson 2011; Pino 2009). First, most respondents were not meaningfully involved even though they possessed indigenous knowledge of crime and crime-related problems in the poor and violent neighborhoods in which they worked. In fact, these respondents were largely unaware of the reform process. One NGO worked on initiatives to reduce gang violence, and another participated in domestic violence training at one model station, but beyond that, NGO leaders could only speak of past coproductive activities with the police, such as sports programs for youth, initiatives to reduce gang violence, and general methodological assistance (Pino 2009). This could be due to the fact that the T&T government does not officially recognize a number of NGOs and community-based organizations for reasons such as not having a social worker and other educated professionals on staff. Wallace (2012) also found in his study involving surveys and focus group discussions of police and local residents that there was a lack of community involvement in police reform efforts and that a majority of both police and community residents saw this as problematic.

Second, respondents were of the opinion that police deviance and corruption levels had not changed after the reform period. The police were still thought to be mistreating citizens, failing in their duty to provide security, engaging in crime control inadequately, responding to criminals capriciously, aggressively policing less serious crimes while ignoring serious offenses, engaging in various forms of corruption, and colluding with criminals (Pino and Johnson 2011; see also Wallace 2012). Police officers also see community residents as part of the problem, indicating that citizens are fractured, have a negative perception of the police, do not respect the police, dishonestly benefit from criminals in numerous ways, and justify their deviant behaviors by citing the need to survive in disadvantaged circumstances (Wallace 2012).

In spite of these perceived problems, a majority of both citizens and police want to engage in coproductive activities in order to reduce crime (Wallace 2012). In fact, vast majorities of both police and citizen respondents in Wallace's (2012) study thought that crime reduction was not just something the police engage in alone. NGO representatives were not rejecting the idea of future foreign assistance, either, but they wanted foreign assistance to arrive in a much more limited and focused way (Pino 2009). For example, they wanted foreign assistance in relation to technical assistance for police investigations, DNA testing, and other technical matters. They thought foreign consultants could also act as neutral and impartial officials investigating accusations of corruption and other forms of police misbehavior. Respondents emphasized, however, that they did want local actors to actually lead reform planning and implementation activities and foreign consultants to facilitate by providing ideas, training local trainers, offering technical assistance, and conducting research (Pino 2009). Put another way, they sought bottom-up strategies informed by indigenous knowledge, which have the potential to improve democratic governance and the chances that police reforms are sustainable. The idea was that a broad coalition of local actors comprised of governmental officials, the police and civil society would lead these reforms while foreign experts facilitated (Ellison and Pino 2012).

In the end, it appears that the T&T government and the TTPS were corrupt, not sufficiently committed to reform, lacked the capacity to carry out reforms, and were politically divided (see Mastrofski and Lum 2008). That being said, the reform plans forwarded by the U.S. team were not tailored to the T&T context adequately. A police force based on the British colonial model was expected to transform into a police service modeled on U.S. service–oriented community policing schemes as well as the reforms in Northern Ireland, under the assumption that the sectarian divide in Northern Ireland was similar to the ethnic divides in T&T. As Ellison and Pino (2012) point out, however, the ethnic divisions between Afro-Trinidadians and Indo-Trinidadians are not analogous to the Unionist–Nationalist divide in Northern Ireland; the countries are in much different positions within the global economic and geopolitical arenas, and they differ dramatically in terms of crime, the drug trade, and the extent of political and police corruption. On top of that, civil society groups were not sufficiently involved in a meaningful way (Pino 2009). The problem is that a particular reform program operating on the assumption that policing occurs in a vacuum outside of local economic and political institutions is doomed to failure (see Pino and Wiatrowski 2006).

Current Policing Landscape in T&T

As it now stands conditions are still not ripe for sustainable police reform in T&T. While the former Minister of National Security, Gary Griffith, claimed that serious crimes, other than murders, were at their lowest rates in 30 years (Clark 2014), as mentioned earlier, violent crime rates remain at a high level, and threats to civil liberties remain a concern in the country. For example, in late August 2011, the government imposed a state of emergency after 11 murders occurred on one weekend (Gabbatt 2011). The government conducted mass arrests of hundreds of suspected gang members, instituted roadblocks, and established curfews for all citizens between 11 p.m and 4 a.m. In early September of that year, the government extended the state of emergency for 3 months, justifying the policy on security concerns and threats stemming from gangs and crime while claiming the curfew had thus far prevented a mass criminal uprising (Associated Press 2011).

The following year, 2012, Jack Warner was appointed as the new Minister of National Security. This was a curious decision because in 2011, after being elected to be the President of CONCACAF (the governing body for association football/soccer in North America, Central America, and the Caribbean) for the sixth time, and while serving as the Vice President of FIFA (the international federation for association football/soccer), Warner was investigated for bribery charges associated with world soccer and had to resign his vice presidency (*Trinidad and Tobago Guardian* 2013). While in the Minister's role, Warner instructed the police to suppress the number of murders and other T&T crime statistics because he thought that the opposition political party (the PNM) would use the statistics to "create more mischief" in a way that would lead to further crimes (Kowlessar 2012). Warner believed that one murder that occurred in Laventille was a direct result of the PNM ending a month-long ceasefire among gangs there. In 2013, the official FIFA report on the bribery allegations against Warner was released, forcing Warner to resign as Minister of National Security (*Trinidad and Tobago Guardian* 2013).

One area where there appears to be some improvement is in civilian oversight of police deviance. Back in 1993, The PCA was created by an act of parliament in order to ensure that an independent body was hearing and compiling citizen complaints (Deosaran 2002). Back in 2009, when the PCA was still active, the 2003 report was the most recently available online at the PCA's website (www.pca.gov.tt), which no longer exists (see below) (Pino 2009). Based on the report, the number of formal and informal complaints had been increasing dramatically, from 769 in 1998–1999 to 1262 in 2002–2003, ranging from battery, criminal damage, failure to perform duties, harassment, impoliteness, wrongful arrest, and extortion (PCA 2003). While there was variation in the number of complaints from year to year, there was never a trend indicating a reduction of complaints. The PCA did not have any real authority to conduct investigations or have any other substantive powers: it was merely a recording device. One member of the Ministry of National Security stated to one of the authors that the PCA was "largely defunct" and that there was no independent oversight body in T&T to hold officers accountable for police deviance (Pino 2009).

However, there is now a new PCA, reconstituted in late December 2010. According to the new website (pca.org.tt), instead of recording all complaints regarding police officers, the current PCA is charged with dealing solely with complaints of "serious police misconduct, police corruption, and criminal offenses involving police officers." Instead of complaints being investigated by the TTPS, the PCA now carries out independent investigations to ensure that the police are not investigating themselves. After investigating, the PCA can recommend action be taken by the Director of Public Prosecutions, the Police Service Commission, or the Commissioner of Police. According to the latest Annual Report available online at the PCA's website (2013), the PCA holds community outreach meetings in addition to engaging in investigations of relevant complaints. During the 2010/2011 period, the PCA received 255 complaints. The next year (2011/2012), the number of complaints increased 33% to 340 and in the following year (2012/2013) increased again 38% to 470. Common complaints have included assault by police (the most common), fatal and nonfatal shootings by police, larceny, and neglect of duty, among others (PCA 2013). Of the 470 complaints received in 2012/2013, 89 were already before the courts, 48 were "completed," and the remaining 333 were active investigations at the time of the report's publication (PCA 2013).

Based on the experiences of the new PCA, various recommendations were included in the 2013 report. Recommendations included the installation of CCTV cameras in all police station areas where police interact with citizens, digitally stored on a remote server to prevent tampering (PCA 2013). In addition, the PCA recommended better record keeping (e.g., general document storage, records on warrants, and upkeep of station diaries), the publication of protocols for document access to PCA investigators and the preservation of scenes where police shootings occur, and enhanced legal awareness training for officers (PCA 2013).

Officers in the TTPS are fighting back against these revived attempts to oversee their behavior. For example, then head of the PCA, Gillian Lucky, complained that police officers were refusing to comply with PCA directives to assist in investigations of police shootings, which apparently increased 100% from 2011 to 2014 (Kowlessar 2014). As of September, there have been at least 38 police shootings in 2014 alone (La Vende 2014). The PCA head also claimed there were long delays between the time of shootings and when the PCA was informed of those shootings, hampering investigations. As a way to potentially reduce the number of police shootings, the acting police commissioner claimed that body cameras would be placed on police officers by September of 2014 (Kowlessar 2014).

A few years ago, after the community policing reforms based on the PFP described earlier were implemented, officers from Scotland Yard had come to assist the TTPS, but according to the T&T Minister of National Security, those officers did very little training work while getting paid a large sum of money (roughly US$150,000 per month) (Clark 2014). While the murder rate in T&T remains at a high level (one-third of which are attributed to gang violence and less than 10% to domestic violence), another problematic trend is that there has been an increase in the percentage of murders committed with firearms, from 70% to 75% (Felmine 2014). These murders were still not being solved: the murder detection rate was only 9%, the same as it was 10 years previously (Kowlessar 2014).

New reforms are now being attempted. The TTPS hired and trained 287 new police at the end of 2014, almost half of them women, bringing the total force to 6617 (Clark 2014). There are also technological improvements being made to the 999 emergency call center (Felmine 2014). The prospects for community oriented and involved policing practices in T&T do not appear to be bright, however. Former New York Mayor Rudy Guliani and New York City Police Commissioner William Bratton, both known for implementing draconian zero-tolerance policing schemes, were scheduled to arrive in early 2015 to conduct an audit of the TTPS geared toward improving investigation methods and forensic testing, as well as to improve the low crime detection rate (Clark 2014).

Conclusion

Based on the preceding analyses, one can see that while numerous police reform efforts have been attempted in the postcolonial period, the police are still perceived to be violent, corrupt, incompetent, and resistant to change. Local and global economic and political barriers, coupled with historical and colonial legacies and high violent crime rates, inhibit systemic change further, and an eager and robust civil society has not been empowered to assist in top-down reform efforts or to help sustain them in any significant way. Foreign consultants are brought in on a regular basis, but the same policing problems remain after they leave, which brings forth further calls for foreign assistance as a way to show that something is being done.

No magic pill (the latest best practices) provided by Western powers will be able to cure what ails policing in T&T. Members of NGOs and individuals within the TTPS and Ministry of National Security all thought that foreign consultants could assist and facilitate, particularly with technical assistance, but they also as a group wanted to have local actors lead reform efforts. However, in order for reforms to be effective and sustainable, it is imperative that T&T taps into its underutilized local capacity and civil society strength (see Pino and Wiatrowski 2006). In addition to rooting out police that have engaged in repression and violence against innocent civilians, police reforms need to be geared toward T&T rather than an off-the-shelf plan created in another context. Furthermore, if foreign consultants or donors are involved in reform planning and implementation, they need to put the country's interests before their own and uphold their commitments, financial and otherwise (Ellison and Pino 2012). Based on lessons learned in a variety of contexts, Ellison and Pino (2012) promote a few more broad recommendations for sustainable reform: effective coordination among different countries, agencies, and other actors involved; accountability and transparency; local involvement and ownership; equal emphasis on both security and human rights; and an emphasis on the long-term rather than short-term goals. This approach may still not succeed if T&T is limited within the geopolitical and economic sphere to govern its own affairs or if the government refuses to approach reform more democratically, with more input and involvement from its citizens. Finally, the police need to have strong, reform-minded leadership without favor toward a particular political party or ethnic group. This approach would be a difficult and long-term process, but I contend that it would have a much better chance of succeeding than what we have seen repeated numerous times in T&T over the decades.

References

AI (Amnesty International). 2006. Trinidad and Tobago: End police immunity for unlawful killings and deaths in custody. http://www.refworld.org/cgi-bin/texis/vtx/rwmain?page=printdoc&docid=445615184 (accessed December 14, 2014).

Associated Press. 2011. Trinidad extends state of emergency for 3 months. *The Guardian*, September 5. http://www.guardian.co.uk/world/feedarticle/9831517 (accessed December 11, 2014).

Bennet, R. R. and J. P. Lynch. 1996. Towards a Caribbean criminology: Prospects and problems. *Caribbean Journal of Criminology and Social Psychology* 1(1): 8–45.

Bennet, R. R. and M. S. Moribito. 2006. Determinants of constables' perceptions of community support in three developing nations. *Police Quarterly* 9(2): 234–265.

Browne, J. 2008. Ramesh to fix SAUTT dilemma. *Trinidad and Tobago Express*, December 10. http://www.caribdaily.com/article/111244/ramesh-to-fix-sautt-dilemma/ (accessed December 15, 2014).

CIA (Central Intelligence Agency). 2014. CIA world factbook – Trinidad and Tobago. https://www.cia.gov/library/publications/the-world-factbook/geos/td.html (accessed December 16, 2014).

Clark, C. 2014. Giuliani, Bratton back next month – Griffith. *Trinidad and Tobago Guardian*, December 13. http://www.guardian.co.tt/news/2014-12-13/giuliani-bratton-back-next-month—griffith (accessed December 14, 2014).

Conway, D. 1998. Misguided directions, mismanaged models, or missed paths? In *Globalization and Neoliberalism: The Caribbean Context*, ed. T. Klak, pp. 29–49. New York: Rowman and Littlefield.

CRPS (Committee on the Restructuring of the Police Service). 1984. *Report of the Committee on the Restructuring of the Police Service*. Port of Spain, Republic of Trinidad and Tobago: CRPS.

Deere, C. D., P. Antrobus, L. Bolles et al. 1990. *In the Shadows of the Sun: Caribbean Development Alternatives and U.S. Policy*. San Francisco, CA: Westview Press.

Deosaran, R. 2002. Community policing in the Caribbean: Context, community, and police capability. *Policing: An International Journal of Police Strategies and Management* 25(1): 125–146.

Ellison, G. and N. W. Pino. 2012. *Globalization, Police Reform, and Development: Doing It the Western Way?* New York: Palgrave Macmillan.

Felmine, K. 2014. Top cop – We're in high gear to stop murders. *Trinidad and Tobago Guardian*, August 22. http://www.guardian.co.tt/news/2014-08-22/top-cop-we're-high-gear-stop-murders (accessed December 13, 2014).

Gabbatt, A. 2011. 100 held in Trinidad and Tobago's state of emergency. *The Guardian*, August 25. http://www.guardian.co.uk/world/2011/aug/25/trini-dad-and-tobago-state-emergency (accessed December 10, 2014).

Griffin, C. E. 1995. Economic restructuring, human rights, state security, and democratic viability in Trinidad and Tobago. *The Roundtable* 84(335): 297–318.

Griffith, I. L. 2000. *The Political Economy of Drugs in the Caribbean*. New York: St. Martin's Press.

Isbister, J. 2003. *Promises Not Kept: Poverty and the Betrayal of Third World Development*. Bloomfield, CT: Kumarian Press.

Klak, T. 1998. 13 theses on globalization and neoliberalism. In *Globalization and Neoliberalism: The Caribbean Context*, ed. T. Klak, pp. 3–23. New York: Rowman and Littlefield.

Klein, A. 2004. The search for a new drug policy framework: From the Barbados plan of action to the ganja commission. In *Caribbean Drugs: From Criminalization to Harm Reduction*, eds. A. Klein, M. Day, and A. Harriott, pp. 9–63. London, U.K.: Zed Books.

Kowlessar, G. 2012. Warner instructs police: Don't reveal crime statistics. *Trinidad and Tobago Guardian*, October 10. http://www.guardian.co.tt/news/2012-10-10/warner-instructs-police-don't-reveal-crime-statistics (accessed December 8, 2014).

Kowlessar, G. 2014. Cops not taking PCA seriously. *Trinidad and Tobago Guardian*, June 12. http://www.guardian.co.tt/news/2014-06-12/cops-not-taking-pca-seriously (accessed December 8, 2014).

Kurian, G. T. 2006. Trinidad and Tobago. In *World Encyclopedia of Police Forces and Correctional Systems*, ed. G. T. Kurian, pp. 900–902. Farmington Hills, MI: Thomson Gale Publishing.

La Vende, J. 2014. Harvey's thoughts on police killings: Cops toting 3, 4 ghosts. *Trinidad and Tobago Guardian*, September 17. http://www.guardian.co.tt/news/2014-09-17/harvey's-thoughts-police-killings-cops-toting-3-4-ghosts (accessed December 13, 2014).

Levitt, K. 2005. *Reclaiming Development: Independent Thought and Caribbean Community*. Kingston, Jamaica: Ian Randle Publishers.

Mandle, J. R. 1996. *Persistent Underdevelopment: Change and Economic Modernization in the West Indies*. Amsterdam, the Netherlands: Gordon and Breach.

Mastrofski, S. 1999. *Policing for People*. Washington, DC: Police Foundation.

Mastrofski, S. and C. Lum. 2008. Meeting the challenges of police governance in Trinidad and Tobago. *Policing: A Journal of Policy and Practice* 2(4): 481–496.

McCulloch, J. 2007. Transnational crime as productive fiction. *Social Justice* 34(2): 19–32.

Miller, J. and N. Hendrix. 2007. Applying the problem solving model to the developing world context: The case of murder in Trinidad and Tobago. *Crime Prevention and Community Safety* 9(4): 275–290.

Nanton, P. 2004. Rethinking privatization, the state, and illegal drugs in the Commonwealth Caribbean. In *Caribbean drugs: From criminalization to harm reduction*, eds. A. Klein, M. Day, and A. Harriott, pp. 120–144. London, U.K.: Zed Books.

O'Dowd, D. J. 1991. *Review of the Trinidad and Tobago Police Service*. Port of Spain, Republic of Trinidad and Tobago.

Parks, R. and S. Mastrofski. 2008. Introducing service-oriented policing to Trinidad and Tobago. Paper presented at the *American Society of Criminology Annual Meeting*, November 14, St. Louis, MO.

Payne, A. and P. Sutton. 2001. *Charting Caribbean Development*. Gainesville, FL: University Press of Florida.

PCA (Police Complaints Authority of Trinidad and Tobago). 2003. *Seventh Report: May 1, 2002 – September 30, 2003*. Port of Spain, Republic of Trinidad and Tobago: Police Complaints Authority.

PCA (Police Complaints Authority of Trinidad and Tobago). 2013. *Annual Report 2013*. Port of Spain, Republic of Trinidad and Tobago: Police Complaints Authority.

Pino, N. W. 2009. Developing democratic policing in the Caribbean: The case of Trinidad and Tobago. *Caribbean Journal of Criminology and Public Safety* 14 (1–2): 214–258.

Pino, N. W. and L. M. Johnson. 2011. Police deviance and community relations in Trinidad and Tobago. *Policing: An International Journal of Police Strategies and Management* 34(3): 454–478.

Pino, N. W. and M. D. Wiatrowski. 2006. *Democratic Policing in Transitional and Developing Countries*. Aldershot, U.K.: Ashgate.

PSC (Police Service Commission). 2004. *Annual Report of the Police Service Commission*. Port of Spain: Republic of Trinidad and Tobago.

Seaby, G. 1993. *Final Report for the Government of Trinidad and Tobago on Investigations Carried Out by Officers from New Scotland Yard in Respect of Allegations MADE by Rodwell Murray and others about Corruption in the Trinidad and Tobago Police Service.* London, U.K.: Metropolitan Police Office.

Townsend, D. 2010. Trouble in paradise: Welcome to the world's newest narcostate. *Foreign Policy.* March 11. http://www.foreignpolicy.com/articles/2010/03/11/trouble_in_paradise?print=yes&hidecomments=yes&page=full (accessed December 3, 2014).

Trinidad and Tobago Guardian. 2013. Warner's rise and fall in PP. *Trinidad and Tobago Guardian,* July 23. http://www.guardian.co.tt/news/2013-07-22/warner's-rise-and-fall-pp (accessed December 6, 2014).

TT Crime Forum. n.d. Crime in Trinidad and Tobago. http://www.ttcrime.com/stats.php (accessed December 17, 2014).

Wallace, W. C. 2012. Findings from a concurrent study on the level of community involvement in the policing process in Trinidad and Tobago. *The Police Journal: Theory, Practice and Principles* 85(1): 61–83.

Wells, W. and C. M. Katz. 2008. Illegal gun carrying and the demand for guns in Trinidad and Tobago: Evidence form a survey of youths in at-risk schools. Paper presented at the *American Society of Criminology Annual Meeting,* November 12, St. Louis, MIO.

Wilson, D. B., R. B. Parks, and S. Mastrofski. 2011. The impact of police reform on communities of Trinidad and Tobago. *Journal of Experimental Criminology* 7(4): 375–405.

Chapter Summaries

V

Chapter Summaries

13

Contents

Chapter 1: An Analytical Perspective on Police Corruption and
            Police Reforms in Developing Societies 229
Chapter 2: Confronting Police Corruption in Developing Societies:
            The Role of the Rule of Law 230
Chapter 3: Emphasizing Anticorruption Training as a Reform Tool
            to Curb Police Corruption in Developing Societies 230
Chapter 4: Ghana: Reducing Police Corruption and Promoting
            Police Professionalism through Reforms 231
Chapter 5: Kenya: Police Corruption and Reforms to Control It 232
Chapter 6: South Africa: A Schizophrenic System for Combating the
            Scourge of Police Corruption 232
Chapter 7: Cameroon: Police Corruption and the Police Reforms
            Imperative 233
Chapter 8: Hong Kong: Police Corruption and Reforms 233
Chapter 9: India: Nature of Police Corruption and Its Remedies 234
Chapter 10: Royal Solomon Islands: Rainbows across the Mountains?
            The Issue of Police Corruption 234
Chapter 11: Argentina: Revisiting Police Corruption and Police
            Reforms in a Captive State 235
Chapter 12: Trinidad and Tobago: Crime, Police Corruption, and
            Police Reforms 235

Chapter 1: An Analytical Perspective on Police Corruption and Police Reforms in Developing Societies

Kempe Ronald Hope, Sr.

Police corruption exists in some form in almost all police services across the globe. However, in most developing societies, this corruption tends to be pervasive and generally reflects the prevailing extent of corruption in those societies at large and the failure or nonperformance of governance institutions in curbing such corruption. In fact, the extent and nature of police corruption in any developing society is a direct reflection of the state of corruption in that society. And, because of the deleterious effects and consequences of police corruption in such societies, police reforms have become an imperative and taken on added significance not only for improving policing to serve the interests of the public but also for enhancing the overall governance environment in said societies. This chapter provides an analytical review and assessment of the police corruption phenomenon and problem in developing societies and the police reforms that have either been embarked upon or that are necessary to control and mitigate the deleterious effects of said police corruption and police misconduct. It draws on the author's vast practical experience as a police reforms adviser to several governments and also reviews the literature with coverage of such topics as what is police corruption, the causes of police corruption, the key indicators of police corruption, the consequences of police corruption, and the required principal elements of police reforms to control police corruption in the developing societies.

Chapter 2: Confronting Police Corruption in Developing Societies: The Role of the Rule of Law

John Mukum Mbaku

Corruption, especially by the police, remains one of the most important constraints to political, economic, and human development in developing and transition societies. Corruption by the police is especially insidious because it not only stunts entrepreneurship and wealth creation but it also deprives citizens of access to welfare-enhancing and life-saving public services. During the last several decades, many developing societies have developed and implemented various reform strategies to confront police corruption. Unfortunately, these programs have not been successful and corruption among the police remains as pervasive as ever. This chapter argues that the failure of many of these anticorruption reforms programs has been due to the fact that they were implemented within institutional arrangements that do not guarantee the rule of law, and one consequence of this is that the police and other public servants and political elites in these societies are not adequately and effectively constrained by the law. Thus, to deal effectively with police corruption, each society must provide itself with governing processes and institutions that guarantee the rule of law.

Chapter 3: Emphasizing Anticorruption Training as a Reform Tool to Curb Police Corruption in Developing Societies

Kempe Ronald Hope, Sr.

Police anticorruption training is important in developing societies to reorient the culture and thinking vis-à-vis corruption among the said police.

Consequently, such training must be aimed at all ranks and levels of police employees including both new recruits and employees previously hired. In other words, the ideal situation is to have comprehensive anticorruption training targeted at new recruits and on-the-job training—sometimes referred to as field, in-service, or post-academy training, targeted at those previously employed. Moreover, most of the anticorruption training that currently exists for the police in developing societies lacks the appropriate focus and is not provided in the manner of a coherent concentration. In fact, it tends to be delivered primarily in the form of police orientation to existing anticorruption laws or other criminal laws in general. It tends not to provide a thorough understanding of the phenomenon of corruption and how it looks in policing practice in the society, nor does it impart even the basic knowledge and skills on how to adhere to professional standards and avoid the temptation of accepting gifts, favors, or gratuities or engage in other corrupt acts. This chapter sets out a basic training framework and approach as a reform tool for curbing police corruption in developing societies. It outlines learning goals and training objectives, proposes a training approach model, suggests training content and coverage, and indicates the expected outcomes from the training approach and process.

Chapter 4: Ghana: Reducing Police Corruption and Promoting Police Professionalism through Reforms

Joseph R. A. Ayee

The Ghana Police Service continues to be perceived as the most corrupt public institution in Ghana as some of the internal and external accountability reforms initiatives that have been implemented have not been able to fully address police corruption and the lack of professionalism in the organization. This chapter demonstrates and emphasizes that the Ghanaian experience of police corruption and police reforms reinforces a number of lessons. First, police corruption is symptomatic of the level of systemic corruption existing in the country. Second, the inability to deal with police corruption is due to the lack of transparency, the absence of checks and balances, inadequate legal frameworks and the rule of law, and fragile institutions. Third, police reforms may not necessarily be targeted toward corruption but to the overall improved performance and transformation of the institution. In this sense, the reforms become a retooling exercise. Finally, like all reforms, the successful implementation of police reforms depends on political leadership, will, and commitment, which the various and succeeding governments did not demonstrate.

Chapter 5: Kenya: Police Corruption and Reforms to Control It

Kempe Ronald Hope, Sr.

In those societies or countries where police corruption is persistent, such as Kenya, it represents a systemic failure of governance where the principal institutions responsible for ensuring police accountability, the observance of ethics and integrity standards, and enforcing the rule of law are compromised and may themselves be infested with corrupt individuals and syndicates. The result is that a chain environment of personal and collective impunity prevails, and police corruption is therefore both perceived and real as running rampant. That, in turn, has considerable negative impacts on justice or security sector development and performance and is a challenge to nation-building, to the maintenance of public order and the rule of law, and to supporting the legitimacy of the state. It further leaves citizens helpless and frustrated and leads to activism (that is not always constructive) on the part of nongovernmental organizations and external actors to advocate on behalf of the citizens for measures to tackle police corruption. This chapter discusses and analyzes the nature and extent of police corruption in Kenya, drawing on the available data and synthesizing the latter to provide a coherent picture and understanding of the police corruption problem and environment in the country within the new and current policing institutional architecture. It then outlines, examines, and analytically reviews and assesses the outcomes of the recent police reforms that have been implemented and offers recommendations on the way forward for curbing police corruption in the Kenyan society.

Chapter 6: South Africa: A Schizophrenic System for Combating the Scourge of Police Corruption

Cornelis Roelofse

Schizophrenia is a mental condition characterized by inconsistent or contradictory elements and behavior. There is no better way to describe South Africa's and particularly the South African Police's approach to the problem of police corruption. Drawing on systems theory and reciprocal moral dualism to undergird the analysis, the chapter reveals the policy inconsistencies and contradictions where words and actions often do not correspond and political and administrative interference are common place. For example, national commissioners of police are now political appointees. Various units fighting corruption have been shut down, and the National Prosecuting Authority's Directorate of Special Operations, which was known as the

Scorpions, was moved from the National Prosecuting Authority and has been incorporated into the police. The Scorpions were renamed the Hawks and a number of senior officers from the Hawks have been suspended. Although South Africa has good laws and codes against police corruption, political interference is hampering efforts to combat the scourge of the said police corruption. However, recent signs and reforms point to a newly found appetite for dealing with this scourge.

Chapter 7: Cameroon: Police Corruption and the Police Reforms Imperative

Polycarp Ngufor Forkum

The police have extra powers meant to assist them to undertake their duties as watchers of the city. Most often, there is the miscarriage of justice and corruption perpetrated by this corps with its resultant consequences. This chapter provides a critical analysis of the depth and intensity of police corruption and misconduct in Cameroon. It details the most common and debilitating forms of police corruption in Cameroon, notably bribery, extortion, and related human rights abuses committed largely by rank-and-file police officers and the embezzlement of public funds, enforcement of a system of *returns*, and abuse of office by senior police officials that drive many of these abuses. This state of affairs has given the Cameroonian police a very bad image and is frequently captured in media headlines. The chapter then examines the police reforms that have either been embarked upon or that are imperative to control and mitigate the deleterious effects of this malpractice and misconduct among the police corps.

Chapter 8: Hong Kong: Police Corruption and Reforms

Dennis Lai Hang Hui

Throughout the past 40 years, Hong Kong has been able to transform itself from a corruption-ridden society to one that is celebrated for its markedly low level of corruption. Remarkably, the Hong Kong Police Force has been able to transform itself from a corruption-ridden organization to a highly professional one. Nonetheless, there are still many reports of corruption cases within the Hong Kong Police Force. This chapter provides a chronological overview of the key cases of police corruption in Hong Kong since 2002 to early 2015 and identifies their general features. It then provides a critical discussion of the institutional mechanisms that have been put in place to curb police corruption in Hong Kong. It focuses specifically on the internal mechanisms of the Hong Kong Police Force and the role of the Independent Commission Against Corruption in developing institutional capacity for controlling the said police corruption. Finally, the chapter identifies the factors that account for the low level of police corruption in Hong Kong and the possible challenges to be confronted in the future.

Chapter 9: India: Nature of Police Corruption and Its Remedies

Arvind Verma

The Indian police organization was designed by the British colonial power to support the Raj and did not incorporate any local accountability. The role of the police was therefore to maintain the British hegemony and deal with any perceived threat to the British rule. Independent India adopted and continued with this system for various historical factors as well as the pressure upon the government due to secessionist threats. At the same time, the democratic polity has also been vitiated by the criminalization of politics that has seen criminals taking advantage of the electoral process to get into positions of power. Political shenanigans have, consequently, thwarted police reforms and resulted in the continuation of the old corrupt and brutal system. Nevertheless, the democratic space now opening up for the citizens has catalyzed creative responses to force accountability from the police and other public officials. This chapter examines the nature of police corruption in India and argues that the democratic polity explains why it exists, why it is unable to control it, and finally how democracy in India is generating new mechanisms to combat corrupt practices. The chapter describes the nature and extent of corruption and then the nature of Indian democracy to explain the relationship. It presents a large variety of attempts to deal with corruption and finally looks into ways in which the citizens themselves are beginning to contest corruption utilizing the democratic space available to them. Lessons for other societies are also discussed.

Chapter 10: Royal Solomon Islands: Rainbows across the Mountains—The Issue of Police Corruption

Garth den Heyer

At the time that the Solomon Islands was granted independence from Britain in 1978, the Royal Solomon Islands Police Force (RSIPF) was widely regarded as an efficient and highly effective police force and a model for the newly emerging states of the South Pacific. However, from the beginning of the tensions in 1998 until the involvement of the Regional Assistance Mission to Solomon Islands in 2003, there had been a progressive decline in the effectiveness, capability, and professional skills of the RSIPF. The force's knowledge and expertise across the range of police disciplines had eroded to the point where the organization was no longer able to effectively fulfill its law and order responsibilities and to the extent that they were one of the influencing agents in the civil conflict. This chapter looks at the role of the RSIPF and the major issues the organization is facing within the context of the Solomon Islands civil conflict and in the wider context of the influence of corruption that is part of the Island's culture. The main issue facing the RSIPF is how to implement a program of reforms that will enable the organization to have the skills and capability to enable it to investigate corruption both within the organization and across the Solomon Islands government.

Chapter 11: Argentina: Revisiting Police Corruption and Police Reforms in a Captive State

Guillermina Seri

Echoing the voices and concerns of Argentine police officers based on field interviews, this chapter dissects the question of police corruption in Argentina as a salient sign of governmental implosion and a facilitator of the expansion of the captive state. More and more state apparatuses across Latin America are infiltrated by criminal networks and turned progressively inoperative as a tool of impunity and lawlessness. In Argentina, corruption has served as a facilitator to the recent rise of drug trafficking and other forms of organized crime that, with the epicenter in the north, the province of Santa Fe, and areas within Buenos Aires, are dramatically transforming the face of the country and altering citizens' everyday life. Parochial, moralistic views of corruption among members of the police and the public and the belief among reformers that *political conduction* of the police will promote transparency and democratic governance are main factors that this chapter discusses as epistemological obstacles blocking the possibility of police reform.

Chapter 12: Trinidad and Tobago: Crime, Police Corruption, and Police Reforms

Nathan W. Pino

It is best to understand policing in Trinidad and Tobago (T&T) within the country's postcolonial and Caribbean context, characterized in part by economic underdevelopment, weak governmental and political capacity, and high violent crime rates that stem largely from high young male unemployment and the country's role as a major drug transshipment hub. In spite of numerous evaluations and efforts at reform, the police remain notoriously violent, corrupt, and incompetent; and recent developments leave little hope that systemic and sustainable changes will occur any time soon. Police corruption and violence in T&T is therefore a considerable problem, and numerous reform efforts have yet to produce sustainable improvements. In this chapter, the discussion centers on the historical, economic, and political context within which policing in T&T occurs, followed by an overview of the crime problems facing the country. Police corruption in T&T is then documented, as well as the various reform efforts attempted over time, including more recent developments in policing in the country. Finally, the chapter ends with concluding thoughts on what might be needed for sustainable and democratic reform of the police, including the needed role of civil society in any future reform efforts.

Index

A

ACA, *see* Anticorruption agency (ACA), Solomon Islands
Acceptance of Advantages (Chief Executive's Permission) Notice 2010 (Hong Kong), 150
Acceptance of law, 35–36, 39–40
Accountability, 26, 104
    civilian oversight (*see* Civilian oversight bodies)
    command accountability, 22–23
    and democratic policing, 18
    Ghana Police Service
        external accountability, 79–80
        internal accountability, 77–78, 80
    HKPF, 149–150
    Indian police, 162, 164–165
    Kenya Police, 88–89, 93
    and openness/transparency, 42–43
    RSIPF, 183, 189, 192
    systems of, 10
ACWG, *see* Anti-Corruption Working Group (ACWG), South Africa
Administration Police Service (APS), Kenya, 86–87, 102, 104
Advisory Committee on Corruption (Hong Kong), 148
African National Congress, 112
African Policing Civilian Oversight Forum (South Africa), 136
Afrobarometer survey, 72, 79
AI, *see* Amnesty International (AI)
Alternative 'imagined communities' of loyalties, 203–204
Amnesty International (AI), 136, 213
Anthropological paradigm, of police training, 113
Anticorruption agency (ACA), Solomon Islands, 190–191
Anti-Corruption Office (Hong Kong), 148
Anticorruption training, *see* Police anticorruption training (PACT)

Anti-Corruption Working Group (ACWG), South Africa, 121
Apartheid, in South Africa, 110–111
APS, *see* Administration Police Service (APS), Kenya
Arbitrary arrests
    in Cameroon, 127–128
    in Kenya, 93
    in Trinidad and Tobago, 212
Argentina
    alternative 'imagined communities' of loyalties, 203–204
    1953 Code of Police Justice, 199
    conditions of labor, 203
    corruption in, 197
    democracy, 201–203
    dismissal of police officers
        massive, 199–200
        rate of, 201–202
    lack of political control, 204–205
    maldita policía, 199
    militarization of police, 199–200
    organization of police forces, 198–199
    pay issues, 201, 203
    perception of police corruption, 202
    political corruption in, 201, 235
    unionization of police, 203
Arslanián, Leon, 199–200
Asset declaration, 19–20
Association of Caribbean Commissioners of Police, 215

B

Background check, during recruitment, 9, 16
    by Kenya Police, 101
    by SAPS, 119
Bad apples theory, 6, 8
Behaviors, police corruption, 7
Béliz, Gustavo, 200
Berni, Sergio, 200

Bilateral investment treaties, of Trinidad
    and Tobago, 209
Black Power Revolt (1970), in Trinidad and
    Tobago, 209
Blair-Kerr, Sir Alastair, 149
Blue code of silence, see Code of silence
Blue wall, see Code of silence
BNI, see Bureau of National Investigations
    (BNI), Ghana
Bratton, William, 221
BribeBusters, 174–175
Bribery
    in Argentina, 197
    in Cameroon, 129–130, 138
    and culture, 10
    in East Africa, 11–12
    in election campaigns, 164
    in Ghana, 73–74
    in Hong Kong, 148
    in India, 158, 160–161, 163
    indices, 11
    in Kenya, 89–91, 95, 97, 104
    and pay/conditions of service, 21
    during recruitment, 9
    in Solomon Islands, 182
    during training, 133–134
    in Trinidad and Tobago, 219
Bureaucratic corruption
    in Cameroon, 38
    in Ghana, 74
Bureau of National Investigations (BNI),
    Ghana, 75–76

C

Cabezas, José Luis, 199
CAG, see Comptroller and Auditor-General
    (CAG), India
Cameroon, 38, 233
    appointment/tenure of office, 134
    arbitrary arrests and detention, 127–128
    community engagement and civil
        society groups, 136
    corrupt system of monetary returns,
        132–133
    creation of new institutional structures,
        137
    democratic policing, 135–136
    extortion
        at police checkpoints, 127
        sexual assault associated with, 128–129
        torture as tool of, 128

high-level embezzlement of police
    funds, 131–132
improvement of conditions and
    welfare, 135
informal sector, extortion and abuses
    in, 130
judicial independence in, 42
oversight bodies, 136–137
parallel reforms, 137
payment to register cases, 129
police protection for sale, 133
recruitment, 133–134
rule of law, 130–131
transportation and logistics fees,
    129–130
zero tolerance, 138
Capacity development
    in democratic policing, 18–19
    Ghana Police Service, 68
    Kenya Police, 100
    RSIPF, 188
Captive state, see Argentina
Case registration fees
    in Cameroon, 129
    in India, 158–159
CBI, see Central Bureau of Investigation
    (CBI), India
CCPEC, see Common Curriculum on Police
    Ethics and Corruption (CCPEC)
Central Bureau of Investigation (CBI),
    India, 166–167, 170
Central Firearms Registry (CFR),
    South Africa, 115
Central Information Commission (CIC),
    India, 167–168
Central Vigilance Commission (CVC),
    India, 167–168, 172
CEPOL, see European Police College
    (CEPOL)
CFR, see Central Firearms Registry (CFR),
    South Africa
Checkpoints, extortion at, 97, 127–128
Checks and balances system, in India,
    158, 165–166, 172
China, anticorruption campaigns in, 153
CHRI, see Commonwealth Human Rights
    Initiative (CHRI)
CIC, see Central Information Commission
    (CIC), India
Citizen movements, in India, 171–172
Civilian oversight bodies, 23–25, 27, 45–46
    in Cameroon, 136–137

in Solomon Islands, 183, 189
in South Africa, 115–118
in Trinidad and Tobago, 216, 219–220
Civilian secretariats for police service, in
        South Africa, 115–116
Civil society, 40
in Cameroon, 127, 132, 136
in South Africa, 118
in Trinidad and Tobago, 219
Civil society organizations (CSOs), in
        Ghana, 79
CLEEN Foundation (Nigeria), 136
Cocoon of silence, see Code of silence
Code of Civil Procedure, 1908 (India), 167
Code of conduct
Kenya Police, 98, 100, 105
RSIPF, 189
SAPS, 121
Code of silence, 12, 14, 71, 158
COI, see Conflict of interest (COI)
Colonial policing system
Ghana, 67–68
Hong Kong, 148–149
India, 161, 234
Trinidad and Tobago, 209–210,
        213–214, 218
Command accountability/responsibility,
        22–23
Command structure, of Kenya Police, 86, 102
Common Curriculum on Police Ethics and
        Corruption (CCPEC), 17, 59
Commonwealth Human Rights Initiative
        (CHRI), 90, 136
Community engagement, in Cameroon, 136
Community policing, 34
Cameroon, 135, 138
forums, South Africa, 116–117
Kenya, 94, 101
Trinidad and Tobago, 215–216, 218, 221
Competitive bureaucracy, in India, 173
Comptroller and Auditor-General (CAG),
        India, 168–169
Conditions of service, 18, 21
Argentine police, 203
Cameroon Police, 135, 138
Ghana Police, 70, 78
Kenya Police, 92
Conflict of interest (COI), 20–21
Constitutional political economy model,
        34–35, 37
Constitutional system, of Solomon
        Islands, 182

Constitution of Kenya (2010), 86, 88
Constitution of the Republic of Ghana
        (1992), 69–70, 77
Constitutions, 37
Ghana Police Service, 69–71, 77
Indian police, 165, 168, 170
Kenya Police, 86, 88, 105
RSIPF, 182
SAPS, 115, 117
Corruption Perceptions Index (CPI), 67, 110
Corruption Prevention Group
        (Hong Kong), 151
Crime Intelligence Unit, South Africa, 120
Crime rate, 14
Ghana, 69
Trinidad and Tobago, 210
Criminal corruption, in Ghana, 74–76
Criminal Investigation Department
        (CID), 186
Criminalization
of politics, in India, 164, 234
of state, 76
Criminal justice
perspective of police corruption, 144
sector reform, in postconflict countries,
        180–181, 191
Criminals
collusion of police with, 34, 75, 148–149,
        214, 218
in elected offices, 164, 175
recruitment of, 38
Cronyism, 112
CSOs, see Civil society organizations
        (CSOs)
Cultural traditions, and police
        corruption, 10
Culture of impunity, 26–27
Curtain, see Code of silence
CVC, see Central Vigilance Commission
        (CVC), India
CVC Act of 2003 (India), 167

D

DCI, see Directorate of Criminal
        Investigations (DCI), Kenya
de Kirchner, Cristina Fernandez, 200
Demand reduction programs, in Trinidad
        and Tobago, 214
Democracy and police corruption, 13
Argentina, 199, 201–202, 205
civilian oversight bodies, 25

Ghana, 66, 69
India, 157–158, 163–165, 171, 175, 234
judicial activism, 169–170
Democratic policing, 13, 22, 57
in Cameroon, 135–136
capacity development in, 18–19
in Ghana, 69
in Kenya, 92, 104
in postconflict countries, 180
Detentions, arbitrary, 127–128, 130
Deterrent, punishment as, 26–27
Developed societies, police corruption in, 8
Dewornu, C.K., 72
Directorate of Criminal Investigations
(DCI), Kenya, 87–88
Directorate of Special Operations, 232–233
Drug trafficking
in Argentina, 198–199, 204–205, 235
involvement of Mexican police in, 34
in Trinidad and Tobago, 210–214

E

EACC, see Ethics and Anti-Corruption
Commission (EACC), Kenya
East African Bribery Index, 90
e-governance, in India, 172
EIOs, see Ethics and integrity officers (EIOs)
Embezzlement of police funds, 131–132,
159–160, 169, 212
Employee confidence, training, 51–52
Encounter killings, in India, 162
Equipes Special d' Intervention Rapides
(special rapid intervention
teams), 135
Equipments, policing, 9–10, 21, 159, 203,
214, 216
Ethics
decision making, 17, 60–61
defined, 60
education/training, 9, 16–18, 151
and oversight bodies, 24
Ethics and Anti-Corruption Commission
(EACC), Kenya, 90, 97
Ethics and integrity officers (EIOs), 19
European Police College (CEPOL), 17, 59
External accountability, 77, 79–80
External oversight committees, see Civilian
oversight bodies
Extortion, 39, 41
in Cameroon, 132
to fund police services, 131

in informal sector, 130
at police checkpoints, 127
sexual assault associated with,
128–129
torture as tool of, 128
in Ghana, 73–74
in India, 159, 161
bribery and, 163
hafta tax, 158, 160
NHRC, 167
in Kenya, 91, 97

F

Failing forward context, 56
Financial disclosure, by police officers,
19–20
Force Committee on Integrity Management
(Hong Kong), 151
Force Discipline Adjudication Unit,
Hong Kong, 145
Forums, community policing, 116–117
Freedom Under Law (NGO), 120
Funds, embezzlement, 131–132, 159–160,
169, 212

G

Garré, Nilda, 200
GDNS, see General Delegation for National
Security (GDNS)
Gendarmerie, 126
Gender balance/mainstreaming,
in Cameroon, 135–136
General crime theory, 114
General Delegation for National Security
(GDNS), 126
Ghana, 231
bribery in, 73–74
bureaucratic corruption, 74
bus shuttle service, 78
colonial policing system, 67–68
constitutions, 69–71, 77
country context, 66–67
criminal corruption, 74–76
extortion in, 73–74
measurement of police corruption,
71–72
oversight bodies, 70, 79
police misconduct in, 71, 74, 76
providing badge of authority, 78
strategies for promotion of

external accountability, 79
internal accountability, 77–78
street-level bribery and extortion, 73–74
Ghana Integrity Initiative (GII), 67
Ghana Police Service (GPS)
    constitutions/legal frameworks
        governing, 69–71
    history of, 67–69
    recruitment in, 9
GNU, *see* Government of national
        unity (GNU)
Godber, Peter, 149
Good conduct, recognition of, 21–22
Governance
    e-governance, 172
    and openness/transparency, 43
    police governance in Hong Kong, 153
    and police reforms, 104
    Solomon Islands, 182, 184
Government of national unity (GNU),
        in Kenya, 98
GPS, *see* Ghana Police Service (GPS)
Grass eaters, 5, 157
Griffith, Gary, 219
Guliani, Rudy, 221
Gunshot-related deaths, in Kenya, 94–95

H

Hafta tax, in India, 158, 160
Hazare, Anna, 170–171
HKPF, *see* Hong Kong Police Force (HKPF)
Homicides, in Trinidad and Tobago, 210, 221
Homo politis, 114
Hong Kong, 233–234
    anticorruption agencies in, 172
    civilian oversight institutions in, 23
    Corruption Prevention Group, 151
    Force Committee on Integrity
        Management, 151
    ICAC
        establishment of, 149
        three-pronged approach, 149–150
    IIO, 151
    institutional mechanisms, 148–152
    key incidences of police corruption in,
        144–148
    Operational Liaison Group, 151
Hong Kong Police Force (HKPF), 143
    conflicts of interest policies in, 20
    and ICAC, 151–152
    organizational reforms of

integrity management, 150–151
    recruitment, 150
Hong Kong Standing Committee on
        Disciplined Services Salaries and
        Conditions of Service, 152
Human rights
    protection, 36, 44–45, 167
    training, 9
    violations, 93, 170

I

ICAC, *see* Independent Commission
        Against Corruption (ICAC),
        Hong Kong
ICAC Ordinance, 149
IG, *see* Inspector-General (IG) of Kenya
IIO, *see* Internal Investigations Office (IIO),
        Hong Kong
Imagined communities, *see* Alternative
        'imagined communities' of
        loyalties
IMF, *see* International Monetary
        Fund (IMF)
IMLU, *see* Independent Medico-Legal Unit
        (IMLU), Kenya
Impunity of police officers, 26–27, 35,
        37–38, 44–45
    in Argentina, 204
    and human rights, 44
    in Kenya, 85
    in South Africa, 112
    in Trinidad and Tobago, 213
Indebtedness, declaration of, 19–20
Independent Commission Against
        Corruption (ICAC), Hong Kong,
        143, 145–146, 234
    Community Relations Department, 150
    Corruption Prevention Department,
        150–151
    establishment of, 149
    and HKPF, relationship between,
        151–152
    Operations Department, 149–151
Independent Medico-Legal Unit (IMLU),
        Kenya, 94
Independent Police Investigative
        Directorate (IPID), South Africa,
        117–118
Independent Policing Oversight Authority
        (IPOA), Kenya, 87–89, 93–95,
        100, 102

India, 234
    accountability, 162–164
    CAG, 168–169
    CBI, 166–167, 170
    checks and balances system in, 158,
        165–166, 172
    citizen movements, 172
    colonial policing model, 161–162
    competitive bureaucracy in, 173
    CVC, 167–168, 172
    democracy, 163–165
    encounter killings, 162
    internal inquiry of police officials in,
        164–165
    judicial activism, 169–171
    kiosk-based complaint registration,
        173–174
    Ministry of Home Affairs, 165
    misuse of funds, 159–160, 169
    NHRC, 167
    organizational culture, 10
    pay of police officers in, 9
    PIL system, 170
    police corruption in
        common practices, 159–161
        efforts to control, 165–169
        nature of, 158–159
    police leadership in, 159–160
    political leadership in, 160, 164
    Public Interest Disclosure (Protection of
        Informers) Bill, 2010, 168
    reasons for police corruption, 161–163
    record keeping system, 163
    RTI Act, 2005, 167–168, 170, 172, 174
    Vigilance Department, 158, 166
    Whistleblowers' Protection Bill 2011,
        168, 170, 172
Indian Police Service (IPS), 158–159,
    165–166
Informal sector, extortion/abuses by
    Cameroon police in, 130
Informant reward system, in Ghana, 78
Inspector-General (IG) of Kenya, 86–87
Institutional integrity, 144, 152; see also
    Integrity
Institutional police building, 188–189
Institutional reforms, 37–38, 40, 100, 184
Instruction content, 55–56
Integrity, 21–22
    institutional integrity, 144, 152
    management, in HKPF, 150–151
    PACT approach, 60

    tests, 25
    training, 16–18
Interagency Task Force (Trinidad and
    Tobago), 215
Internal accountability, 76–78
Internal Affairs Unit (IAU), 87–88, 101
Internal Investigations Office (IIO), Hong
    Kong, 151
International Monetary Fund (IMF),
    208–209
I-paid-a-bribe (website), 175
IPID, see Independent Police Investigative
    Directorate (IPID), South Africa
IPID Act 2011, 117–118
IPOA, see Independent Policing Oversight
    Authority (IPOA), Kenya
IPOA Act, 2011, 88
IPS, see Indian Police Service (IPS)

J

Jamaat al Muslimeen (Trinidad and
    Tobago), 209
Judicial activism, in India, 169–171
Judicial independence, 36, 41–42
Judicial institutions, 34–35, 38, 40

K

Kaléé Kaléé (mass arrests), 128
Kastom (Solomon Islands), 191
Kenya
    APS, 86–87, 102, 104
    bribery in, 89–91, 95, 97, 104
    community policing in, 94, 101
    Constitution of Kenya (2010), 86, 88
    current policing institutional
        architecture in, 86–89
    democratic policing in, 92, 104
    extortion in, 91, 97
    gunshot-related deaths, 94–95
    human rights violations, 93
    IPOA, 87–89, 93–95, 100, 102
    multiyear strategic plans, 100
    NPS, 86, 97, 99–100, 103–104
        IAU, 87–88, 101
        Police Code of Conduct and
            Ethics, 100
    oversight bodies, 23, 88–89, 97
    police corruption in, 89
        traffic police corruption, 92, 97
    police misconduct in, 88, 94–95, 102

police reforms in, 97
The Ransley Report, 92, 95, 98–99
recruitment in, 92, 95–97, 101
Kenya Association of Women in
    Policing, 100
Kenya Human Rights Commission
    (KHRC), 90
Kenya Police Service (KPS), 86–87, 102, 104
    capacity development, 100
    code of conduct, 98, 100, 105
    command structure, 86, 102
KHRC, see Kenya Human Rights
    Commission (KHRC)
Kiosks, for complaint registration, 173–174
Kirchner, Nestor, 200
KPS, see Kenya Police Service (KPS)

L

Laissez-faire mode of colonial
    capitalism, 149
Law, see Rule of law
Leadership, see Police leadership; Political
    leadership
Leadership Code Commission (LCC),
    Solomon Islands, 187
Legal stability, 44
Legitimacy
    of government/state, 12–13, 85, 104
    of police, 61, 66, 144, 192
Liabilities, declaration of, 19–20
Lifestyle audits, 19–20
Literacy, and police reforms, 190
Logistics fees for investigation, 129–130
Lorenzetti, Ricardo, 204
Lucky, Gillian, 221

M

MacLehose, Murray, 149, 151
Mahama, John Dramani, 66
Maldita policía, in Argentina, 199
Marginalized groups, acceptance of law
    by, 40
Martyrs' Day, in Ghana, 78
Massive dismissals, in Argentina, 199–200
Mather, Shaffi, 174
Mbeki, Thabo, 111
Meat eaters, 6, 157
Media
    and police corruption oversight, 118
    social media, 174–175

Mexico
    pay of police officers in, 9
    police corruption in, 33–34
Middle management, role in police
    reforms, 190
Militarization of police
    in Argentina, 199–200
    in Trinidad and Tobago, 215
Model station programs, in Trinidad and
    Tobago, 216–217
Monetary return system, in Cameroon,
    132–133
Multiyear strategic plans, in Kenya, 100
Mutual legal assistance treaties, of Trinidad
    and Tobago, 214–215

N

Narcoorganizations, 204
Narcotics, and Ghana Police Service,
    75–76, 79
National Advanced Police School
    (Cameroon), 133
National Anti-Corruption Action Plan
    (Ghana), 67
National civilian secretariats for police
    service, in South Africa, 115–116
National Democratic Congress (NDC),
    Ghana, 66
National Human Rights Commission
    (NHRC), India, 167
National Parliamentary Portfolio
    Committee (South Africa), 115
National Police Service (NPS), Kenya,
    86–88, 97, 99–101, 103–104
    IAU, 87–88, 101
    Police Code of Conduct and Ethics, 100
National Police Service Commission
    (NPSC), Kenya, 86–88, 95–97,
    100, 105
National policing plan (Ghana), 68–69
National Prosecuting Authority (NPA),
    South Africa, 110, 232–233
National Task Force on Police Reforms
    (NTFPR), Kenya, 98–99
National Union of Freedom Fighters
    (Trinidad and Tobago), 209
NDC, see National Democratic Congress
    (NDC), Ghana
Neoliberalism, 203, 208
Nepotism, 17, 92, 112, 133
New Patriotic Party (NPP), Ghana, 66

NGO, *see* Freedom Under Law (NGO)
NHRC, *see* National Human Rights
      Commission (NHRC), India
Nigeria, 38
   pay of police officers in, 9–10
   predatory policing in, 4
   self-help associations in, 34
Nipping points, in Cameroon, 127
Njangis (savings clubs), 130
Northern Ireland, police reforms in, 218
NPA, *see* National Prosecuting Authority
      (NPA), South Africa
NPP, *see* New Patriotic Party (NPP), Ghana
NPS, *see* National Police Service (NPS),
      Kenya
NPSC, *see* National Police Service
      Commission (NPSC), Kenya
NPSC Act, 2011, 86–88, 105
NTFPR, *see* National Task Force on Police
      Reforms (NTFPR), Kenya

O

Occupy Central Movement (Hong Kong),
      153
Office of the Public Service Commission
      (OPSC), South Africa, 122
Ombudsman, 164, 170–172
Ombudsman Act 2014 (India), 171
On-the-job anticorruption training,
      54–55, 231
Openness of law, 36, 42–43
Operational Liaison Group (Hong Kong), 151
OPSC, *see* Office of the Public Service
      Commission (OPSC),
      South Africa
Organizational culture, 10, 80, 181
Organizational structure
   of HKPF, 150
   of RSIPF, 185–186
Oversight bodies; *see also* Civilian oversight
      bodies
   in Ghana, 70, 79
   in Kenya, 88–89, 97

P

PACT, *see* Police anticorruption training
      (PACT)
Parallel reforms, in Cameroon, 137
Parliamentary Committee on Defence and
      Interior (Ghana), 79

Participating Police Force (PPF), Solomon
      Islands, 184–185, 187
Pay of police officers, 9–10, 21
   Argentina, 201, 203
   Cameroon, 138
   Ghana, 78
   Hong Kong, 152–153
   Kenya, 92
   Solomon Islands, 186
   Trinidad and Tobago, 214, 216–217
PBL, *see* Problem-based learning (PBL)
PCA, *see* Police Complaints
      Authority (PCA), Trinidad
      and Tobago
People's National Movement (PNM),
      Trinidad and Tobago, 209, 219
Perception surveys, 10–11
Perón, Juan Domingo, 199
PFP, *see* Policing for People (PFP) model
PIL, *see* Public Interest Litigation (PIL)
      system
PNM, *see* People's National Movement
      (PNM), Trinidad and Tobago
POBO, *see* Prevention of Bribery Ordinance
      (POBO), Hong Kong
Pockets of corruption theory, *see* Bad
      apples theory
Police abuse
   Argentina, 204
   Trinidad and Tobago, 213
Police Act of 1861, India, 162
Police Act (1972), Solomon Islands, 189
Police Act (Act 68 of 1995), South Africa,
      116–117
Police anticorruption training (PACT),
      230–231
   anticipated outcomes, 59–61
   approach, 55–57
   content and coverage
      other police employees, 59
      recruits, 58
      senior police employees, 58–59
   learning goals and objectives
      other police employees, 55
      recruits, 54
      senior police employees, 54–55
Police Central Disciplinary Board
      (Ghana), 76
Police Complaints Authority (PCA),
      Trinidad and Tobago, 216,
      219–221
Police conservatism, 135

Police corruption, 5–8, 144
  causes of, 8–10
  consequences of, 11–14
  functional definition of, 5
  indicators of, 10–11
  measurement of, 71–72
  types and dimensions of, 6
  typology, 144
Police Council (Ghana), 70, 79
Police–criminal nexus, 34, 75, 148–149,
    214, 218
Police deviance, in Trinidad and Tobago,
    207, 212–213, 218
Police ethics, 17, 23, 58–59, 61
Police Force (Amendment) Decree
    (Ghana), 67
Police Force (Disciplinary Proceedings)
    Regulations 1974 (Ghana), 70
Police General Orders (Hong Kong), 150
Police–judicial collusion, in Ghana, 74
Police leadership, 23, 57
  Cameroon, 128–129, 131, 133
  India, 158–160
  of senior police officers, 17
  South Africa, 118–120
  Trinidad and Tobago, 212, 215
Police legitimacy, 61, 66, 144, 192
Police misconduct, 4, 10, 16, 24
  Cameroon, 126, 136
  Ghana, 71, 74, 76
  Kenya, 88, 94–95, 102
  Solomon Islands, 189
  South Africa, 110, 117, 122
  Trinidad and Tobago, 212–213
Police Ordinance (Ghana), 67
Police–public partnership, 117
Police–public relationship, 13, 153, 192,
    211–212
Police (Discipline) Regulation (Hong
    Kong), 150
Police Service Act 350 of 1970 (Ghana),
    67–70, 77
Police Service Instructions (Ghana), 70
Police Service Regulations, 2012 (Ghana),
    70–71
Police Service (Administration) Regulations
    (Ghana)
  1974, 70
  2012, 74
Police shootings, investigation of, 221
Police Training College (Cameroon), 133
Policing for People (PFP) model, 216

Political corruption
  Argentina, 201
  Hong Kong, 153
  India, 160
Political leadership
  and anticorruption agencies, 172
  control over police, 204–205
  in India, 160, 164
Portfolio Committee on Safety and Security
    (South Africa), 115
Positive behaviors/ethics, 60
Post buying, in Cameroon, 134
Postconflict countries, police reform in,
    180–181
PPF, see Participating Police Force (PPF),
    Solomon Islands
PPF–RSIPF Joint Corruption Targeting
    Task Force, 185
Predatory policing, 4, 92
Predictability of law, 36, 44
Prevention of Bribery Ordinance (POBO),
    Hong Kong, 145, 147, 149
Prevention of Corruption Act, 1988
    (India), 167
Preventive measures
  capacity development in democratic
    policing, 18–19
  civilian oversight institutions, 23–25
  counteracting and managing conflicts of
    interest, 20–21
  declaration of assets/property/liabilities
    and lifestyle audits, 19–20
  enhanced command accountability and
    responsibility, 22–23
  ethics and integrity officers, 19
  ethics and integrity training, 16–18
  good conduct recognition and
    rewards, 21–22
  pay and conditions of service, 21
  recruitment and selection
    procedures, 15–16
Proactive models of civilian oversight, 24
Problem-based learning (PBL), 55–56
Professional standards, 17, 19
  promotion, in Ghana, 77
  of RSIPF, 189
Professional Standards and Internal
    Investigations Section (PSII),
    186–187
Property declaration, 19–20
Protection of Human Rights (Amendment)
    Act, 2006 (India), 167

Provincial civilian secretariats for police service, in South Africa, 115–116
Provincial legislatures, South Africa, 115
Psychological predispositions, in recruitment, 113
Psychological tests, during recruitment, 9, 16
Public accountability, and anticorruption programs, 153
Public confidence, 11–13, 26–27, 61, 80, 94, 104, 110, 185, 188, 212
Public Interest Disclosure (Protection of Informers) Bill, 2010 (India), 168
Public Interest Litigation (PIL) system, in India, 170
Public perceptions, 8, 10–11, 13, 73–74, 118–119, 121, 138, 197, 211
Public policies, openness and transparency in, 42–43
Public Protector (South Africa), 118
Public sector corruption, 13, 74
Public Service Commission (South Africa), 118
Punitive measures
  increased detection and investigation, 25–26
  punishment as deterrent, 26–27

R

RAMSI, see Regional Assistance Mission to the Solomon Islands (RAMSI)
Random integrity testing, 25
Rape by Cameroon police, 128–129
Reactive models of civilian oversight, 24
Reciprocal moral dualism, 113–114, 232
Recognition and reward policy (RRP), 21–22
Record keeping system, 163, 220
Recruitment
  in Cameroon, 133–134
  gender-based discrimination in, 135
  in Hong Kong, 150
  in India, 165
  in Kenya, 92, 95–97, 101
  and police corruption, 9, 15–16
  in South Africa, 112–113
  in Trinidad and Tobago, 214
Recruits, PACT for
  content, 58–59
  objectives, 54

Regional Assistance Mission to the Solomon Islands (RAMSI), 184–185
Regional Police Councils (Ghana), 79
Resources for police officers, 9–10, 21; see also Equipments, policing; Pay of police officers
Respect for law, 35–36, 39–40
Responsibility, command, 22–23
Rights, see Human rights
Right to Information (RTI) Act 2005 (India), 167–168, 170, 172, 174
Roadblocks, extortion at, 92, 97, 127
Royal Solomon Islands, 234–235
  corruption in, 182–184
  RAMSI, 184–185
Royal Solomon Islands Police Force (RSIPF), 179–180, 183, 234–235
  anticorruption investigative capability, 186–187
  CID, 186
  civilian oversight, 189
  Corruption Squad, 186–187, 190
  establishment of anti-corruption agency, 190–191
  Fraud Squad, 186–187
  major issues with, 185–186
  organizational structure/leadership, 185–186
  PPF–RSIPF Joint Corruption Targeting Task Force, 185
  Professional Standards Unit, 189
  PSII, 186–187
  reforms, 187
    challenges, 191
    implementation, 190
    role in Guadalcanal–Malaita conflict, 182
RRP, see Recognition and reward policy (RRP)
RSIPF, see Royal Solomon Islands Police Force (RSIPF)
RTI, see Right to Information (RTI) Act 2005 (India)
Rule of law, 34, 68, 230
  in Cameroon, 130–131
  elements of, 35–36
  judicial independence, 41–42
  openness and transparency, 42–43
  predictability, 44
  and reform strategies, 45–46
  supremacy of law, 38–39

S

SAPA, *see* South African Press Association
    (SAPA)
SAPS, *see* South African Police Service
    (SAPS)
SAUTT, *see* Special Anti-Crime Unit of
    Trinidad and Tobago (SAUTT)
Security and Intelligence Act 1996
    (Ghana), 70
Security threats, in Kenya, 104
Selection procedures, during recruitment,
    15–16, 150
Self-help associations, 34
Self-regulation, *see* Internal accountability
Senior police officers
    in Cameroon
        embezzlement, 131–132
        monetary return system, 132–133
    leadership of, 17
    PACT for
        content, 58–59
        objectives, 54–55
Sexual assault, associated with extortion in
    Cameroon, 128–129
Sexual exploitation/abuse, in
    workplace, 136
Sex workers, in Cameroon, 129
Ship rider agreements, of Trinidad and
    Tobago, 214
Singapore
    anticorruption agencies in, 172
    civilian oversight institutions in, 23
    recognition and reward policy in, 21–22
Socialization process within police, 113
Sociological–criminological perspective of
    police corruption, 144
South Africa, 38–39, 232–233
    background, 110–112
    civil society and media, 118
    community policing forums, 116–117
    Crime Intelligence Unit, 120
    Independent Police Investigative
        Directorate, 117–118
    national and provincial secretariats,
        115–116
    national parliament and provincial
        legislatures, 115
    police misconduct in, 110, 117, 122
    reciprocal moral dualism, 113–114
    systems theory, 112–113

South African Human Rights
    Commission, 118
South African Police Service (SAPS), 38–39,
    110, 115, 117, 122
    code of conduct, 121
    police leadership issues, 118–120
    recruitment, 112–113
South African Press Association
    (SAPA), 112
South Sudan, 39
SP, *see* Superintendent of Police (SP), India
Special Anti-Crime Unit of Trinidad and
    Tobago (SAUTT), 215, 217
Special Division for Service Control (Police
    of Police), Cameroon, 136
Statement of values, 71
Sting operations, 25
Stop-and-check operations, in
    Cameroon, 127
Strategy for Integrity Management
    (Hong Kong Police Force), 151
Street-level corruption, in Ghana, 73–74
Street vendors, bribes from, 130, 159
Subordinate officers
    delinquent, handling, 173
    transfer and posting of, 159
Superintendent of Police (SP), India, 164
Supremacy of law, 35, 38–39
Supreme Court of India, 167, 169–170
Syndicated corruption, in Hong Kong,
    148–149
Systems failure, in postconflict
    countries, 181
Systems theory, 112–113, 232

T

Target Committee on Corruption
    (Hong Kong), 148
Tea money, in Hong Kong, 148
Terms of reference (TOR), 98–99
Terrorism, in Kenya, 104
The Ransley Report, 92, 95, 98–99
Third-degree method, in India, 162
TI, *see* Transparency International (TI)
Torture
    by Cameroon police, 128, 131, 136
    by Kenya Police, 93
Traffic police corruption
    in Ghana, 73
    in Kenya, 92, 97

248

Index

Training
ethics/integrity, 16–18
of new recruits, 113–114
on-the-job anticorruption training,
54–55, 231
PACT (*see* Police anticorruption training
(PACT))
and police corruption, 9
preventive measures in, 16–18
of recruits, in Cameroon, 133
socialization during, 113
Transparency International (TI), 10–11
GII, 67
Transparency International—Kenya,
11–12, 90–91
Transparency of law, 36, 42–43
Transportation fees for investigation,
129–130
Trinidad and Tobago, 235–236
bilateral investment treaties of, 209
civilian oversight bodies, 219–220
community policing in, 215
crime in, 210–211
Crime Policy Commission, 216
current policing landscape in, 219–221
drug trade in, 210–211
economic and political context, 208–210
fatal shootings in, 213
foreign consultants, 218
gender inequality in, 209–210
incompetence of police in, 213
investigation
of police abuse, 213
of police shootings, 221
model station programs in, 216–217
mutual legal assistance treaties, 214–215
PCA, 216, 219–221
police reforms, 214–219
coproductive activities, 218
lack of community involvement, 217
ship rider agreements of, 214
state of emergency in, 219
Trinidad and Tobago Police Service (TTPS)
internal disciplinary procedures, 212
militarization of police, 215
police deviance in, 212–213, 218
police leadership, 212
public–police relationship, 211–212
Truth, Justice and Reconciliation
Commission (TJRC), Kenya, 91

TTPS, *see* Trinidad and Tobago Police
Service (TTPS)

U

UNC, *see* United National Congress (UNC),
Trinidad and Tobago
UNCAT, *see* United Nations Committee
Against Torture (UNCAT)
Undercover operations, 26
UNHRC, *see* United Nations Human Rights
Committee (UNHRC)
Unionization of police, 203
United National Congress (UNC), Trinidad
and Tobago, 209
United Nations Committee Against Torture
(UNCAT), 93, 136
United Nations Human Rights Committee
(UNHRC), 93
United Nations Office on Drugs and Crime
(UNODC), 99–100
Usalama Reforms Forum (Kenya), 136

V

Values-based framework, in
HKPF, 152
Vetting
in Cameroon, 133–134
in Kenya, 101
during recruitment, 16
Vigilance Department (India), 158, 166
Vigilantism, 34
Violent mobilization, 41, 43

W

Wantokism (Solomon Islands), 191
Warner, Jack, 219
Welfare of police, 135
Westminster constitutional system,
in Solomon Islands, 182
Whistleblowers' Act (Ghana), 67
Whistleblowers' Protection Bill, 2011
(India), 168, 170, 172

Z

Zero tolerance policing, 138, 221